LOVE IS ALWAYS

Love Is Always

Michael Miles

WILLIAM MORROW AND COMPANY, INC.
NEW YORK

Library of Congress Cataloging-in-Publication Data

Miles, Michael, 1940–
Love is always.

1. Miles, Michael, 1940–   . 2. Catholic Church—
United States—Clergy—Biography. 3. Celibacy—
Catholic Church.   4. Catholic Church—Doctrines.
I. Title.
BX4705.M5529A35 1986   282′.092′4   [B]   86-2378
ISBN 0-688-06218-0

Printed in the United States of America

3 4 5 6 7 8 9 10

BOOK DESIGN BY PATRICE FODERO

*For Joan, who taught me the meaning behind
the Apostle's words:
"In the end there will be only these three
which endure;
faith, hope and love. The greatest of these is*
Love."

ACKNOWLEDGMENTS

Writing this book has demonstrated to me once again how inter-dependent we all are.

The men, women, and children of Resurrection Parish, by initially opening their hearts to the unexpected, opened a new way. Without them, this story could never have happened.

There are particular individuals mentioned within these pages who gave so much of themselves that part of them is forever part of me. Some among them have gone the extra mile, encouraging this book along its way to life. They know who they are. I am forever grateful.

Special thanks to Bob and Toni Adams, Bill and Patty Peters, Charles Hamp, and again and again to Bob Perry and Tim Warner, who urged me to revisit the mountain and share what together we saw up there. The kind counsel of Rhoda Lerman and the patient assistance of Brenda Putnam are also appreciated.

The contribution of Carl Brandt, who put his deserved reputation at the service of this book, was invaluable. His wisdom, inspiration, and downright humanity have been sheer gifts.

Thanks also to my editor, Bruce Lee, whose creative insight, sense of balance, and quick wit made the process far easier than it might have been.

ACKNOWLEDGMENTS

Throughout the long, solitary moments of writing this book, I felt the presence of numerous other priests, other women, and am indebted to them in ways I don't fully understand. Indebted to individuals like Frank Bonnike—as well as those I know by name only, like Theresa Kane—who have never ceased to chase after the morning star.

Most especially, I am grateful to our children, Michelle, Sean-Michael, and Shaleen, who had to put up with a father snatching bits and pieces of time away from them to record a drama which they may someday come to see as very much their own.

CONTENTS

When evening came, he was there alone, while the boat, by now far out on the lake, was battling with a heavy sea, for there was a head-wind. In the fourth watch of the night he went towards them, walking on the lake, and when the disciples saw him . . . they were terrified . . . and cried out in fear. But at once Jesus called out to them, saying, "Courage! It is I! Do not be afraid."

It was Peter who answered, "Lord," he said, "if it is you, tell me to come to you across the water." "Come," said Jesus. Then Peter got out of the boat and started walking towards Jesus across the water, but as soon as he felt the force of the wind, he took fright and began to sink. "Lord! Save me!" he cried. Jesus put out his hand at once and held him.

—The Gospel According to Matthew

Part I

*These are morning matters, pictures
you dream as the final wave heaves
you up on the sand to the bright light
and drying air. You remember . . .*

—Annie Dillard,
Pilgrim at Tinker Creek

When everything comes together, September in south-western Montana is sheer magic. As the crowd began to swell for the nine o'clock mass, a Sunday sun popped out between the frosty fingers of the Spanish Peak range, inching along the floor of the Gallatin Valley, leaving in its wake a gentle mist that rose like incense over garden squash, cattails, and aspen leaves.

A slight buzz rose and fell from the congregation within Bozeman's Resurrection Parish and finally settled into a steady hum over the sea of faces, scarves, and baby bottles.

As a nation we were in our bicentennial year, watching the Yankees and Cincinnati advance toward the World Series, while political winds tossed Jimmy Carter like a tumbleweed across our landscape toward the White House.

Events of the previous day had left me at once exhausted and euphoric. Now, adjusting a stole over a Roman chasuble as I moved down the aisle, I felt like a child rushing home from school, anxious to share the joy of a first golden star.

"In the name of the Father, and of the Son, and of the Holy Spirit." The mass began. Later, as a slender, athletic woman finished reading the epistle, I stepped before the congregation, the quiet punctuated by an occasional cough or an infant's squeal.

Within me a picture emerged from a scrapbook of memories. An earlier time, when at the age of twenty-six I knelt on the polished marble floor of the sanctuary. Bathed in a kaleidoscope of light break ing through the seminary's stained glass, I promised never to marry. Pledged to observe the law of lifelong celibacy as a condition of entering the Roman Catholic priesthood. Now, less than a decade later, my voice choked up.

"Before today's homily, I would like to share another kind of good news with you—something most of you knew was coming. A friend once told me that until your first child, you really don't know what it means to say, 'God creates.' I know now what he meant. Yesterday morning—well, Joan finally had the baby. A daughter—all seven pounds three ounces of her. We've named her Michelle Raelene. The 'Ray' is after Bishop Hunthausen."

Spontaneously the bass player strummed a few chords, and the room spilled over with twinkles and ready smiles.

Moments later, as I elevated the bread and wine over the altar, an abrupt movement toward the back of the church caught my attention. A wiry woman was turning, whispering something to her husband, who responded with a quizzical look and a slouch of his shoulders. I didn't see them again until after mass when, amid handshakes and hugs, I noticed them speaking with the other priest just before the woman shot a final look in my direction and rushed out the door.

I'd never known Tim O'Mera when he wasn't a priest, first as my philosophy professor in college and now as co-pastor of Resurrection. Through more than twenty years, the burly redhead had become a close friend. More often than not, we discovered what we meant to each other through laughter. Right now he wore the frown he used to display in class when pondering the esoteric nuances separating being and essence.

He motioned me toward his office, closing the door.

"That couple I was talking with just moved here from New York. She said she had never seen a member of the clergy so taken with a baby; wondered whose it was. When I told her it was yours, she was flabbergasted. Her husband asked if you were married. I said you were, then she pipes in—'And he's a Catholic priest! I thought the married ones got kicked out!' "

Then Tim lightened up. "Apparently this was their first time here. She wasn't at all negative about it, just astonished. She kept shaking her head, saying she couldn't believe it."

He settled into a high-backed rocker, still frowning.

"By the way, I didn't want to bother you at the hospital yesterday.

Curtiss called." The rocker began to move to an intense rhythm as Tim outlined the bishop's message. Once again he was insisting that Rome would not tolerate our situation at Resurrection, and that some of his own clergy were demanding my dismissal. While we had received such warnings before, this time Tim was more concerned.

"I don't know who's complaining. The bishop will never say. They're men without faces. We can only assume they're the same bunch who've fought change all along. But with you—well, it's different. Maybe you're symbolic of change. Who knows? It's not your marriage that they have a problem with, it's that you were allowed to stay. From their perspective a married priest is bound to throw into question much of what they've stood for all their lives. Ah, hell," he said, shaking his head, "I don't know. In any event, they can be genuine bastards."

I felt like a balloon with a slow leak.

"What else did he say?"

The rocker stopped. "Just two other bombshells, that's all. These guys circulated a petition among themselves. Sent it to Rome. Then —you aren't going to believe this—he mentioned the Vatican sent a monsignor here disguised as a layman. Just to check things out and see if you existed."

"The Vatican? Here? So it's finally come to this." My stomach started into a slow roll.

The rocker began to creak again.

"At first, the bishop sounded as if he thought Rome's move was clever. Then he realized he said too much and backed off."

There was a knock on the door. Tim stepped out. In his absence I drifted back to another interruption, months earlier.

It was shortly past six in the morning. Joan and I teased about who should get up and cross the chilly floor to answer the phone.

I recognized the voice of Blake Robins, a priest at the university parish in Missoula.

"Well, he's been named."

"Named?"

"Our new bishop. Want to guess?"

I didn't.

"You won't believe this one. Ready?"

I wasn't.

"Elden Francis Curtiss. Ever heard of him?"

I hadn't.

"Par for the course," he grunted. "Rome asks the whole diocese to go through the process of suggesting candidates and then appoints someone none of us ever heard of!"

Blake went on to repeat the morning newscast announcing the appointment of the rector of a small seminary in Oregon as the bishop-elect of Helena. Over a year before, our previous bishop, Raymond "Dutch" Hunthausen, had been elevated as Archbishop of Seattle. Though the prolonged delay in naming his successor was unusual, the news of the appointment came as a relief. The suspense was over.

I returned to lie next to Joan. A sliver of light, peeping through the blind, moved across the ceiling. Joan rose up on her elbow, listening as I told her the news, then touched her lips against mine.

I wondered if she remembered Dutch's parting comment just before leaving for Seattle. There was an unfamiliar melancholy in his voice.

"Don't worry about me. This is a promotion. I'll be okay." He hugged Joan, started to leave, then hesitated. "I'm worried for both of you. Whoever he'll be, the attitude of my successor is important. There are some who see you, Mike, as having your cake and eating it, too. Sometimes it seems they won't rest until this whole experiment is crushed and you with it. Be careful."

Joan pulled at the sheet. "Hey, come on. A penny for your thoughts."

I felt nothing other than an uneasy emptiness.

"Whoever Curtiss is and what he's been told about us, we'll just have to wait and find out."

In less than two weeks we would get the chance.

The invitation to Oregon came as somewhat of a surprise. The bishop-elect wanted to clarify a few matters.

Placing the suitcase in the car, I held Joan close. She was as soft and warm as the comforter which had draped us through the night. In her fourth month, Joan's early weeks of morning sickness were behind us. She placed my hand against her abdomen, the orange flecks in her eyes dancing.

"Careful, mister. You'll wake Pee-Wee."

Later, driving in the dawn chill toward the airport, I wondered if the bishop-elect had ever been involved with a woman . . . felt her warmth against his own.

The world seemed to shrink the farther south I drove away from Portland. Route 213 jutted off Interstate 5, winding past dairy farms and weathered Burma Shave signs toward the tiny community of Mount Angel. On the outskirts of town, the seminary sat atop a knoll like a medieval villa captured in a time warp. Although declining enrollments forced most seminaries in neighboring states to close, it clung to life —the heir of institutional death all around.

A paunchy student lifted the skirt of his cassock and, breathing heavily, led me up a stairway into the waiting room adjacent to the rector's office.

"Father has been terribly busy," he puffed. "Calls are coming in from everywhere. We're all so thrilled. Imagine—he'll be a bishop!"

He reminded me of a teenager about to embark on a first date.

Precisely at ten o'clock the door swung open. In clerical black, Curtiss seemed all collar and cuffs, much smaller than the picture his voice suggested. The papers said he was forty-three. I stepped into the office, antiseptic and bland save for a glistening statue of the Sacred Heart against a far wall.

Curtiss's arm traced a sweeping arc over a gray metal desk. "Letters of congratulations. They're pouring in. Even telegrams. I can't keep up with them!"

Hyped by the flurry of attention, he launched into a rapid-fire monologue on the seminary's reaction to his appointment. Eventually coming up against the rush of his own momentum, he stopped abruptly—shifting an inner gear.

"Enough of this. We don't even know one another." He sat behind the desk, picked up a stack of letters, and leaned forward. "Not all of these are comforting. A few are from priests in the Helena Diocese." He looked up, flashing a smile. "My diocese, I should now say. Anyway, these men warn that the number one problem I'll face is a parish which can't even be considered Catholic. Ring a bell?"

Wanting this first time together to go well, I didn't respond.

Motioning me toward a chair, as one accustomed to command, he adjusted his heavy-framed glasses and continued.

"They're especially alarmed with the parish's so-called 'married priest'." With a steady glare, he shook a finger in my direction. "Let me tell you, some of the older fathers are seriously scandalized!"

"There are a few of them who've been upset all along," I replied, taken back.

"Whatever, it's important to listen to them. I respect the ol' bucks and around here at least they've learned to trust me."

"I care about them, too. If it weren't for their example, at least some, I'd never have become a priest."

"Whoa! Don't hold them responsible," he said through a pencil-line smile. "Most of the ones I hear from won't rest until you're pushed out of the sanctuary into the last seat of the last pew."

"I'm sorry they're upset. Maybe that's the price of change."

His eyes rolled upward as he leaned across the desk. "Change! You mean revolution! My God, I was astounded to hear you even existed! How'd you ever get away with it?"

I loosened my tie, wondering what he saw in me. Weakness? Arrogance? A hint of defiance?

He shifted gears again.

"Archbishop Hunthausen called to congratulate me. He speaks highly of you and the parish. What's its name?" he asked, the shadow from the venetian blinds spreading across his face.

"Resurrection."

"Ah yes." He leaned back, chuckling. "I don't mean to sound disrespectful, but I have to question the archbishop's judgment."

In a whisper, glancing at the closed door as if fearful someone might hear our shared secret, he suggested that Hunthausen had not endeared himself to Rome over us. "Far from it."

I felt the hairs on the back of my neck stand up.

"Well, they must have seen something good. Seattle was quite a promotion."

He abruptly switched the subject, focusing for a moment on his new diocese, which he felt was "way out," and directed too much by the laity.

Our conversation see-sawed back and forth, like two fencers, each circling about an intriguing and intimidating opponent. All at once, Curtiss took a stab at what for him lay at the heart of things.

"Tell me. Weren't you sincere when you promised celibacy?"

He didn't wait for an answer, but continued.

"I'm committed to it myself. Have been since first entering the seminary."

"When was that?" I asked, recalling my days in college, the dating and normal attachments of young men.

"Right after high school. Though I decided long before then. But we're getting away from my point," he said, toying with a cuff link. "Quite honestly, I can't understand how a man can claim to be fully committed to Christ and the service of the church while getting tied up with a woman."

"Maybe you have to love someone to see how," I said with a frosty smile.

He bristled, a vein showing faintly blue beneath an eye.

Although it seemed tactless, I plunged into the debate, mentioning that marriage, if anything, had enhanced my own ministry; that Jesus himself did not demand celibacy even of the apostles; that in the first twelve hundred years of the church, marriage was permitted for priests before the papacy levied a law forbidding such unions.

"It was a carry-over from monasticism," I said, taking a deep breath. "I'm sure you know all of this as well as anyone . . . it's just that while I appreciate the value of celibacy, it should never be the criterion for whether one can be a priest or not. Whether or not a person possesses gifts to serve others, has a passion for the gospel . . . seems lots more important, I would think."

Curtiss interrupted, his tone cool but controlled. "No one forced you to vow chastity. You could have dropped out before you were ordained. Besides, it's not a question of what you think anyway. It's for the church to decide and us to obey the dictates of the Holy See."

"Blindly?"

"The law is clear. We can't have that parish thinking you're a married priest."

"But I am a married priest!"

He stood, waving off my attempt to cut in. "I know the whole bit . . . once we receive the sacrament of Holy Orders, we're priests forever . . . I'm talking about the law, and the Church of Rome will not tolerate people becoming laws unto themselves!" He was shouting but didn't seem to notice.

Resolute, he began pacing back and forth in front of me. "Tonight I fly to Reno for a meeting with the Holy Father's delegate. His personal representative, for godsakes! Let me tell you right now, at the top of our agenda is this diocese which sometimes apparently sees itself as an island."

A steady buzz interrupted us, a reminder that another appointment was waiting. Trying to gather up the questions whirling about within me, my eyes rested on the plaster Christ behind him, its almost feminine fingers pointing to the ring of thorns around the pierced heart.

"I just hope you take the time to get to know us all."

As I stood, Curtiss extended a firm hand. "Don't worry. I'll make no judgment about your situation until I've witnessed your 'catholicity' firsthand. We won't throw you to the dogs." He hesitated, smiling. "At least, not yet!"

I feigned a smile in return. "Just know that if you try, you'll have a whale of a battle on your hands. The people at home will go to the wall over this.''

"Let them," he shot back. "So long as they're willing to pay the price once they get there.''

Opening the door, I lingered over a photo of what he then pointed out were his parents. Staring back at me was a short couple, posing stiffly for the camera. Anxious to end on a cordial note, I mentioned the peculiar resemblance couples occasionally take on after a lifetime together. Aware that he had not inquired about Joan, I dropped her name into the farewells.

"Ah yes. Your wife.'' He cleared his throat, looking down while stroking the carpet with the tip of his shoe. When I mentioned she was pregnant, his head jerked up. He flushed crimson. "Well! This thing is much farther down the road than I had imagined,'' he said, moving by me to greet a group of nuns in full habit outside the office. In the flurry of their excited banter over the bishop-elect, I eased by and went outside into the heavy humidity.

As I flew home that evening, the conversation continued to press upon me.

While the sun faded into the Pacific and we tipped a wing turning east, I couldn't shake off the certain feeling that any hope for the future was about to fade.

Tim returned to the room; the memory of Oregon had passed through me in an instant. Moments later, as we proceeded down the aisle toward the altar for the next mass, he slipped me a note. "You're supposed to pick up some diapers on the way to the hospital, *Father*.''

The OB wing was hushed. As I eased open the door to room 201, Joan, wearing a canary negligée, was watching a swirl of leaves dance against the window, Michelle cuddled against her breast. Tiptoeing in, I managed to brush a kiss across the back of her neck before she noticed me.

"You've got two women who need you now,'' she said, lifting Michelle into my arms. "Here. She doesn't weigh much more than one of those leaves.'' She sat up against the bed. "Do you realize that this young lady is almost twenty-four hours old and she hasn't danced with her dad?''

Suddenly a heavyset nurse pushed open the door. "Excuse me, Father. They've been paging you . . . a car accident. Poor guy down-stairs is barely hanging in there. He needs a priest.''

I eased Michelle back into her mother's arms.

Descending the stairs two at a time, I entered Emergency, its metal doors cold to the touch. Except for a couple of nurses and a physician working over a stretcher in a far corner, the room was empty. Motioning me over, one of the nurses mentioned that he was being prepped for an air ambulance.

Although about thirty, the victim struck me as no more than a child. There was little sign of blood, or of the usual aftermath of carnage. No trace of injury. Except for his pale blue eyes fixed on the glaring lights overhead, he might have been asleep.

"Can you hear me?" I asked quietly, leaning over him.

Nothing.

I brushed back a shock of fine hair matted against his forehead. It was moist, warm, just like Michelle's. Not until the bright rivulets of blood trickled across my palm, settling in little pools at my fingertips, did I see the naked gash.

"You're going to be okay now. Let me pray for you."

Withdrawing a small vial of oil from my jacket and tracing a sign of the cross just below the wound, I pronounced the ancient words of anointing.

"May almighty God have mercy on you, forgive you . . . bring you to life everlasting."

A nurse behind me muttered, "Amen."

"May the almighty and merciful Lord grant you pardon, absolution, and remission . . . May the blessing of almighty God, Father, Son, and Holy Spirit descend upon you and remain forever."

"Amen."

His pupils dilated as a foamy ridge of pink bubbles oozed between his lips. Startled, I stepped back as the physician examined him, then drew the stiff sheet over his face. There would be no hasty trip in the air ambulance. He was dead. Shaken, I went back upstairs to OB.

Not until later, in breaking the news to his parents, would I discover that the man had divorced then married a second time outside the church. His mother especially treasured the news that a priest had been there in his final moments; finding solace in the assurance that what they had been taught to perceive as his sin, was in the end perhaps understood by a God not nearly so hard on him as some mortals might have been.

From earliest memory, time has both fascinated and haunted me. Among my fondest recollections are those of sweltering summer evenings on Grandpa's back porch, when I lay snuggled on his lap. I can still smell the creosote. Grandpa was a locomotive engineer for the Northern Pacific Railway—just about the finest thing a man could ever be.

One evening as we stared out into the black Montana sky, he pointed to the Big and Little Dippers hanging over the Beartooth Mountains. Not until he told me of his great-grandfather pointing out identical constellations over Galway Bay when he was a child, did it dawn on me that there was anything anywhere older than my grandpa Tim. At that moment, the twinkling stars gave me the first hint of an immense river of time. The world seemed larger and I, much smaller than before.

Whenever a star fell, Grandpa said someone had died. A soul was on its way to heaven. If anyone had asked me, I would never have dreamed that he, too, would die. When his star finally did slip from its niche in the Big Sky, it landed with a thud against my heart, there to smolder as a constant reminder that someday mine also would fall.

Later, as a man, I lay beneath that same sky, prostrate and still, on the sanctuary floor in the parish of my childhood while a choir chanted the solemn litany of the saints. When I rose, kneeling before Bishop Hunthausen to feel his hands, heavy upon my head, conferring the priesthood, I felt a belief destined never to leave me. Knowing that whenever my star fell, it might—just might—fall into God.

Three years after ordination, the heavy trampling boots of war continued to soak up blood in Vietnam. Richard Nixon was cruising midway through his first term. The winds of change unleashed by the Second Vatican Council were buffeting the Church of Rome with increasing velocity, and much as two grains of sand passing through the nape of an hourglass, a woman's life and mine were about to brush against each other.

It began with Bishop Hunthausen's suggestion that I move from my position as professor of theology at our small Catholic college in Helena, to that of campus pastor at the state's largest university. The opportunity came as a welcome surprise. The period at Carroll College had been comforting, certain, though, because I was one of several clerics on the faculty, a bit too rote and predictable. With the move I would be alone, facing a far different atmosphere at Montana State University.

The first few months in Bozeman moved quickly, laced together by an attempt to transform the Catholic Newman Club, which served a limited cadre of students, into a full-fledged parish. One which included the faculty and reached out to the city itself. Inch by inch the transformation began, revealing itself opaquely as new faces melted in among the familiar. One face in particular stood out.

She started coming regularly to the late afternoon mass in Danforth Chapel. One day, we had forgotten to turn up the heat and a damp chill was in the air. As we huddled around the altar, someone blurted out, "Not only can we hear your words, Father, we can see them, too!" The chapel rocked with laughter. Since coming to Bozeman, I was happier than ever before.

"Behold the Lamb of God . . ." Again, I found myself looking toward her before turning back to the bread and the cup. ". . . who takes away the sins of the world."

Though neither of us had spoken since our initial meeting early in the summer, she continued to intrigue me.

It had been one of those lazy summer afternoons, draped in yellows and greens. Bees bumped against flowers; so, too, quite by accident, had our lives. We were introduced. She smelled of fresh grass. Her waist-length hair was as black as a raven's wing; her voice, soft, sure. Never had I seen anyone so full, so confidently woman. The moment passed, clung to me. Now, as with each day, I looked forward just to seeing her.

"The Body of Christ." I placed the Eucharist in her hands, cradled before me like a cup of fine bone china. We touched. Her walnut-colored eyes rose to meet mine, turned down again. I glanced away.

Following the mass, she wrapped a soft orange scarf about her hair and started to leave.

"Dr. Doyle? Ah . . . Joan?" The words were out before I knew it. "I think you walk the same direction as I do. Want some company?"

She smiled. "I live just a few blocks from you. You go by my place every day."

I was flattered she even noticed. We stepped into the quiet purple evening. Within minutes, Joan was talking about life on a Wisconsin farm.

"As kids, we used to name the cows. They were like people to us. Darn ol' Ethel was my favorite. Dad used to say she looked like she was just daring any one of us to milk her." She giggled—her breath against the dusk—offering a glimpse of the little girl who still lived within her. She went on with particular delight about her family, the decision of her brother to become a priest.

"We were typically Irish—always putting priests on a pedestal."

Her voice trailed off. "Then again, maybe they wanted it that way. We warned Gene he'd better not try any of that high-and-mighty stuff on us . . ." She stopped in front of her house. "It's nice to see that you have a human face behind the cloth. You know, it's really a bit disarming."

So was she, I thought.

That night, crawling into bed, I saw her face between the pages of my breviary. Finally, unable to concentrate, I clicked off the light, but not the unfamiliar stir within me.

Over the next several weeks, as fall slipped into winter, our walks together became more frequent as bit by bit we poured out our stories and shared our dreams. More often than not, I found myself slowing the pace, taking a mini-vacation from the stimulating task of starting a new parish. Sometimes, when a late appointment at the university prevented Joan from coming along, I walked home by myself, disappointed. Following one such occasion, I suggested that it wasn't good for her to walk home alone at night.

She didn't break stride. "No worry. Scott usually comes by and picks me up."

My knees buckled. "Scott?" I felt like someone had kicked me in the stomach. My reaction surprised me. A stunning professor of counseling, and single to boot! What, after all, did I expect?

"He's with the Forest Service. The other night we went out to a place called Buck's T-Four. Everyone was doing what they call 'cowboy jitterbug.' You should have seen him, he was so-o funny and so-o serious." Lost in the memory, she appeared oblivious of its impact on me. An unfamiliar melancholy swept over me. I didn't say anything more. As for Scott—Joan never mentioned him again.

Maybe I should have known better, faced up to the rush of feelings which rose and fell within me each time she came into view. Only a decade before, even the presence of a priest and a woman together might have raised a red flag, started tongues wagging. Yet as the 70s dawned, the church was still struggling to recover from the initial shock waves of the Second Vatican Council which had turned almost everything inside out. What was once certain became uncertain; the fixed became fluid; the secure, laden with risk; black and white, an amorphous gray. Those of us trained in the wake of such change felt encouraged to skate upon thin ice into the unpredictable future rather than cling to the shores of a passing era. The seminary was our training ground, its memories as fresh as our ideals.

*   *   *

It was only four years ago, yet another lifetime—

I peered north from the seminary windows as a March wind swirled across the thin ice covering the Mississippi. The river wound its way west along the edge of Dubuque, Iowa, before disappearing behind a slender bluff. To the east, evening shadows stretched across the rolling hills into Wisconsin, where less than twenty miles away a young woman, then unknown to me, the wind stinging her cheeks, broke a bale of hay, pitching it to hungry heifers. In the morning, Joan would join her family at St. Matthew's for Sunday mass. At the same hour, I would kneel before the altar and, with a simple *"Adsum,"* take another step closer to the priesthood by accepting the law of clerical celibacy.

I looked away from the window. The first-floor hallway of Mount St. Bernard's was blaring with exaggerated conversation and nervous laughter; the strict rules of silence all but ignored this night before our third-year theology class took the plunge into Major Orders.

Chuffer pushed open my door. A former dental student from La Crosse, Wisconsin, he would later serve as a priest in the slums of Bolivia. "Hey, why so monkish?" He slipped into my room, violating still another rule that would not be easily tolerated if noticed by the rector.

"Tomorrow is no big deal. Relax. They say the archbishop's knife is quick and sure. He snips your balls off like apples from a tree."

I reached across the bed, grabbed a pillow, and hurled it toward him. "Hell, Davidson. It's easy for you to say. We all know you were born without them in the first place!"

Despite the banter, we both knew the step we were about to take was a more precarious one than it had been with previous generations. Reverberations from the Second Vatican Council were just beginning to rattle doors closed for centuries. While the law forbidding marriage for priests remained firm, it was increasingly subject to debate in an atmosphere which was conditioning us to expect the unexpected. Earlier in the week, a cryptic message bearing the rector's seal had provided an example.

"Effective immediately, Fr. Valarian Costello will no longer meet with his classes. Announcement of a replacement will be forthcoming."

Practically before the ink was dry, rumors spread through the seminary that the popular Dominican had been in an accident, come down with a terminal illness, or even worse—left the priesthood.

That evening, a few of us met in our weekly group-dynamics practicum, directed by Matthew Vaughn, a priest from nearby Aquinas Institute. Although he and other Dominicans had little influence over our day-to-day existence at St. Bernard's, they were exclusively responsible for our education. The lanky former basketball star of Notre Dame scanned the group, waiting out our pensive silence. Finally, Dick Pepper, a classmate who had abandoned plans for a legal career to enter the seminary, popped the question which preoccupied us all.

"What's the story with Val?"

Matthew filled us in on what was becoming a familiar scenario. Costello had wanted to tell us himself, but the archbishop insisted he leave quick and clean, to avoid scandal. He would marry Sister Dianne in a month or so. Pepper, like a kettle bursting with steam, exploded.

"Shit! His timing is just great. Here we are taking 'sub' in a few days and ol' Val jumps ship. Maybe we can have a double ceremony on the same date—his and ours." He removed his glasses, wiping them slowly as if in doing so he would erase Val's decision. "Anyone want to look through these things? Look what I see. It's the pope announcing his wedding to his housekeeper."

The room erupted with laughter. Then, as though a zipper had been pulled over the indiscretion, we stopped. Someone muttered, "First Mueller leaves like a thief in the night, and then a novice master and even the prior here at Aquinas. Geez . . ."

We were nervous. News media reports of priests who had exchanged their collars for wedding bands were becoming more frequent. There were forecasts that the exodus would reach crisis proportions within a few years.

On the edge of the circle, Josh Gorton, his coffee cup drained, tore at the Styrofoam, pitching bits and pieces onto the floor. Despite the seminary's traditional rule that cautioned against particular friendships, over the years we had become close friends.

"Josh?" This time it was my own voice. "I think I know what you're feeling. But it might help if we knew for sure."

"Oh, nothing really," he said in the mellow manner which endeared him to us all. He tossed away the cup. "What the hell are we supposed to think? Val was my spiritual director! Here I am talking with him about the celibacy bit and all the while he is planning to run off with one of the nuns!" His eyes glistened. "He didn't let on that anything was happening. Not even a good-bye. Oh, I know the good archbishop didn't want him to shock us poor innocents. Damn, what a system! It's just that he was such a good priest. So human. Look what it got him. He falls in love and bingo, one more padre in the trash bin.''

Henry Whistler chimed in, his normally cherubic features furrowed and intense.

"Yeah, here we are, caught in the middle. On the one hand, you Dominicans''—he glanced at Matthew—''are saying we should be human priests. Not just stuff ourselves into a mold. All we hear anymore is we are supposed to get off the clerical pedestal and get involved in the lives of others. We're not ordained to fill a slot or meet the church's past expectations . . . and . . .''

While Henry struggled for words, I remembered a recent conversation I had had with Vaughn while strolling across the half-mile green which separated Aquinas from St. Bernard's.

"It's an exciting time for the church. As a priest, you'll do well,'' he said, a spring breeze snapping and popping at his white habit.

"Let's hope so. If for no other reason than to add a dose of love to the troubled brew of the world,'' I said, fingering the letter stuffed inside my jacket. Its hurried script bore further testimony to my brother's ongoing nightmare in Vietnam.

Vaughn stopped, his wide eyes, younger somehow than the lean face they dominated, fastened upon me.

"Where do you get yours?''

"I'm not reading you.''

"Love. Where do you get the dose in your own life?''

His frankness threw me. Sounding defensive, I mentioned something about family and friends.

"Is it enough?''

When I alluded more confidently to the reservoir someday to be found within fellow priests, he nodded.

"Maybe. Whatever, without it we dry up. Dead men don't have much to offer others.''

We leaned back into the breeze, which caused the monk's cowl to bellow like a tiny parachute at the nape of his neck.

Henry had found his voice again, its high pitch drawing me back into the circle.

"Cripes, it's scary. If I ended up like Costello, it would kill my folks, or . . .'' He paused. "They'd kill me!''

Another ripple of laughter.

"What the hell do you mean, 'end up like Costello'?" The sheer strength of Pepper's question was intimidating.

Stung, Henry flushed.

"I didn't mean it that way. Yeah, it's better to take the chance of being open, much better than ending up like some of the turkeys we see around us, but my parents are plain farm folks."

He tapped a cigarette against his wrist, lit up, exhaling tiny rings like miniature halos. "So many priests are like islands . . ." He trailed off, lost in his own reflections.

Undaunted, Pepper took up where Henry left off.

"Remember when we first came here? What a zoo! That steel curtain in the dining room?"

We remembered all right. The nuns and college girls who prepared our meals used to pass food to us beneath the curtain, cafeteria-style; only their hands were exposed.

"Then Stark here"—Pepper pushed at Jim's shoe; Jim was the only one among us who had been in seminaries since grade school— "he gets the idea that we should know what's behind it. When you slid the thing up, I thought the rector was going to have a stroke. What a disappointment. All the while we thought those were levitating hands and here they were attached to honest-to-God women all along!"

"Gave us a chance to practice custody of the eyes," Stark teased, adding as an afterthought, "Some custody. When those coeds peeked out, every face in the place was staring back at them."

"Sheer lust," Pepper quipped.

Stark was enjoying himself.

"Whether in thought or deed, it doesn't matter. Either way, a violation of the virtue of chastity. Which, by the way, becomes a sacrilege if we happen to be in Major Orders . . . which, I might point out, will be the case this time next week."

"Whew," Whistler sighed. "Just under the wire," and we all enjoyed the humor before returning to the matter of Father Costello.

For the next hour, we released the tide of emotion brought to the surface by Val's departure. Clearly we wanted to be priests. We were willing to accept celibacy as the price of admission. However, we refused to see women as a threat, always to be kept at a distance. None of us wanted to live sterile lives with love reduced to a Sunday word, spoken for others. While we intended to make it as celibates, our primary goal was to become effective priests. It sounded fine. Still, we were more than anxious about the road ahead.

Eventually Chuffer turned, pushed Henry playfully on the shoulder.

"Hell, Hen. Quit worrying about what's coming. Val wasn't the first and he won't be the last. Let's just take it a day at a time. Besides, no woman in her right mind is going to come chasing after you. No way. You're home free!"

Another round of cathartic laughter.

The session had gone on longer than usual. As we began snapping our collars back into place, Gorton picked listlessly at the fragments of his cup. Hurling them into the wastebasket, he scurried out ahead of us without saying a word.

Now, a week later, I said good night to Chuffer and went downstairs. The chapel was dark but for a soft glow surrounding the tabernacle at its far end. Feeling my way between the carved shoulders of the pews and a stucco wall, I genuflected and entered the choir stalls within the sanctuary. Over the years I had come to treasure such moments snatched from the night. Moments when the damp must rising from oiled oak, worn hymnals, and leather kneelers spoke of the familiar. In the stillness, broken only by the occasional swish of a cassocked figure sweeping by, I found a peculiar comfort. It was there, as I knelt before the tabernacle, that the world's uncertain chaos was held at bay. Where life itself somehow found its center and held.

As my pupils accommodated to the darkness, I could make out the archbishop's cope folded in layers next to embroidered white gloves and a beaded miter. Like me, they waited, impatient for morning. On the one hand, the prospect of living out a lifetime of celibacy was sobering, especially given a church bursting with change. Then again, any concern was vanquished at the thought of advancing yet another step toward the priesthood. After all, I thought, the choice of giving myself over to a life without wife and family had been made years earlier with the decision to enter the seminary. Having dated throughout college, I knew then the cost of achieving the goal I sought above all else. A price levied as a measure of total dedication. While only a fool would turn a deaf ear to the rising din questioning the church's discipline, I would embrace the law, trusting its wisdom.

I leaned forward, facing the altar, pressing against the padded rail. Through the pearly-white cloth draped over the tabernacle I stared at the image of a host and chalice etched upon its door, and felt a quiet certitude. Though only a vessel of clay, I would trust God to do the molding as He had done with countless others before me.

Relaxed, I sat back, flicking on a single spot above the stall, and finished the day's breviary.

The next morning, we newly consecrated subdeacons posed

beneath the stern gaze of a statue of Saint Bernard. A photographer's lens, focusing upon the white and gold chasubles which clothed our anxious zeal, captured the moment, cutting close to the bone. Dick Pepper, squinting into the sun, older somehow than the day before; Henry Whistler, squat, roly-poly, an oversized alb protruding from beneath his chasuble; Josh Gorton, smiling awkwardly toward his parents with just a hint of sadness. All of us, like Moses, determined to somehow climb Yahweh's mountain. None of us knowing then that our training had led us to expect and hope for so much more in the church than we would find. Nor that the years ahead would be strewn with crushed dreams, broken hearts, and disillusioned expectations. That, much like soldiers preparing for battle, stirred to a high pitch, some would be dashed feebly against the walls of power. As the shutter clicked, twenty miles south across the river, Joan was talking with the aged pastor on the steps of St. Matthew's. Neither of us aware that within a few years our paths would cross, and our lives would never be the same.

Four years passed. Early one evening, a group from Resurrection assembled to help plan a Sunday liturgy. No longer behaving as though Joan did not exist, at one point I mentioned that she grew up on a farm twenty miles from where I had studied for the priesthood.

Jane Harlow, an always outspoken housewife, proved true to form.

"All those years neither of you knew one another. Sounds like more than fate to me," she teased. "Must be the Holy Spirit. Better watch out, Joan, Father will have you signing up for the convent."

Joan blinked, rested her eyes on me. "No way." She grinned. "All it means is that he was supposed to be a farmer." I flushed, but no one seemed to notice. Not even Joan.

Later, as the sound of the car engines and muffled voices faded, a blanket of uneasy loneliness settled over me. At times, the late-night silence of the rectory was soothing, even therapeutic. Not so this night. I went to the phone, hesitated, and then dialed. Joan's voice was immediately warm as she agreed to join me on a hike the following morning. Suddenly the room didn't seem so empty, or the day so long.

Strolling along Snowbank Meadow, we passed a broken wagon wheel embedded in the creek bank. I wondered what memories it held, what lives it once carried west. Who were they? What drove them toward a new beginning?

Joan knelt next to the wheel. "Dad used to say that these are like life itself. Each spoke leads to another. All part of something bigger." She scraped away moss from the hub. "What makes a wheel strong is its center. Like people, don't you think?"

As I reached to help her stand, her hair brushed against my cheek. It smelled of the land, of October.

Toward midday, we scurried over a slippery log stretching to a small waterfall. There we climbed atop a large boulder and nestled into its center opening, which cradled us like a giant hand. Over a lunch of cheese and bread, we watched a gentle breeze tear leaves from the aspen trees overhead and spill them into the swirling stream.

Joan broke off a piece of bread and shared it before passing along the one cup we had for our wine, just as a beaver slapped his tail with a loud *whack* and slithered across the creek bottom, out of sight.

Stretching and settling back against the boulder, she closed her eyes. "October smells of the earth more than any other month. It triggers memories. I can smell October at home now. When we were kids, Dad used to get up and start a fire, then we'd all join him around the kitchen stove for the rosary. I can still feel the floor on my knees. Sometimes we would try to skip a decade, but Dad always caught us." She sat up, looked at me but somehow through me. "They were good days. After the rosary we would dash out for chores. The mornings were so chilly that Mom claimed even Jack Frost stayed indoors." Her eyes were smiling. "I was the tiny one and so always got to go with Dad to the milk barn."

She sat up, wrapping her arms about her knees. "I've always kidded my brother Gene that he decided to become a priest to avoid all the work!" Slicing an apple, she handed me a sliver. "How about you? Why did you—how do they say it—embrace the cloth?"

Like the wagon wheel, the answer had several spokes. A lump settled in my throat, and before long I was telling her about one of them; about Jamie Fitzgerald. We were the closest of friends. Out in the shed behind Buzzy Turner's house we had a secret place, our haven from the adult world. While growing up, we used to go there and play cowboys and Indians; maybe catch mice in a jar. One day Jamie opened his small hand to reveal his uncle's pocketknife. It had a pearl handle; just about the most beautiful sight either of us had ever seen.

"I can still see his green eyes, sparkling with excitement. We decided to carve our names side by side on the wall of the shed." My voice started to quiver. "In the years that followed, we used to return to that wall just to see if the names were still there. I suppose we thought that so long as they were, everything would remain the same. But it didn't. We were twelve or so when the accident happened.'' My voice trailed off as the wind spilled a basket of leaves into the creek.

Joan stroked my arm while I recounted the events of that ugly afternoon. While Bruce Harper toyed with his dad's 30.06 rifle, it discharged and blew Jamie away in a maze of blood and bone. People said it was over in an instant. Jamie couldn't have felt a thing, or so they said.

The hardest part was the funeral parlor. Fastened to Jamie's collar was the same bow tie he had worn for our children's choir. I overheard someone say that the dead continue to grow fingernails. I couldn't see his; the flowers hid them. The funny curl in his soft blond hair which used to spill over his forehead was gone. For weeks afterward, I used to wake up at night seeing his face flickering against the vigil light, his hair all slick and pasty. The words of our last recital wouldn't leave me. ''Oh he's gone, he's gone away, for to stay a little while. But he's coming back if he goes ten thousand mile . . . Oh, who will tie my shoe? And who will glove your hand and who will kiss . . . ?''

I stopped, swallowing hard as a butterfly touched down on the rock, fanning its bright yellow and black wings before gliding away.

''Anyway, after that I'd go to the old shed alone. Every time I looked at our names . . . touched them . . . it helped. It was there that I first knew that my life would end someday, too.'' I stood, shrugged. ''So maybe that's where the seed was planted. Who knows?''

''Seed?'' Joan whispered.

''The priesthood. Sure, I was too young to think about it then, but growing up . . . you know, later . . . I had a desire to do something special with what was left of my life. Something that would outlast it.''

That evening as we drove through Paradise Valley along the Yellowstone River, the aura from a pumpkin sun held everything around us in harmony. Joan helped me with the Sunday homily. It would have much to do with our day; with the season's promise and fullness of life. With Jesus, an October man. Along the way, shadows flickered in her eyes. I wondered if she felt the easy bond between us as the sun shimmered then slipped behind the now purple Gallatin Range.

All Saints' Eve. Slipping the small chalice alongside a copy of the Scriptures, I closed the suitcase, lamenting that the Agriculture Auditorium was already too small. Within months, like seed long dormant, the parish suddenly flowered; even the evening mass was bursting at the seams.

"Hey, Father," a gangly sophomore yelled out. "You have to haul that thing around with you all the time? You ought to call this place Saint Suitcase Parish." Not waiting for a response, he began to wheel a horse skeleton from behind a curtain onto the spot where the makeshift altar had been moments before.

"Now that mass is over, ol' Bones has to get set for tomorrow's Vet class. I watched him during your sermon, Father. He was hooked. He didn't move a muscle."

Promising him one hundred additional days in purgatory for the crack, I scurried out into the frigid, gusting wind, already late for dinner with the priests.

For three-quarters of a century, Holy Rosary's spire marked the sole Catholic parish in Bozeman. Its pastor, much like the edifice itself, formed along traditional lines, fixed in place, crowded by change from without, cracking along fault lines from within. Stepping through the rear entrance into Father Paul Metzner's living room, I felt a combination of affection and unease.

When we had met years earlier, I liked him at once. However, since assuming my position as pastor of an emerging city parish, there was now a slight fray in our relationship, one which would unravel even further during the evening.

A half-dozen clergy, drinks in hand, filled the room, engaging in the easy banter of men comfortable among peers, confident of their roles in a select brotherhood. Glancing around at the universal black, I regretted not stopping along the way to change out of a sweater into a collar.

Metzner's young assistant tapped me on the shoulder. "Glad to see you," Don said, brushing back a shock of sandy hair with one hand and handing me an hors-d'oeuvre plate with the other. "Paul's here somewhere, buzzing around like a bee in a jar. You know, All Saints' Day, the traditional dinner, the whole bit. He's so electric we don't need lights. Oh, there's something I should tip you off about. I've had an uneasy sense that since you arrived, Paul has . . ."

Just then, Metzner zipped in to herd us into the dining room. Before long, our dinner conversation was bouncing back and forth along familiar lines. One priest, a ruddy-faced Irishman whom we all knew drank too much, too often, guided us through the appetizer with the details of his coming journey to Hawaii. As chaplain to a travel tour, he would go free, provided he helped enlist enough Catholics to go along.

Meanwhile, Don moved around the table, pouring wine whenever Paul looked toward him, which was often. We exchanged stories and myths from days passed. The room swelled with a mixture of nostalgia and mirth which only those inside the clerical world could appreciate. Suddenly Don's elbow brought me up short. From across the table, Paul was addressing me.

"Of course, you young priests must find all of this talk about the past terribly boring." He cleared his throat and pushed himself toward the edge of his chair. Around the table, scattered conversations halted. Paul obviously had something he wanted to say. I shifted, felt the warmth of the wine draining away.

"Mike thinks the Newman Club ought to be a full-blown parish. We've had only one in town all these years and it's been more than enough. The kids up there ought to stick to building floats for Homecoming and sock hops." He laughed, cleared his throat again. I started to say something about the bishop also desiring a second parish, but Paul rolled on.

"From what I hear, you're replacing individual confession with general absolution. You permit Protestants to take communion. Artificial birth control is a matter of choice." He paused, looking around the table. "Tell me now. Do we really need another parish in town?"

The room took on a stillness as if someone had suddenly turned off the sound track of a film. I was stung, feeling a flush of anger rush through me.

Recognizing the somber mood, Paul tossed a smile across the table. "Come on now, I'm only teasing. Besides, with you in town, people are going to church twice as much. Lots of those who go to your place get confused, what with no kneelers, no pews—and what was it the other day?" He groped for a moment. "Ah yes. Dance. That was it." He looked around the table, confident of support. "Would you believe it, once people finish at this new 'parish' they feel that they haven't been at mass at all, so they come here and go again. Like I said, since Mike's coming to town, mass attendance has doubled."

The Irishman straightened up, tittering while reaching for more wine. Picking up a knife, Paul began dividing a meringue pie. "Hey, I'm just joking. Besides, there's more than enough work in the church to go around for us all."

Someone changed the subject and we managed to get through dinner without further incident. Once outside, I felt like I had just emerged from a suffocating elevator.

Don walked me to the car. "Come on, don't take that crap seriously. It's just that Paul knows a few families from here—some of whom he considers pillars of the parish—have started going to your place. He's used to having his turf and resents anyone who appears to be trespassing. Every time he hears someone quote your sermons, or ask why we aren't offering adult education seminars or giving women leadership positions like Resurrection, he gets antsy. Don't worry, though, he's more smoke than fire. Besides, even though you're a threat, in his own way he likes you."

Paul and I were far different from one another, yet in certain ways, we were the same. Deep down, I felt a bit protective of my turf also; even a twinge of pride at being a pastor so young. Like him, I could be strong-willed and stubborn. Still, for the first time, I had seen a side of him which disturbed me.

The clock on the rectory wall was just tolling midnight when I arrived home—too late to call Joan and say good-bye. Early in the morning, I was scheduled to leave for Montana State Penitentiary.

All Souls afternoon was steely gray. From Highway 10, which crested before descending the two miles into the city of Deer Lodge, I could see the guard towers of the prison. Established in 1871 to house offenders against the peace of the Montana territory, it dominated the landscape. A rugged boulder-packed wall formed a twenty-foot-high, three-foot-thick skin around the penitentiary. Spherical guard towers protruded at each of the four corners of the red-brick cell house.

It was dusk when I pressed the bell at the main gate. A sergeant whose belly drooped over the butt of his pistol emerged from a hut to inspect my credentials. Satisfied, he signaled overhead and a key was lowered by rope from the tower above. We stepped inside and strolled across the courtyard just as a light blinked on and began its methodical arc across the walls.

Later, as the deputy warden led me up the spiral stairs to Gallery 6, where other members of the retreat team would be housed, he asked me about the four-day Cursillo I would help direct.

"Cursillo means 'little course' in Christianity," I said as he took the stairs two at a time.

There would be forty cons making the retreat, and this time the experience would be unique. Five of us from the retreat would live in the cell block itself.

"Ever slept in a cell?" the deputy warden asked as we entered the catwalk.

"Nope. Except in the seminary."

"Can you imagine? Some of these poor bastards have been in the same cell longer than you and I have been alive."

As we moved along the walk, bordered on one side by a rusty iron rail, I recalled a recent news report of a trusty who had committed suicide by hurling himself over the rail onto the concrete deck below.

I stepped into Cell 212. A cubicle housing a narrow metal bunk, sink, and bucketlike commode. A guard at the end of the corridor threw a switch and the door slammed shut with a dull clang.

The sound brought back a buried memory. It was the first week of kindergarten. Not until all the children were gone did I realize Mother had forgotten to pick me up. The school janitor suggested that I walk home. I was afraid to ask him which direction to go. When the heavy door closed behind me, I felt utterly alone.

Alone again, I listened to the life sounds of imprisoned men—a toilet flushed, a harmonica player hit a high note.

A voice from the far side of the cell block blurted out, "Stan? Who's the motherfucker they put in next to you?"

A faceless voice shouted back, "Watch your mouth, asshole. Ain't you got no respect? The guy's not pulling time. He's a free man. Besides, he's a priest, for Chrissake!"

When the lights went out, the cell block took on the blackness of a mine shaft, punctuated only by the lonely arm of a searchlight sweeping across the windows overhead.

The next four days passed in a blur of conferences and liturgy surrounded by the oppressive atmosphere of confinement. But in the waning moments of the day, when night took the prison's bruised lives into its dark belly, I would begin to pray, only to end up thinking of Joan. Whereas I normally dismissed or denied such intrusion, the intense surroundings brought her sharply into focus. Though the church cautioned against the problem of Eve, I had seen too many priests caged in a terrible isolation. I leaned back in my bunk, unwilling to resist all thought of her. We could remain friends. Why not?

It was late when I tapped on her door. Since leaving the prison a few hours earlier, I still felt the haze of cigarette smoke biting at my eyes. The smell of sweat, of khaki and anxious men, still stung my nostrils. A tinge of exhaustion crept over me. Nevertheless, I wanted to see her—needed to. Inside the room the gentle flicker of burning candles against the knotty-pine walls made Gallery 6, Cell 212, seem at once a lifetime away, yet immediately present.

Joan pressed at her hair, wet from the shower. She poured tea as I spilled out the emotions of the week, filtered through a sieve of stories which in their telling brought to mind again what an extraordinary life the priesthood offered.

Where else would I witness a con boss publicly pleading for forgiveness from his peers and in their absolution catch a glimpse perhaps of the elusive face of God? Where but in the life now mine would I encounter the "cannibal killer" in his moment of grace? Who, seething with an undefined intensity, withdrew a voodoo doll from beneath his shirt only to hurl it against a wall directly behind me, where it exploded into a mass of debris, and in so doing, managed to shatter his cult of rage. In what other life would I recognize my own humanity, yet in raising a hand of compassion over others, reach for a world beyond ours?

In the soft light, Joan's eyes widened, filled with tales of steel bars, nightsticks, and broken men.

"Well, thank God you're out of there," she said, her voice cracking. "You know what struck me while you were talking? Just how much you love it."

"It?"

"The priesthood. I see it in you all the time. You know what? I think you love being a priest more than you know. It's not just a job with you. It's who you are and it shows."

She leaned back against a sofa pillow, her voice softer. "To tell the truth, I'm glad you're a priest. Happy not only for myself and the people around you, but most of all for you."

While I needed to hear it, in another way, I didn't. Perhaps I enjoyed her too much. A thought I at once denied. A denial made necessary by the priesthood we both knew held such sway. Noting that the candles were about to burn out, I apologized for cutting her short, then said good night.

Once alone, I continued to picture Joan, her damp hair, the smell of fresh soap. Eventually I found myself staring at the words of the Apostle Paul etched on a plaque above my bed, a gift at ordination.

"I thank Christ Jesus our Lord . . . who judged me faithful enough to call me into his service."

Slamming shut the rectory's bedroom door, I waited for the clang of steel which never came. The ensuing darkness was punctuated by the memory of searchlights sweeping across cell blocks, casting shadows like spiders' legs, as I fell asleep with a voice from a distant world still ringing in my ears.

"He's not pulling time. He's a free man."

The earth tilted away from the sun toward December.

The parish center's recreation room was a maze of snow boots, cider cups, and wall-to-wall people. On the verge of Christmas, we had just completed a discussion of the Apostle Luke's infancy narrative and the role of a most unlikely woman, invited to chase a star and say yes to the birth of God.

In the course of the evening, I found myself repeatedly drawn to Joan, as though seeing her in focus for the first time. From across the room I could sense her softness and fresh innocence. The session wound down to the wistful words of John Lennon "When I find myself in times of trouble/Mother Mary comes to me/speaking words of wisdom/'Let it be.' "

Normally I would have fought off the gentle flow of feelings swelling within me. This time, I let them be.

A soft snow continued to fall. When Joan fastened her coat and started out the door, I tapped her shoulder.

"It's gorgeous out there. I'll walk you home."

Outside, a muffled stillness gave the impression that we were alone in the world but for the blinking Christmas trees. As we passed beneath a towering blue spruce, a branch touched by one too many snowflakes sagged, spilling a mini-avalanche over us.

"Martin Luther probably pushed that branch," I teased. "He thought of the world as barren except for the love of God which he compared to fresh-fallen snow."

Scooping up a gloveful of powder, Joan tossed it at me. "Here's a bit of love, then."

Children again, we pelted one another with snowballs. Running, she slipped, falling into a drift, her laughter a frosty mist. I lifted her up. We stood beneath the streetlight like two figures within a crystal paperweight, her eyelashes shimmering as if with dew. Reaching to brush away the moisture, I suddenly felt the warmth of her lips against mine. Ours was no longer a children's game.

We walked again. The silence shattered only by the voices of guilt pounding within me. Why had I been so foolish? So damned presumptuous? She had trusted me, allowed me to come close, and I had wasted it. My feelings raged. What would she think? I was a Catholic priest, taking advantage of her trust. I wouldn't blame her if she never spoke to me again.

Then again, I had to admit that holding her was natural and honest; in ways, so right. I was happy at the thought. Still, it had happened too fast. Our lives seemed much like a phonograph record, its needle jarred abruptly, forcing the movement away from an easy melody. Prepared to apologize, I braced myself.

Stepping onto the porch, Joan unlocked her door, turning with a sparkle in her eyes.

"Don't look so guilty," she said, clasping my hand. "I was thinking about those parachuting flakes . . . at once the same and so unique. Much like love." She inched forward and lightly touched her lips against mine before opening the door and stepping inside.

Back home, I flung myself onto the bed. A rush of anger scorched through me. Anger at myself, for I knew well the fate of other priests and women who dared to reach for Catholicism's forbidden fruit. Once it had been so easy to treat the issues surrounding celibacy from a distance. Such fruit might turn bitter in the mouths of other priests— not mine. They might make the error of falling in love; not me. It had all been so simple before her kiss—when the world was black and white, now suddenly blood-red. Just before sleep pulled me down into its troublesome corridor, I resolved to get hold of myself and chalk the whole episode up to a naïve mistake which wouldn't happen again.

Throughout the following weeks, I pretended that Luther's snow had not fallen over our lives. I no longer joined Joan after the evening mass. My conversations with her were guarded, strained, as if by resorting to an act of sheer will, an impregnable fence could be strung between us. Still, her face leaped into my consciousness throughout the days, stared back at me from my dreams. Just before Christmas, the carefully constructed wall between us cracked, then crumbled altogether.

When she answered the phone, it was clear that Joan had been asleep. "It's nearly midnight," she said with a trace of concern. "Is something the matter?"

"We have to talk."

She agreed to put on some tea.

Like an actor with rote lines, my speech was set. I would admit to strong feelings for her; natural enough. After all, priests weren't disembodied spirits. Still, my indiscretion probably embarrassed, even shocked her. If so, an apology was in order. Well, things were under control now. End of speech.

Joan opened the door, brushing back a strand of hair which spilled across her wine-red robe. She asked for my jacket. I declined.

"I'll only be here a second." My voice was empty. She noticed.

"Hey, it's okay. I don't like seeing this bother you so much." She leaned back against the knotty-pine wall.

"You know what? When you called, I decided there's something I've just got to say." A soft smile spread across her face.

"I just don't believe God gives us lovable people in our lives and then asks us not to love them. So . . . it's time you know just how much I love you." She looked down at the lush green carpet, then back up, moving closer. "There. I said it, by darn. Know what else? It felt pretty good!"

Despite myself, it felt pretty good to hear, too.

Reaching up, she brushed a fingertip across my cheek. "I love you as a man, but also as a priest. Trouble is, I don't want to hurt either one."

All resolve slackened as knots began to unravel about my soul. "Oh, but I needed to hear that."

As if reaching across a vast chasm, grasping hold lest we both tumble into the abyss, she came, featherlight, into my arms. "I love you, too. Why has it taken so long to admit it?" I asked.

I kissed her forehead, the tip of her nose, gently touching her trembling lips. Stepping out the door, I eased it closed between us. From that moment on, both of us were all too aware that wherever we were, it was where we had to be, yet dared not to be.

The next morning, Joan flew east for Christmas, leaving me to wrestle with Jacob's God. Twin phantoms of euphoria and rage visited me throughout the days into the nights. In darker moments I tumbled into a cloudy rage at the sudden weight of mandatory celibacy. Faced with the shattering love of a woman, the discipline seemingly inviting its victims to die. Was it right to spurn the Joans of this world in the name of one to come? It sounded so unfair. In any event, all attempts to push aside my feelings for her failed. But what to do, where to turn? The church would stand firm, if need be ruthlessly, against the magic of man and woman. That is, if that man happened to be a priest. The alternatives were clear. Shape up or ship out. If pushed to the latter, the stained priest sneaked away or departed the ministry in ridicule. Parishioners would be informed of the scandal of still another abandoning his call.

In less volatile moments, when I was able to pull myself into a more objective state of mind, the problem was no less oppressive. Now that we had faced up to what had been lying dormant between us all along, it was time to admit the mistake and sever our relationship. Yet the most profound segments of our personal experience seemed to call us to accept the gift of love. After all, it was the central message of the gospel of Jesus. To flee from each other would be a violation of all that was true. Yet any thought of leaving the priesthood was inconceivable. Where did it leave us? What was the meaning of a love fated to wander along the dark edges of life? My wrestling continued.

Christmas Eve—the auditorium was dark but for a pale blue light spreading translucently over the congregation.

"Joseph listened to the message of his dream. For all outer appearances, he should've walked away from her, but in that deepest part of himself, which he didn't fully understand, he believed that nothing was impossible. So he took the risk, made a choice, chased a star to a stable, and there discovered his God."

As I continued with the homily, the words came from somewhere beyond me. "His story is our story. We're invited to move beyond the secure, the fixed—chasing the Bethlehem star—taking a chance on love and permitting the birth of God. What is our Bethlehem? Where is our star? Is the impossible, possible? For each of us, a different answer. For all of us, the same invitation . . ."

During the elevation of the Eucharist my own words slapped me in the face as once again a stir of free-floating anxiety wrapped me in its fine web. Although the star seemed to beckon, I desperately needed to understand which road led to Bethlehem, and decided to get some help.

Our planes might have crossed in the air. As Joan's touched down in Bozeman, my Northwest flight taxied to the ramp at O'Hare Airport.

Chicago carried with it fond memories, primarily because of the corduroy-clad, auburn-haired figure who scurried across the lobby toward me. Since working with Bob Upshaw years before on the city's South

Side, I had struck up an immediate, now rich, friendship with him. A member of the Dominican Order, he was rumored to be a likely choice of his peers as provincial of a ten-state region. It was because of this ruggedly handsome priest that the depth of the gospel had first confronted me. He wrapped me in a bear hug while I feared, yet prayed, he would confront me again.

For the better part of the day, I poured out the story. Throughout, Bob never questioned the reality of our love. Indeed, he seemed to delight in it. Not until our final hours together while strolling along the lakeshore did he offer the counsel I had traveled so far to hear.

A blistering wind stirred up whitecaps, splashing a cold spray over us. Upshaw tugged at his collar, drawing it higher.

"You've made the one mistake the institutional church won't tolerate—you've fallen in love. Oh sure," he said, frustratedly slapping a hand against his thigh, "too often you can be a tyrant, a drunk, a do-nothing. Hell, in some places you can be an active gay and they'll look the other way. However, for a priest, the love of a woman is anathema. It shouldn't be like this, but it is."

Reaching down, he found a stone, skipping it across the lake.

"I don't know what to say, and yet I think we both know something has to be said. Yeah, you're in love. Joan sounds wonderful. I don't doubt it one moment, nor that she loves you, too. But that's not the question."

My emotions settled into a slow quiver.

"Well then, what is?"

"You know as well as I do," he said, flashing a quick smile.

The blood flushed against my temples.

"You're talking about the priesthood."

He nodded.

"I suspect you're a good priest. Ever since we first met—when you were still in the seminary—it's all you've talked about."

While I wanted to focus on Joan, defend our love, plead for its validity, Bob turned the tables. As the moments passed, he continued to press in on me. When I surrendered my own agenda and started spilling out my feelings about being drawn to ordination early in life and about the growing certitude it was the only path for me, he reached over, gently placing an arm about my shoulder.

"That's in the past. What I'm interested in is the present. Okay? You've never said, at least to me, what the priesthood actually means to you." He paused as the wind gusted, swirling a trace of snow along the walkway, and added soberly, "You know . . . deep inside."

We walked on in a comfortable silence, waving to an old man on a park bench flipping breadcrumbs to a couple of puffed-up pigeons. In the distance behind him, the expressway was coming to life with the evening rush.

"Well," I said finally, picking words out of the air, "I've never felt drawn to the world of pinstripe suits, two-car garages, and martinis before lunch. It's not enough. Measuring success by what's in a bank account seems like so much fluff. What I do now allows me to be part of people's lives. Ah . . . the counseling . . . helping them out when they need it . . . means a lot. You know, just being there for people, in whatever way."

"You sound like a social worker," he prodded. "There's got to be more."

"Well, sure, but it's hard to put into words."

"Try just one. First thing that comes to mind."

"Freedom," I said, half under my breath.

"Freedom?"

"Yeah, helping people see that being Christian isn't all about sin and guilt but about life. Freeing them from worrying about going to hell, about being sinners . . . just because they aren't perfect . . . because they're human. You know, maybe they practice birth control or their marriage fell on its face or they simply happen to be women in a masculine church. Whatever. They can still respect themselves . . . God does."

"Go on," Upshaw said, kicking back a small ball which had rolled away from a group of kids playing along the walkway.

"Hopefully, this doesn't all sound like I'm reading a script off the back of a holy card," I responded, smiling for the first time since the airport.

"It doesn't."

"It's just that so many people seem to see being part of the church as a burden, whereas the gospel is all about being set free. To love life and themselves. It's not about damnation but heaven. Not how bad, but how good they are. That they're worth something."

"More precious than many sparrows," he added. "And being a priest gives you the chance to say what you think?"

"No," I replied, struggling for words to wrap around the feelings within me. "Not what I think, but what the gospel says."

Once again we slipped into an envelope of silence that lasted for

several blocks. I thought of Grandpa and falling stars. Of Jamie Fitzgerald, our initials scratched on a rotting shed wall. Of wanting to live
out a life which somehow contained within itself the seeds of another.

"Bob?"

"Uh-huh."

"I'm still finding out what being a priest means to me, but maybe
I can touch upon it by saying what it's not. It's got precious little to
do with the robes . . . the collar. Although I must admit it feels good
to be looked up to. To have people all astir when 'Father' is around.
You know, to be somebody. But that part wears thin pretty fast," I
said, unsure where the train of thought now spilling out was going
next. "Do you ever feel driven sometimes? Somehow the thing starts
to get in one's bones."

"What thing?"

"The gospel. Being a priest for me is tied in with talking about,
teaching about, the gospel. Maybe that sounds corny, but . . ."

Upshaw shook his head, waving off any such suggestion.

"Well, when I preach on Sunday, it's like there's a hunger out
there . . . not for what being a member of the big, institutional thing
we think of as the church . . . but for what it means to be Christian.
For the nitty-gritty of what the Catholic faith is all about." I looked
back over my shoulder, far down the lakeshore where the old man was
probably still feeding the pigeons. "No matter what the setting . . .
Sunday mass, discussion groups, one-on-one . . . whenever I tell the
gospel story and try to unravel its meaning, it's like people are as
hungry for it as those pigeons were back there for bread."

"So you identify being a priest with sharing the gospel?" Bob
responded, zipping up his jacket and waiting for me to go on.

"Yeah. It sounds so obvious when you say it. I'm not talking about
using the *Baltimore Catechism* as a yardstick, or jumping through all
the hoops associated with being Catholic. Not to make light of all that,
but somehow the ministry has something to do with stripping all those
layers away and getting to the heart of a faith folks lived and died for
all these centuries."

I stopped, looking out across the lake toward a buoy bobbing up
and down, its rhythm keeping time with my own.

"There's more?" Upshaw asked.

"I just don't want to sound so bloody pious," I said, hesitating.

"Ah, don't you wish! Look, Michael my friend, you are so far
from being pious it's an embarrassment to me . . . the church . . .

your friends,'' Upshaw teased again, pushing me ahead of him. In our years together we had laughed often. It felt good to do so now. I changed the subject, recalled earlier times, and in their memory we gave vent to an uninhibited joy. Before long, Upshaw pulled us back into the present.

"So you don't want to sound like a Jesus freak, but there's more?"

"Yeah. Sure. It's so easy to act like we've got God on the shelf and all we have to do is pull Him down whenever we need to do our priest thing. There's magic but no mystery. Nothing more to learn. Once ordained, we're home free and it's just a matter of saving everybody else. And there's more yet! It's so easy to forget about Jesus himself. So convenient to keep him locked up in a tabernacle or off in his heaven somewhere. But to believe in a person, not just a memory, who is alive and who wants me to come alive, too? Well, that's something else altogether."

Grabbing Upshaw by the jacket, I drew him up short. Behind the lenses, his eyes were as gray, as alive as the waters alongside us.

"What I'm trying to say is so obvious, yet for some reason took so long to get out. Being a priest has everything to do with Christ. I have fewer answers today than when first ordained . . . Hell, far more questions. But it all boils down to him, and letting part of his life into my own and maybe into others, too. I'm talking about here and now, not some distant far-off time beyond the clouds."

I had started to tremble, unsure whether it was the evening chill or my insides. Bob just kept looking at me, then let out a long, slow sigh.

"Okay, enough said. There's a lot I'm uncertain of, too, Mike, but one thing is clear—no matter how you put it or what words you use, it all boils down to the priesthood being your life. It's not just a job. From what you've said, Joan understands that, too. I'm afraid if you were to leave, you would be running away from who you are."

The mood shifted. Behind him the clouds hung leaden over the lake. Suddenly uneasy, I wanted to shout, "Out with it! Come on, what are you saying?" But I knew full well what it was.

Removing his glasses, wiping away droplets of spray clinging to his heavy eyebrows, Upshaw faced me dead on. Never had I seen him look at once so hesitant and yet so sure.

"Ideally you could marry and keep on with your work. But that's not the real world of the church we live with. You've got to accept the facts and, well frankly, not be so damn naïve. Mike, if you leave the priesthood to marry, it could destroy you. If you want to remain a priest—and it's clear you do—there is only one way to go. You've got to say good-bye to Joan. Never see her again, starting today. If you look for an easier way out of this, a more piecemeal approach, you'll only get more involved and ultimately there'll be no turning back. You'll end up bailing out of the priesthood just like all the others."

The distant lights of the Sears Tower twinkled on, its windows like so many cats' eyes on the horizon. Alarmed, I started to protest, my words carrying on the breeze into the city, to whoever would listen.

"Cold turkey! You're asking us to reach for stones, not bread. What the hell! Peter was married; so, too, most of the apostles. Abandon Joan? For whom? The pope? You talk about love as if it can be set aside like a worn toy. The church is just great! They told us at the Council to become more human, to become all that we can be. Then when we fall in love, an uninvited stranger, waiting in the wings until the last moment, drags out a script of imposed celibacy, spewing his lethal lines from a dead era. Forget it!"

Bob reached over, placing his hand on my arm. Blinking back the tears, I brushed it away.

"Didn't Jesus call God love? Didn't he have one commandment above all others? He'd never have survived the system. What is Rome so uptight about? It's got something to do with keeping women at a distance and in their place. If they marry a priest, next thing you know, they'll want to be one! I can't believe you'd suggest it, you know, cold turkey! Whose side are you on anyway?"

Despite my frustration, I knew he was right. Leaving the priesthood would most likely destroy me and ultimately her. Though severing all connection with Joan would be like taking a knife to both of us, there was really only one choice.

The following morning, after apologizing to Bob for my outburst, I called Joan from the airport. It would not be necessary to meet the plane. No, we would not have dinner together. On the end of the line her voice was flat, followed by a long silence. Choking up, I whispered I loved her but could never see her again. Before she could respond, I hung up.

The retreat from love was agonizing. As I waded through the days, there was no escaping the vacuum left by Joan's absence. Depression crept over me as on cat's paws. No longer would I look out from behind the altar and find her eyes; no longer journey through a day in anticipation of her presence; no longer carry within me a sense of wholeness. Still, it was the nights—feeling guilty at leaving her alone, wondering whether she had been sucked under by the whirlpool of feelings that swirled within me—which hurt the most. Work was hollow. I sought escape in books, only to find her between each page. Time and again, I turned to prayer, only to come up with a dry well. Through it all the phone sat quietly upon the desk. I came to detest it. Where once its ring announced Joan, its silence mocked me. Hating and fearing it, I longed for it to ring.

The moments of stillness before dawn were less ulcerous than the nights. In the buffer zone between darkness and light I repeatedly turned to the gospel for the comfort that eluded me—until a frigid Tuesday in February.

Through frosted windows, the streetlights switched off one by one.

Fumbling through the pages of the New Testament, I settled half-heartedly upon the First Letter of John.

"This is the message as you heard it from the beginning: that we are to love one another; . . . our love is not to be just words or mere talk, but something real . . ."

Across the street a milk truck stopped, the driver scurrying up to the porch with his delivery. I thought of the family inside the house.

"God is love and . . . anyone who lives in love lives in God, and God lives in him."

In that fractured moment, with night evaporating into day, the words leaped out and the darkness within me began to fade. How could I, in the name of ministry, avoid the gospel itself? Dare stand before the congregation Sunday after Sunday, speaking of a God who promises to come whenever we love one another while at the same time spurning love itself? Why was what I preached to others so wrong for Joan and me? Why did the choice between priesthood and being human have to be so ultimate? Where in such a scenario was the promise that sprang from the lips of the resurrected Christ? "I am Alpha and Omega, the First and the Last. Behold, I make all things new!"

I descended the stairs and put on the coffee, for the first time in weeks, anxious for the day to begin.

After Joan's first-period class, a few students remained behind chatting with her. Unaware of me, she swept up a bundle of papers, starting down the hallway. "Joan?" Halting, she didn't turn.

"Please, we've got to talk," I stammered. She rushed down the hallway, zigzagging through a maze of students toward her office, along the way dropping a few of the papers. I picked them up, feeling the moisture of teardrops, and raced after her. She slammed the door.

"Joan? Please."

I knocked. Silence. Whatever I expected, it wasn't this. I knocked again. Nothing. Deflated, I turned away as the door opened.

She had lost weight; her eyes were bloodshot. We entered the office and fell into each other's arms. Her body shivered, quieted, then shook again.

"Oh, Lord, but I've missed you. Longed to see you but so afraid to," she whispered. Releasing me, she stepped back, her hands still on my shoulders.

"I know you need to be a priest, but I can't help loving you."

The dam within me, which began to crack with the dawn sky, now fractured even more.

"I'm not sure of very much anymore," I replied, "but staying away from you just isn't in the cards. To kill our love can't be right. If that's the price of a divine blessing, then God can't have much of a heart."

She reached up, placed a finger against my lips.

"Shh . . . come on now. It's not God's fault. It's the times and that vow you took!"

"Not a vow, a promise!" I erupted. "One makes vows to God. One makes promises to the church. Priests promise to observe the law of celibacy. Man's law, not God's. Maybe it's splitting hairs, but there's a difference. It's just that I'm tired of hearing about all these priests breaking their vows. That's so much garbage!"

Joan moved away, staring blankly out the window, then gave a slow sigh. "I'm sorry. So it's the law, a promise, whatever. It amounts to the same thing. We're stuck." She spun around. "You're a good priest. We can't let what's happening take you away from it. These past weeks have been awful. Oh, but I needed to hear you. Touch you. Be held." She paused, as if to shake off her words. "Sometimes I wish we'd never met."

Despite a lump settling in my throat, I tried to convince her that after all, she had a life to live. There were other men. Someday, marriage; a home and family. Celibacy hadn't been part of her package, why then should it now be her cross?

"Listen to me, Michael. I'm not interested in anyone else. It's you I love, but don't know how to live it out, or where it'll all end."

"Catch twenty-two! I can't leave the priesthood, but to lose you is to die inside . . ."

"We'll take it a day at a time," she said, coming over and laying her cheek against my shoulder.

"You mean it?"

"Only if you're willing."

I nodded; her cheek felt hot, flushed.

"But we'll need some help from above . . . or wherever. If God really is love, then it's in the bag."

"No more cold turkey?"

"No more. A day at a time," I muttered, wondering where such a calendar could possibly lead. "But how long can you hang in there?"

She laughed, barely. "Hey, mister, I'm in this all the way. For the duration, if you are."

I was, though still fearful for her. We stood there holding one another without another word.

Choices constitute the fabric of our lives. In choosing not to abandon each other, we chose at the same time to live a hyphenated existence. To avoid rumors, especially among the city's Catholics, we took measures not to draw attention to ourselves. The irony of concealing love from Christians did not escape us. Still, the potential for gossip was real, and if we were to prevent the horse of controversy from bolting out of the barn, we had to be careful.

Whereas once we might have strolled freely together, now discretion smothered spontaneity. In a more innocent time, we might have gravitated toward one another, now caution kept us at a distance publicly. To the casual observer, we appeared no more than mere acquaintances, if that. Such pretense was not without its own price, and in subtle ways made a victim of the very relationship we sought to protect.

The accidents of geography have more than once tipped the scales of history, influenced the course of nations. The accidents of each individual's particular time and place likewise carry in their wake significant consequences.

Were it not for the good fortune that Joan's home sat back from the street, away from all but the most persistent observer, we would not have found a haven, or endured our otherwise goldfish-bowl existence. There, in her small cottage, nestled behind a row of apple trees, we discovered a freedom that provided the tape that held the passing months together.

Coping with intimacy in our own personal lives proved nearly as difficult as dealing with the outside world. While the need to conceal affection drove us underground, such efforts in turn caused the surprising strength of our desire to express that same affection to each other to surface. Before long, we both knew we had to draw a line which we would not cross. Examining our confusing, occasionally contradictory reasons for doing so was like peeling back the skin of fresh fruit only to discover yet another layer. Any notion of intimate sexual involvement had been and would remain decidedly out of bounds to each of us. For my part, I had little stomach for toying with her life. What if, in a worst-case scenario, we were forced someday to sever our bonds? The prospect then of cutting Joan loose, leaving her bruised and used while returning to the comfort of my clerical nest, was repugnant. However, despite such exercises in moral gymnastics, in the end our choice emerged not so much from any notion of sin as from what for us constituted the truth. So long as we were stuck with celibacy, neither of us was willing to live a lie. Nor were we willing to set up the possibility that the bony finger of righteousness might someday be pointed in our direction, accusing us of sleeping with falsehood all along. Though there was no guarantee that such conviction would win out over the sometimes volcanic nature of passion, the line was drawn. A barbed wire against the nakedness of our own humanity.

For her part, Joan embraced the priesthood I clung to; whether assisting me with an accelerating load of counseling, helping out with frequent retreats, or serving as a speaker for adult education programs, she was always there. However, it was in the vital area of composing the themes and in the actual celebration of liturgy that our talents and interests seemed to jell. Before long, Joan was invited by Resurrection's newly elected parish council to oversee the music, decor, and audio-visuals for all Sunday masses. But her most significant contribution proved to be with Sunday homilies.

Routinely we read and discussed the Scriptures together before each weekend, Joan coaxing me throughout to relate the message to everyday life. Following each mass, she was my most persistent critic. Through the use of stories or relating personal experience, the sermons seemed to take on a more human texture. The results were undeniable as my preaching and entire approach to ministry took on a more down-to-earth, compassionate style.

Despite our hyphenated existence, it did provide a degree of predictability; that is, until the bishop called.

"Vance Mudd is on the verge of leaving the priesthood, but he's willing to give it one last shot. He asked to be with you. He knows you're short-handed, and right now he needs to be needed. He'll be there mid-March."

There was no choice but to accept the bishop's decision. Not until I placed the phone down did its full impact catch up with me.

"Dammit to hell, why now, of all times?" I thought, kicking the wastebasket across the floor. Trying to keep our balance on the slippery deck was awkward enough. Now the slight privacy Joan and I enjoyed was certain to be forfeited.

Then a flush of guilt. After all, we were classmates. Friends! Vance was hurting, as revealed on the night we sat before a blazing fire sipping Scotch while he spilled out the suffocating loneliness. Relying at first on the "brotherhood of priests," he expected it would pass. I could still see him angrily stirring the fire.

"Brotherhood? What a joke. Too many of them aren't close to anyone. Not as close as they are to their cars, their TVs. Then again, maybe I've got B. O." His attempted smile fell over his lower lip like a dead weight. "I don't mean to sound bitter. Maybe it's just that lots of priests have been living alone so long they don't know how to let another person get in. There are exceptions, but God, it terrifies me to think I'm headed in the same direction."

Before I could respond, he pulled a shade over his despondency. "Oh, what the hell. Let's forget it. Who cares anyway?"

Now the crisis had caught up with him. With us. He was reaching out and I was finding it an imposition; another ingredient hurled into the simmering stew of my own life. That evening, ashamed of my feelings, I wrote and told him he would be welcomed with open arms. Deep down, I didn't mean a word of it.

The instant Vance arrived, my resentment dissolved. I was stunned to find a skeleton of the man who had gone off to graduate school less than a year before. The juices of life were all but drained from his skin, milked down to the roots of his wiry black hair. Fixed behind protruding cheekbones, his eyes telegraphed a festering torment. In the days and weeks ahead, our conversations lanced the boil, spilling out a struggle he no longer concealed. So that our efforts might focus on his groping toward decision, I referred to Joan only as a friend. However, as time wore on, it became obvious that any attempt to conceal our love would erode my natural rapport with Vance. Besides, he had to have noticed I felt something far more than friendship for her.

Shortly after Easter, the opportunity to say something arrived. It was one of those afternoons when summer, attempting to push spring aside, sweeps the world with a magnificent wind. On impulse, Vance put together a yellow kite, fastened on it a slender tail of ribbon and rags and the two of us raced out to a vacant field, there to play with the mythological "Gods of the Air."

Ankle-deep in clover, squinting into the sun, Vance toyed with the twine as the kite lunged toward puffy clouds overhead. In the past weeks, he had eased up, no longer compelled to crawl within himself and close the shutters. With laughter drifting back into his soul, the pasty pallor had almost vanished from his complexion.

I hesitated, the kite dancing directly above us. "Vance, I need to say something."

"So speak, Zarathustra," he said in his distinctive, booming baritone.

"Well, there's really not much to say; then again, a lot. It's about Joan."

Unraveling the twine, he sent its protesting captive into a lazy arc. "She's a doll, really she is. I can't imagine why some guy at the university hasn't snatched her up."

"Someone has." I swallowed. "We've been in love for more than a year now. I've . . . well . . . wanted to tell you about it, but didn't know how."

He kept peering at the kite, drawing it in and out with a mesmerizing motion.

"You know, I had a hunch there was something special between you two. Oh man. You have no idea how I prayed it was true. Mike, I'm happy. For both of you." Turning with a face at once sad and touched with delight, he added, "You're one of the lucky ones, fella. Truly."

Much as the clouds overhead were thrust along by a jet stream, his immediate acceptance pushed me forward. Confessing my desire to remain a priest, I catalogued the choices we'd made and our decision to hold fast to one another. Throughout my apology, he sat quietly, eyes fixed on the floating yellow diamond.

"Anything I can do to be supportive, just let me know."

"You've just done it."

He frowned. "My only concern is that you will put Joan second to your work. We clergy are fairly ego-centered and you're a bit compulsive to boot. They drilled that thing of Saint Paul's into us pretty well—about being all things to all people. Well, no one of us can be." He paused, a familiar sadness behind his words. "Not most of us, at least. Anyway, just don't end up neglecting your own lives and wasting love."

I started to agree, but he swept my comments aside.

"Maybe you understand, but I'm not so sure. I've known you for a long time and what I'm trying to say is . . ."

Just then a gust of wind tasting of damp clover tore at the kite, snapping it from his grasp. Within seconds, nothing was left but a distant speck drifting off and away. We started to laugh as in an earlier, more certain time.

"What I'm trying to say is—life is short, amigo. For what it's worth, fly your kite while you still can."

From that moment on, I knew we would do so; that riding the winds free—at least in Vance's presence—would be good for us and also for him.

As the buds of spring unfolded into summer, so, too, did our lives. The mushrooming needs of the parish dissipated somewhat as the university recessed and the city embarked on the annual ritual of un-packing hiking boots and sleeping bags. Still indecisive about his future, Vance headed west to be with his family. For Joan and me, the summer provided a gift of time we came to cherish.

By July, we quickly fell into a pattern. Each morning, after an early morning rendezvous on Joan's patio, I set out into another day of counseling, marriage preparation, and hospital calls. Returning at dusk, we celebrated mass in the seclusion of her living room, followed by dinner and my departure for the rectory. The certitude of our routine, tranquilizing. Her presence throughout lending luster to its moments.

They were champagne days, though at times our hidden love was suffocating. Whenever we felt the walls were closing in, we escaped the city, usually for a hike in the woods. Whether descending a trail into the Yellowstone or scaling a rock face in the Hyalite Range, our excursions touched upon a sense of the primal, provided a way for us to breathe free—well, not always.

In July 1806, William Clark's party separated from that of Meri-
wether Lewis and set up camp where the Madison, Gallatin, and
Jefferson rivers converged. They called the site, which formed the
headwaters of the Missouri, Three Forks. Proceeding overland through
a lush valley destined to become the home of Bozeman, they arrived
at the base of a wall of mountains. There, a young Shoshone woman,
still with papoose, pointed out a pass through its rugged peaks, enabling
them to continue their journey eastward.

The climb from Fairy Lake took us three hours. By the time we
reached Sacajawea's Peak, the rays of an August sun spread over the
entire valley far below. To the west, beyond Three Forks, stretched
the Tobacco Root Mountains; behind us, to the east, towered the
Crazies. Perched on a rock shelf, uncapping a bottle of wine, we shared
a lunch of brown bread, cheese, and apples.

"I wonder what Adam and Eve felt like," Joan said, the bandanna
about her neck whipping lazily in the warm wind. "I feel like we're
the only people in the world right now." She sliced another piece of
apple, handing it to me. "Hey, you don't think of me as the temptress,
do you?"

I couldn't tell if she was serious or joking. "What you offer isn't
forbidden fruit, at least not by the God I believe in."

"I know, only sometimes I worry about you; about where this will
take you if . . ." She stopped. I leaned over and kissed her as she
stretched out on the rock shelf, her head cradled in my lap, gazing
into the perfectly cloudless sky.

"Come on now. We'll find a way," I said, just as her eyes fluttered
and closed.

My thoughts drifted down the mountain toward a plateau in the
distance. It was there that Sacajawea reportedly stood with Clark to
point a pathway through the massive range. According to legend, she
motioned toward the peak we now rested upon, advising that if they
proceeded directly toward it, they would come across a rutted buffalo
trail leading to the wild, often perilous Yellowstone River. What seemed
improbable was not. They did, indeed, find a way.

Next to me, Joan was still but for the easy undulation of her breasts.
Held there in the breath of sleep, she seemed vulnerable, somehow
tamed. Where, I wondered, would it all lead her? Wherever it was,
in that instant I felt as never before a responsibility for this woman
now tamed by love.

As afternoon shadows slithered upward along Sacajawea's spine,

I woke her and we began our descent, leaving the serene isolation behind.

The footpath encircling Fairy Lake converged with a logging road. When the Jeep appeared, we waved, stepping aside to allow the two men to pass, just as one of them shouted, "Mike, hey, Mike!" They stopped, backing toward us.

I released her hand, mumbling to Joan, "Dammit. We can't go anywhere," angry at myself for how cautious and protective of our relationship I had become.

"For Pete's sake. No one's going to raise an eyebrow seeing us on a hike," she said, and started toward the Jeep just as I recognized the driver.

"Why," I thought, "if we have to run into someone in the middle of nowhere, does it have to be a priest!" Then again, if it had to be, Ernie Stenzel was at the top of my list.

We exchanged small talk, and when Ernie introduced his friend, I reciprocated with something innocuous about Joan, nothing more. Moments later they were on their way when suddenly the Jeep lurched to a stop and Ernie called out to me. I trotted up the road, to find him leaning from the cab, deadly serious.

"I couldn't help but notice and wouldn't be able to leave here with a clear conscience if I didn't say something."

My nerves quivered.

"Seeing her in those hiking shorts," he said, pointing back toward Joan. "Well, your mother has damn nice legs!" A broad smile spread over his face as the Jeep jumped forward and he was gone.

By the time I reached Joan, the smile from Ernie's face covered my own, his quip darting through the membrane of exaggerated caution which threatened to envelop us. While we had to be careful, we didn't need to be paranoid. Besides, I thought, as Joan wrapped her arms through mine, "Mother" does have nice-looking legs!

Such tender distractions were eclipsed soon enough by the reality of our circumstance. In September, Vance returned along with the usual migration of students converging upon the university. We expanded the mass schedule and kicked off the fall with a series of workshops and retreats. Along with tenure and a promotion, Joan received an additional load of classes and therapy sessions. All too soon, we found ourselves immersed in the schizophrenic world of hidden love and rigid expectations, once again clinging to a papier-mâché raft tossed upon an uncertain sea.

Though our commitment to one another acted as cement against circumstances that might otherwise unglue our lives, it wasn't enough. In the long haul we hungered for something to hope for; a future in which what was closed to us might be open, the impossible, possible. The international Synod of Bishops was about to convene in Rome and give focus to that hope.

The agenda for the nearly two hundred delegates streaming into the Eternal City called for a discussion of the ministerial priesthood, setting the stage for what the world's press predicted would be a protracted debate on the explosive question of clerical celibacy. After all, the crisis sweeping Catholicism was unavoidable. What had once been a trickle of departures among the clergy was now a rising tide. Though Rome refused to release statistics, it was estimated that over fifty thousand priests had left the ministry within the five years following the Second Vatican Council.

Despite Pope Paul VI's steadfast insistence on the maintenance of mandatory celibacy in the encyclical *Sacerdotalis Caelibatus*, the issue refused to go away, surfacing earlier in the year with dramatic impact when the Dutch Pastoral Council broke ranks, serving notice that observance of the discipline should no longer be considered a condition for the priesthood. The Cardinal Archbishop of the Netherlands promised to press hard for his country's position in the Synod.

A major study sponsored by the American bishops themselves discovered that the majority of priests favored a change in the law and expected it within the near future. The same expectations existed in other countries throughout the world. The writing was on the wall. Submitting to public pressure, the pope reluctantly agreed to place the smoldering issue on the Synod's agenda.

On the eve of the Synod, a poll in the United States revealed that the majority of Catholics favored a married priesthood. Consequently, while even the most optimistic observers refused to entertain the possibility that the assembled hierarchy would endorse optional celibacy outright, the signs were there for those of us clinging to the slender threads of hope. Despite myself, I began to daydream about what marriage could mean. Our hassle would be over. We would emerge from underground, basking in the full light of a white-picket-fence world. Joan picked up on my mood, taking it a step further. Change was on the way; just a matter of time.

However, as the proceedings wore on, headlines from Rome were empty of such promise.

Midway through the Synod, *L'Osservatore Romano*, relying upon unnamed sources, suggested that efforts to consider a voluntary celibate priesthood in the Latin Church appeared to have died early in the closed session.

Despite such warnings, Joan's spirit didn't falter. "The bishops aren't blind. They want what's best for the church—they have to. In the end, they won't let the loss of so many good men continue. I just know they won't." In the face of my eroding confidence, she teased, "Come on, Father—where's your faith?"

In the end, cynicism won the day. The much-discussed possibility of marriage for ordained men was, in fact, never seriously considered. By early November the Synod adjourned with an overwhelming majority of the bishops opting to sustain the status quo, issuing a terse statement—"The law of priestly celibacy existing in the Latin Church is to be kept in its entirety."

Paul VI, in his closing remarks, put the genie firmly back in the bottle. "In the Latin Church, there shall continue to be observed, with the help of God, the present discipline . . ." The pope emphasized that all debate on the issue was henceforth considered closed to Roman Catholics.

Joan's vulnerability was partially my fault for suggesting the Vatican assembly might pave the way out of our dilemma. Even more, it was born of an innocent trust of the institution, a confidence woven since childhood into the fabric of her Catholic life. Consequently, she took the Synod's punch head on, convinced thereafter that what might be the most humane and, from her perspective, the best course for the church was not necessarily a factor for those at its highest levels.

The night we heard that the flame of change had flickered out in Rome, Joan had a dream. She lay in a coffin, looking up from an open grave. A black-robed figure, swinging a censer of incense, leered above her before kicking the earth upon her with silken slippers. She started to suffocate, her cries strangled in cakes of clay. The sky went out. She woke screaming, the innocence which cost her so dearly, forever vanquished.

All the while, Vance seemed oblivious to the Synod and our reactions. Since returning from California he had grown increasingly somber and pensive; at times strung as tight as the wires of his beloved piano. His laugh contained a hollow ring, while empty Kaopectate bottles kept tally of the turmoil churning inside him. His assistance in the parish declined in proportion to his energy. My own emotions swung from empathy to a fear which goaded me to flee from him, lest in his wrestling I would recognize my own. Clearly the ice jammed up within him was starting to splinter. Just before Thanksgiving, it shattered.

Turning the Volvo into our driveway, I saw Vance silhouetted against the bay window, swaying back and forth to the muffled sounds of "Zorba the Greek." Catching him at such a naked moment, I felt a flush of embarrassment sweep through me. The music shuddered to a halt. Before he could set the needle down again, I opened the door. Drenched in perspiration, his eyes still holding the dance, he swept across the room to embrace me.

"I talked to the bishop this morning," he said enthusiastically. "Once I actually heard myself tell him I was going to leave, it was easy, and felt so right! I'm sure it hurt him. But he said he would help in any way and he really believed that the Spirit was part of my decision. I called my family this afternoon. They're all supportive . . . it's just that I felt so constricted, so imprisoned. Mike, for the first time in ages, I feel free. I feel myself!"

We celebrated the decision into the early morning hours. Vance wanted to remain a priest, of that he was fairly certain. Yet he found himself caught in a truncated life-style, gradually being destroyed by what he felt were rigidly defined roles and the ever-present specter of celibacy.

He walked the stony road of decision; in the end it came down to the question of remaining and seeing the bonds of his humanity shattered in the process, or getting out. The choice was clear. Within two days, his faded blue Cutlass packed from floor to ceiling with everything from Plato to Chopin, he said good-bye.

Later, alone in the singular insulation of night, I outlined the explanation for Sunday. Resurrection Parish would hear the truth. Vance had not rejected the church, or them, in following the dictates of his heart. He would seek laicization, thereby putting down the duties of a priest and assuming the status of a layman. Those reared with catechetical certitude would remember "Once a priest, always a priest." Nevertheless, he would not be permitted to function as one. Surely someone would ask if he was about to marry. Not at all. Could he? Of course, now that he'd agreed to leave the priesthood.

I gazed blankly into the living room, picturing the shadow of Vance dancing against the walls. His departure, like a delayed shock wave, began jarring loose a reservoir of feelings. Who was I trying to kid anyway? At least, he had the sense to face reality and get out. Who was I to presume to swim upstream, forcing Joan to do the same? Was I wearing blinders, unable to see we were in a no-win situation? Whereas Vance moved on, we remained paralyzed.

A ripple of anger raced through me. "Meanwhile," I thought, "he pats me on the back and drops the whole parish in my lap! How could I have been gullible enough to believe the Synod would act, standing by, permitting Joan to be kicked in the stomach that way?" We were trapped in a circle of iron; there would be no golden key to set us free.

On second thought there was an easier way; at least, one more certain. Why not just pull the plug and get out? Just serve notice to the bishop and bid it all farewell?

Casting a glance out at the driveway where Vance's car had been just hours before, I felt a tightness pressing in upon my chest. Just the suggestion of departing the priesthood left me empty. Then again, with the results of the Synod and the intransigence of the hierarchy, the writing was on the wall.

Abruptly the stillness of the house crashed in upon me. Crumpling the beginnings of the homily into a ball, I hurled it toward Vance's piano resting mutely in the corner; then I wandered over to its vacant stool.

"Dammit, I should cut the cord and be done with it," I thought, fingering a few hollow notes. "After all, the priesthood is all I've known. Maybe there is another life out there somewhere—anywhere."

With Joan's income we would easily survive until I found something. Our options were wide open. My degrees provided access to university teaching. There was always law school. Somewhere I had read that ex-priests were considered excellent prospects by corporations. Best of all, by getting off the merry-go-round we were on, we could wed at once. Neither of us was getting younger, and if we were to have a family with children running around inside a white-picket-fence world, time was running out.

I slammed a fist against the keyboard, spinning around on the stool only to come up against my reflection in a wall mirror. There was a haggardness to the image before me, but something more. Beyond the glaze of blue, deep within the pupils staring back at me, there was a steadiness, a hint of certainty. Mutely I sat there, face to face with myself in an altogether empty room, knowing it was no use. No matter how sound the reasoning, pulling the plug on the priesthood wouldn't do. Once again, I knew that somewhere along the line, something had touched me, seized me. Not only did I want to remain a priest, I needed to. While Vance saw some light and was on his way out, imagining such a course for me brought nothing but blackness. To flee would be like taking a knife and tearing through layers of flesh to pry out a fine pearl, leaving in its place a gaping wound. Vance had done what was right for him; for me, there was simply no way.

Not until moments later, wandering by his empty room, did I notice the card.

Mike and Joan:
    Thank you for helping me to believe again. To laugh again. To remember that I, too, am worth loving. Most especially, thanks for setting me free to be myself. Although your future is uncertain, don't ask any less of yourselves always remembering:
    "The glory of God is the flower that has conquered the rock!"

I read the note again, slipped it between the pages of John's gospel, and flopping back on the bed, slept there fully clothed until morning.

February. While grizzly bear hibernated in their dens, herds of elk, ice clinging to their undersides, migrated down to the foothills in search of stubble buried beneath the crusted snow. A century earlier, a Sioux family, wrapped in a buffalo robe, might have peered from their tepee at a flock of geese knifing through crystallized air above the Yellowstone, mindful that spring was many moons away. Winter always lasted too long under the Big Sky.

Since the Synod in Rome, a winter mood had swept over me, burying my pent-up feelings, which eventually broke through on Valentine's Day.

We were decorating the parish center. Drake Shepler, a graying professor, was struggling to string a scarlet banner proclaiming "See How They Love One Another" above the altar. No sooner had he descended the ladder than the banner tore loose and for a second time slid in a heap to the floor. Exasperated, he crumpled it up, shouting, "Hey, Father, this thing is more trouble than it's worth."

I stood glaring at him, seething inside, before bolting through a doorway into the hall, where I began to shake, confused by what was becoming a pattern of overreaction to trivial matters. I took a deep breath, then another. Settled down.

Over a year had elapsed since Joan's commitment to stay with me. That was before the Synod. The Vatican was not about to bend. Clearly, I thought, it was time to leave fairy tales behind; to break off with Joan and set her free.

That evening on the way home to the rectory, I stopped by to see her. The penetrating heat from a wood stove melted away the winter chill but not my resolve. Each time I sipped the steaming Irish coffee, whipped cream attached itself to my moustache, bringing giggles of delight from Joan and promises that the next trace would have to be kissed away. I was in no mood to play.

"There we were—Valentine's Day, for Pete's sake, and I have to bite my tongue to keep from jumping all over Drake. For nothing, nothing at all!" I backed closer to the stove. "Ever since the Synod, I'm not handling things well. I'm on pins and needles half the time. Our lives are as frozen as the ground outside. It's not fair, especially to you."

Waiting, Joan leaned forward, wrapping her arms about her knees. A log popped like a rifle shot.

"I'm so bloody jumpy lately. It's all because of us. This thing has been dragging on for almost two years. It was one thing to ask you to wait on the bishops. On Paul the Sixth. Talk about leading you on with a carrot of hope! I should have known better than to rely on people like Cardinal Krol, or McIntyre. And the Italians in the Curia! Well, now there's no excuse. Even the carrot is gone!"

I was on an emotional roller coaster, pacing back and forth like a drill sergeant before a raw recruit. "You're a beautiful woman and there are men out there who would be damn lucky to run into you. You could get married. Have a family. Live a normal life."

Joan pulled her knees up against her chest. "Look at you," I protested. "This mess is like taking a razor to your veins and watching your life dribble away drop by drop. Being stuck with me is a dead end. Not all our talk about a changing church, about dreams coming true, is worth a hill of beans. That may be how it comes out in the movies, but in the real world, no way!"

I stared through the frost caked upon the window, turning away to face her again. "We can't go on. If I really love you, then I've got to let you go. You've a whole life to live"—my voice cracked—"but you hitched your wagon to the wrong star."

Spent, I sat next to her cross-legged on the carpet, toying with the coffee mug. I expected to see in her a sadness, maybe tears. Instead, she was livid with anger.

"That's just great. Just great." She struggled for control. "What gives you the notion there's a rope around me? That you've got this poor little waif shackled to you, who now in your infinite wisdom you have decided to set free?"

There was a white heat in her voice I had never experienced before. I tried to speak. She shook her head in protest.

"No, no. Wait. Now you listen to me! You love me, do you? Well, isn't that just dandy! Has it ever occurred to you that I love you, too? Freely. Without your permission! And what is all this . . . this"—she clenched her fist, searching for a word—"this drivel about me meeting another man? Settling down happily ever after? I've known other men. Don't you know by now it's you I love? I'm not some desperate maiden looking around for a handsome prince." She sniffled, fought back a rush of tears.

Shaken by her passion, I reached for her. She pushed me away. "Just let me be. I'm in this because I want to be. All the way. I refuse to believe that the only way to receive God's blessing is to destroy our love. What kind of God would want that? If you don't want me, just say so. But don't come in here with all this bull . . . as if I'm a kept woman! You can't set free what you don't own."

The slow drip of a kitchen faucet measured the long silence between us, the anxiety within me slipping away. Through the flickering light I caressed the furrow on her forehead. Whispered, "I deserved that. Oh yeah. As if I could walk away from you in the first place. I tried it once. No go. It's just that I'm so tired of watching what this is doing to us . . . especially to you. What are we waiting for? All we're doing is drifting. No plan, nothing. It'll take a miracle and I'm fresh out. But just the thought of losing you, well, it's . . ." My voice broke off and fell away.

Why couldn't I face up to reality as other priests all over the world had done? Surely many of them, facing similar circumstances, didn't want to leave the priesthood either. However reluctantly, they knew the church held all the cards, and so packed their bags and moved on to new lives.

"The day Vance left, I thought we should just say the hell with it and get married. Not when the law changes. It won't. Not when the powers that be decide to quit counting the number of angels on the head of a pin. They won't. Not when the pope says it's all right. He won't. Maybe we ought to just walk away from it all.''

Joan stood, her back to me, blowing into a Kleenex before spinning around, her eyes red as the coals in front of me. "Oh, Michael. Thank you. I needed that. If I thought for one moment that you could do it and be happy, we could be gone tomorrow. But think what you're saying. You are talking about leaving the priesthood. If only you could see your face. How do you feel right now?''

I wasn't sure, but whatever it was, it wasn't good.

"We both know you couldn't leave. I've watched you with the people. You've got a gift for making the gospel, their faith and mine, come alive. Look at the parish. It's doubled in size this year alone!''

She sat next to me, caressing the back of my neck with her fingertips.

"Being a priest isn't just a job with you, or a suit of clothes you can put on and take off whenever you like. It's in the marrow of your bones. It's your life. You just can't get laicized. God, how I hate that word! Sounds like something the Curia would come up with. You couldn't leave who you are. If you tried, part of you would never recover.''

I rested my head against her breast, the only sound that of her heart. She was right, the prospect of getting out left me cold. Finally, after several minutes, Joan jumped to her feet, went into another room, and returned with a frayed Salinger paperback.

"Here. Remember? You once told me you'd do it for the Fat Lady. Let me see, it's marked here somewhere.'' She leaned into the fire for light. "Yes, here it is, where Zooey's talking to Franny. . .

Seymour'd told me to shine my shoes . . . I said they couldn't see them *any*way, where we sat. . . . He said to shine them for the Fat Lady. I didn't know what the hell he was talking about . . . He never did tell me who the Fat Lady was . . .

This terribly clear, clear picture of the Fat Lady formed in my mind. I had her sitting on this porch all day, swatting flies, with her radio going full-blast from morning till night. I figured the heat was terrible, and she probably had cancer . . .

'Yes, yes, yes. All right. Let me tell you something now, buddy. . . . Are you listening?'
Franny, looking extremely tense, nodded. . . .

'I'll tell you a terrible secret—Are you listening to me?—
don't you know who that Fat Lady really is? . . . Ah, buddy.
Ah, buddy. It's Christ Himself. Christ Himself, buddy.' ''

Joan bit her lower lip, wiping her eyes. "The Lady's still there,
she's why you've got to hang on. Why I'll stay with you. Not for the
Vatican! Not because of their crazy law, but in spite of it. Stay for
the kids on campus who love you. For the people in the parish who
are just beginning to get excited about the church." She stammered,
her mind racing ahead of her, then smiled. "Stay for old Forrest who
tells me he's quit falling asleep during sermons for the first time since
he was a boy."

She tugged at my sleeve. "Stay for me. We'll wait. Something
will happen. It's come down to the Fat Lady. We'll both do it for
her."

Her lips came to mine, flushed and full. Tasting of salt, sealing
our resolve to wander again into the long valley. There to wait and
cast an anxious eye toward a God who might or might not come.

Time creeps on turtle's legs when measured in waitings. We wait
in lines, at stoplights, for snow to melt, for spring to come. We wait
to be born. To die. Life is a patched quilt of waitings. Without any
signs for a way beyond impasse, we waited. Locked on dead center.

At the same time, the parish, enthusiastic with the prospect of a
renewed Catholicism, wasn't waiting; it continued to burst into life.
With the growth came an avalanche of counseling, sick calls, weddings, and baptisms. It came as no surprise when, determined to provide help, Bishop Hunthausen called to suggest that Tim O'Mera join
me. The bountiful humor of the burly Irishman, who before becoming
a priest had worked in the underground mines of Butte, would strike
a responsive chord with Resurrection.

Just before saying good-bye, the bishop added a personal note.

"Part of the reason he asked to come is you fellas get along so
well."

True enough. Ours was a friendship rooted in my undergraduate
days. Because of the inspiration of men like O'Mera, then newly
ordained, my "vocation" had surfaced.

Hunthausen hesitated, weighing his words.

"There's more. He's been a bit . . . ah . . . restless lately. Nothing
major. Just thinks working with you will help. Tells me you seem to

have your act together. Coming from Tim, that's quite a compliment.''

My spirits sagged. "Act together?" I thought. "God help us. If only he knew!'' I resolved then and there not to make the mistake of closing the windows and drawing the blinds over our lives, and tell Tim about Joan at once. He would have to know how unsettled I truly was; that if he was looking for stability, the last place he would find it was within me.

Turning away from the phone, I noticed the headline in the paper.

34 THEOLOGIANS TAKE BOLD STAND

I skimmed through the first paragraphs. An international group of the most noted Catholic theologians chose to address a statement to those who felt their expectations for renewal of the church all but cut off by the high walls of Roman intransigence; the document's principal author, Germany's Hans Küng.

> Whenever the Church exercises power over men instead of ministering to them, whenever her institutions, doctrines and laws become ends in themselves, whenever those in authority offer their personal opinions and concerns as divine commands, there the Church's mission is betrayed, there the Church distances herself both from God and man, there the Church enters into crisis.

"So what's new?" I muttered, frustrated, crumpling the paper and hurling it into the wastebasket. Three words of the wrinkled text stared back at me: "Don't give up!"

Curious, I retrieved the article and read on. The thirty-four admitted that waiting for change to emanate from the top down was proving to be futile. They urged those anxious to find ways of living within the church to cease complaining about the Vatican and the bishops and to act decisively, even daringly, themselves. "Don't give up . . . never losing sight of the goal, i. e., a Church that is more open, more human, more credible. In short, that is more Christian.''

They were right, but intentions were not enough. I tossed the document away only to find its message seeping through the cracks of my days. "Seek provisional solutions. Act decisively, creatively, even daringly." But how? Where? The questions hounded me, but with them came a sense of the answer. Lying back, permitting the church to make even the most fundamental decisions, was a temptation for Catholics, especially the clergy. I would step off the merry-go-round to nowhere, see for myself the kind of church emerging in scattered pockets of Europe. Perhaps focus on Holland, maybe even approach Hans Küng himself—somehow do something to find a way for the twin loves, Joan and the ministry, to survive.

Father Nat Taylor outlived nearly all his contemporaries. By the time I arrived for the funeral, a large crowd had assembled in the dilapidated church to bid him farewell. As was the custom, priests sat together in the front, senior clergy taking the first pews.

Kneeling, I scanned the rows of priests in front of me. Pasty baldness, a dapple of gray here and there. Hairlines serving as a chart through time of what we were all becoming. To the far right, a row of middle-aged priests known for their staunch resistance to change. Scattered among the assembly, four or five whose flushed skin and streaked eyes told the story of alcoholism. Then, too, there were those who seemed to have the pieces of the priestly puzzle all together.

For an instant, time collapsed. I saw myself in the future. Gray, palsied, and terribly alone. Waiting my return to the earth, there to crumble back into dust. Where would my life lead? Which place on the clerical chess board would my soul occupy before the long knife of death cut me down?

The bishop proclaimed the words of Ecclesiastes. "Remember before darkness comes . . . before the silver cord has snapped or the golden lamp broken . . ." He descended the steps before the altar, standing next to Nat's casket. ". . . Before the pitcher is shattered at the spring, or the pulley cracked at the well . . ."

My hands were clammy. Time wouldn't wait on further indecision, which even now threatened to throw a pall over Joan and me. I decided to speak to the bishop immediately, suggesting I take a journey, which, while vague, at least promised an escape from the rigor mortis of inertia.

The funeral cortege wound its way to a hillside overlooking the rooftops of Anaconda. A smokestack, dubbed the world's tallest, rose from a smelter off in the distance, dwarfing the tombstones at our feet. A dog scurried through the cemetery, stopping beneath a budding birch to relieve itself.

Nat would rest in the priests' plot, which contained a surprising number of graves. Silent witness to the overshadowing presence of the church throughout the tumultuous years of the mining community.

Criss-crossing below were the streets over which the bishop had driven a beer truck before entering the seminary. In the distance, the house he grew up in, with a family peeled straight off a Norman Rockwell canvas. To the north, the overgrown football stadium where he had distinguished himself, or so the old-timers like to say, as the best quarterback the city ever spawned.

The bishop's tone was somber, that reserved for the final reaper.

"Deliver us, O Lord, from everlasting death . . . Teach us to see your good and gracious purpose working in the trials which you send upon us."

We joined in the doxology. "*Per omnia saecula saeculorum*. Amen." Hunthausen removed the cross from the casket, turned to offer it to the family, and realizing there was none, slid it into his overcoat. Already the priests were ambling down the hillside toward the parish hall, where the ladies would serve cocktails and the traditional clergy brunch.

The bishop lingered next to the grave, chatting with the mortician, then laughed gaily, slapping him on the back with his square, truck driver's hand, and started after the flock of clergy.

"Dutch!" I shouted. "Do you have a minute?" I knew he would. He always had.

He stopped, looking back with the kindly expression of a favorite uncle. "We can talk on the way to brunch. Hop in the car."

In a way, he was like his Volkswagen. Short, squat, unassuming, but with more energy per square inch than anything on the road. A bishop born quite unexpectedly in the calm dawn of Vatican II, who over the years continued to maintain an utter lack of pretense.

By the time he'd backed around the hearse and ground the gear into first, I was spilling out a bag of feelings. After two years without a break at Resurrection, I was tired, needed to get away. He nodded, perhaps sensing that here was still another priest living in the fast lane but losing touch with himself. He listened as I outlined the request.

Over the summer there were a couple of seminars in Holland, which everyone knew was in the forefront of church renewal. Afterward, I might go to France, maybe Germany. Hunthausen knew the Dutch Church was a burr under the Vatican's saddle. I looked for bristles along his neck. There were none.

"Schillebeeckx will be on the faculty, and . . ."

"He signed that recent statement?" the bishop asked.

"You saw it?"

"Yes. Very good. I listened to him during the Council, and to

Küng. Küng wrote it, didn't he?'' A furrow spread over his face. "Unfortunately, they're in hot water with the Curia.''

We stopped in front of the parish hall. "Go ahead. It sounds like an exciting summer.'' He smiled without a hint of caution, his trust as always disarming. For an instant I nearly told him the primary reason for getting away—of Joan and our pressing need to get off-center. I didn't. Couldn't. Maybe Hunthausen the man would understand, but there was little chance Hunthausen the bishop ever could.

Our final weekend together before separating for the summer, Joan eased into the Volvo alongside me as we headed west along Highway 10.

"I'm so tired of hiding the way we do,'' she said, unpinning and shaking her hair down over her shoulders. "Here I am, a grown woman, sneaking out of town like a parolee. Sometimes I hate our lives.''

We needed to escape the guarded existence of Bozeman. In so doing, we found the day yielded its own tonic of liberation. Whether searching for beaver dams along Prickly Pear Creek, picking bouquets of mountain flora, or cooling off in the soft spray of a waterfall, we laughed a lot at and with each other. By the time we reached the tiny logging community of Lincoln, the moon was full. We lingered there over dinner beneath a buffalo head which Joan insisted resembled her uncle Harry.

We had stretched the day too long, and were a bit unnerved when the matronly proprietress of Leeper's Motel informed us that the only room available had one bed. Bozeman was three hours away. We took the room.

Before settling down, we strolled through the soft, warm night among the jack pines. The moon, danced through the trees, casting them in a veil of mellow blue. A twig snapped. We froze as two whitetails stepped into a meadow less than ten yards away. The buck's antlers shimmered in the light before he wandered off into the darkness with his doe. Within forty-eight hours, I would be wandering the streets of Amsterdam alone. We turned back to the motel.

Jittery, I leafed through a magazine while Joan undressed and slipped under the covers, from all indications perfectly at ease with our situation.

"Come on. Don't look so sheepish. If we were going to do something, we would've before now. Just climb in and get some sleep.''

She was right, yet I felt guilty. What would the parish think? The bishop? More important, what did I think? Bombarded with questions, my mind rolled into a tailspin.

I switched off the light, took off my sweater and Levi's, and inched into bed. Eventually Joan propped herself up on an elbow, facing me. "Psst," she teased. "If you don't move in, you'll fall off the edge." She leaned forward with a quick kiss. "Just pretend I'm not here." Turning to the wall, she was asleep within minutes.

For over an hour I lay there, staring at the ceiling, wondering just how long we could take such chances, rely so heavily on our resolve. A ray of moonlight managed to peek through the curtains, spreading itself along Joan's hips and across her back like a silken sheet.

Certainly I wanted her; ached to hold her close; caress the soft lines of her body and tell her what at times words could not. Why not give rein to the desperate longing, float free of all that bound us and surrender to the deep waters of passion? After all, who would know?

I leaned over, kissing her softly on the nape of the neck. She smelled of the earth, of another, far simpler time. I reached to draw her close, only to see the faces of nuns from my childhood. We were eight shiny-faced grades in two rooms with two nuns. The earth was flat. Christ hung on the walls, but for us, God lived in the convent, cloaked in black. Before the sisters' strict discipline and quick-brogued tempers, children aged prematurely. We both loved and feared them. Now, through the tunnel of time I heard the whisper of their robes, the rustle of beads. It never dawned on me that they were genuine women. Still, life told us so whenever we listened, as it did once when I wandered by Sister Clare's office and drawn by her sobbing, dared to peek inside. She sat alone with her tears. Growing up, I wondered if she still wept alone; or if she was dead now, whether there was anyone to notice and cry over her.

I felt the steady warmth of Joan's breath. Wondered what the nuns would think if they could see me now.

"We'll hold the line, dear sister," I whispered with what might have been a prayer. Abruptly the guilt passed. With Joan's cheek pressed against my shoulder, I faded into sleep, the Fat Lady squeezed close between us.

The day Tim arrived, we moved through revolving doors. He anxious to plunge into the parish; I, to get away. During the drive to the airport, he confessed that the rumored relationship between himself and a woman had been true; it had gone sour.

"Things just didn't work out." He didn't say more, nor did I ask.

"Sometimes, I'm convinced that it's unhealthy for most of us to go through life without a woman," he chuckled as we pulled up in front of the terminal. "Then guys like you come along who seem to have it all together, steaming through the single life so easily. Blowing all my presumptions sky-high!"

I decided to explain that I wasn't steaming along all that well, but knew it could wait and turned my attention to the long flight across the country and over the Atlantic.

A Dutch child, who had sat next to me on the plane, waved good-bye as we passed through customs at Schiphol Airport and scurried across the lobby into the arms of his parents. An attractive brunette, squealing something in French, brushed by to embrace a boyfriend struggling to maintain a slender balance between his satchel and a now crumpled bouquet of tulips. With the exception of myself and a chunky business type, nearly everyone else on KLM Flight 612 had someone meeting them.

The bus hummed along through the faint morning mist, turning onto Vijzelstraat for Amsterdam. I thought of Joan, at that moment most likely nestled in the same Wisconsin bed which at one time or other had held all ten of her parents' children. In a few hours, she would be herding cows into the milk barn. One day into the journey and already her absence left a gaping hole.

On the flight over I had tried to leaf through the pages of my own faith. I was momentarily buoyed by the inkling that God's destiny for us might indeed lie in the journey, the quest itself. After all, there was the promise "Seek and you will find. Knock and the door will be opened." Yet what if such discovery eluded us? While others appeared to reach up on a shelf to pull down and dust off their God with firm certitude, I could not. In any event, I knew far less of the divine than the church confidently claimed for itself.

By the time the bus jerked to a stop in front of the Hotel Delphi, most of my confidence was jarred loose. At best, it was a long shot that there was a needle hidden in Catholicism's haystack, much less that I would find it. My only hope was that if the needle did exist, it would find me.

Hours later I tried to focus on the lecture of Professor Edward Schillebeeckx, finding it difficult to imagine that the gentle, somewhat shy priest addressing the conference participants was considered a threat by the Roman Curia. He looked and acted more like the neighborhood librarian, his flat gray eyes illuminated behind rimless spectacles.

Following the Second Vatican Council, during which he surfaced as a major theologian of renewal, Schillebeeckx publicly lamented the Vatican's reluctance to modify its stands on contraception, divorce, and the role of women as an example of an institution unwilling to abandon the status quo. Esteemed by the Dutch hierarchy, he soon emerged as a spokesman throughout Europe on the necessity of placing grass-roots pressure on the institutional church to respond to the signs of the times.

Immediately following the lecture, Schillebeeckx left the room for a cigarette. Moments later I joined him outside in the street. Before long, we were chatting about the exodus from the ministry by priests throughout the world. Aware that he had written a book on celibacy, I asked him what, if any, impact a change in the law might bring to the mounting crisis facing the church.

He ran a hand through his crop of white hair, staring out over the flat skyline. "Here in Holland, we used to ordain a couple of hundred men a year to the priesthood. Now there is no one. The loss of numbers is not all bad. I'm convinced we are on the edge of a transformation in the church's ministry. With fewer priests, men and women may climb out of the pews and take up their calling as Catholics—in this sense there is no vocational crisis at all. Not many of us here want to see a return to the clerical church . . . but"—he inhaled, continuing in measured English—"we will always need priests. Those whose gifts and witness provide unique leadership. For such people celibacy is such a stumbling block!"

As he turned to face me, his gray eyes narrowed and he exhaled with the resignation of one repeating a threadbare story.

"I believe celibacy has a place and is of some value. But not if what is supposed to be a gift of the Spirit is forced upon everyone. People change in life. They fall in love. Of course, young people just refuse these days to lock themselves into something so rigid." He cited a poll that reported that over eighty percent of Dutch Catholics would accept a married clergy.

"Why is Rome so stubborn?" I asked.

A gentle smile crossed his face. "The Romans say that if there is a change, the Curia knows that most priests would have two popes— one in the Vatican and the other at home."

I laughed. He turned serious again. "Celibacy maintains a particular caste in the church, set aside from everyone else. Maintaining it has more to do with control and power than anything else.'' He sighed. "Still, Paul the Sixth told our own Cardinal Alfrink that his successor would be forced to change the law. Poor, tormented Paul. He just doesn't have the energy to resist the Curia.''

He stubbed out his cigarette with a twist of frustration, glancing up at a Peugeot approaching along Apollolaan. "He probably doesn't have the conviction, either. Since his decision forbidding birth control, he's afraid to do anything lest he make another mistake. Well, here in Holland, there are priests and parishes who aren't waiting for his successor!''

Curiosity aroused, I started to inquire further, but the sedan pulled alongside the curb and Schillebeeckx excused himself to catch a plane for London.

During the remaining days of the seminar, my interest in the Dutch Church—reputed to be Catholicism's most progressive—grew. Before departing for France, I arranged to return later for a theological symposium in Leiden, the city of Rembrandt.

In Paris I stayed in the monastery above the Dominican publishing firm Les Éditions du Cerf. The environment proved to be an international zone, a way station for clergy passing through the city enroute to any number of destinations throughout the world.

Daily, our conversations touched upon everything from the plight of the Vietnamese in Hanoi to the poor in the backwaters of the Amazon. Regardless of the geography, a common denominator continually manifested itself—the church's mission was being jeopardized in numerous ways, not the least of which was the shrinking number of priests.

In Paris alone, the evidence was everywhere. Religious houses, now reduced to little more than rest homes for a clerical past. Seminaries, empty of youthful promise, their very sterility reminders of the crisis pressing upon Catholicism. Cathedrals, where gargoyles screamed down in protest at tourists blinking back with their cameras' eyes, seeking to capture them as relics of a distant age—and nothing more.

Throughout it all, I missed her. I saw her everywhere. Like the time near Montmartre.

While I was in a cafeteria, waiting out a sudden cloudburst, I noticed a young Frenchwoman scurrying across the Rue des Abbesses, taking shelter beneath an awning. She brushed off her coat, while the rain pelted the canvas, spilling in random sheets over its lip. I recalled another time.

Climbing alongside a waterfall, Joan discovered a cavern concealed behind its spillway. Once inside, she gazed out triumphantly through the waters. Now and then I could see her peering back at me from behind the cascading veil. I shouted, but she couldn't hear, nor could we reach out and touch through the wall of raw beauty.

Now, staring at the woman who looked back and smiled before hailing a taxi, I felt Joan's presence. Again, unable to speak or touch.

Eventually a packet of her letters caught up with me.

> Every day now, I'm either driving the rake or baler. I'm tan all over except for under the necklace you gave me. When I take it off, it's like someone branded me . . . That's it. Branded by the one I love! By mid-afternoon I start watching for the mail truck. For as long as I can remember, Dad walked down to pick up the mail. The first time he saw a European postmark, he didn't say anything, but now he's suspicious. So I've got my younger brother intercepting them for me! Gosh, here I am a grown woman and it's the first time in my life I've ever been secretive with my folks. I don't like it. Still, if Dad knew you were a priest, he would not understand. That's putting it mildly!

From Mainz, the Rhine flows southeast to the medieval city of Worms. To the soft-spoken Jesuit, I might have been just another tourist curious about the cathedral whose three Romanesque towers had overshadowed the town square for nearly a millennium. Discovering that I was a priest, he escorted me through the heavy wooden door into the sanctuary, paused next to a scarred statue of Saint Anne holding her daughter Mary, who in turn embraced the child Jesus.

Martin Luther first stopped in the same cathedral after Emperor Charles V summoned him to Worms to defend himself against charges of heresy. Known to have had a lifelong devotion to Saint Anne, he had probably knelt and prayed where we were standing.

We walked down the center aisle, standing beneath an oak pulpit which protruded like a ship's bow from the wall overhead.

"Some say Luther preached here just before Charles convened the Versammlung."

"Please?"

"The general assembly of the estates of the Holy Roman Empire,"
he replied, surprised I had missed what for him was not a footnote in
history. "Can you imagine? He was about our age—refused to recant
his position at the Diet, which ultimately led to the split with Rome."

I asked whether he felt Luther intended to divide the church.

"Nein. Definitely not. In fact, he told the emperor he wished only
to help reform it. He felt the church had strayed from the Scriptures,
and was relying more on the whims of man than the word of God."
The priest sighed, as if bearing the weight of the Reformation upon
himself. "Poor Martin. He saw the break with Rome as tragic, but
unavoidable."

He unlocked the wrought-iron gate, inviting me up the short stair-
case into the pulpit.

"Do you think Luther would break with Rome today?" My voice
echoed over the pews below.

"Nein, I think not. He'd probably still be an Augustinian priest.
Every essential reform he stood for was embraced by the Second
Vatican Council. Of course, the Council went beyond Luther in many
respects."

For a moment I imagined the fiery friar poised, a firm grip upon
the pulpit's rail. Looking out toward the flickering vigil lights, I could
feel his presence . . . almost hear him pronounce the words sealing
his fate in Worms—*"Hier steh' ich, ich kann nicht anders.* Here I
stand, I can do no other." The goosebumps which spread over me
had little to do with the damp chill of the cathedral.

I stroked the cool railing. Wondered if the monk standing in this
place five hundred years earlier could have envisioned the tumult which
would follow him throughout his life. Wondered, too, about Katharina,
his wife.

We stepped outside, for a moment blinded by the brightness. Sitting
on a bench in the town square, the lanky cleric brought up Luther once
again. "Some say the spirit of Martin himself has reappeared in the
church, is reincarnated just a few kilometers from here."

"Tübingen?"

"Ja. Father Hans Küng teaches there. At the university." He
squinted into the sun. "He's regarded by many as the greatest Catholic
theologian since the Reformation." He shrugged. "I prefer Rahner
myself. He's more scholarly. Then again, Küng speaks to the person
in the street, whereas most theologians only talk to one another."

I checked my watch. It was time to leave.

"Küng has a few of the hierarchy here upset. Especially Archbishop Ratzinger in Munich. He's even got the Curia after him." He stood. "I don't know what to think about him. He's sincere. No one questions that he truly loves the church. It's just that sometimes I feel we've had enough changes for a while without him stirring things up."

He smiled, shook my hand vigorously. "Come to think of it, I'd better watch myself. People said the same thing about Luther. They even said it about the Lord in his time."

Since arriving in Europe, I had been tempted to go to Tübingen. Now it was clear that Munich would have to wait. That evening, after boarding a gold-and-black train marked "Heidelberg-Pforzheim" and switching cars in Stuttgart, I stretched across the seats and slept. Before long, I was wrestling with the identical dream of a few nights earlier. I was standing upon a high glass tower. A slender rope swayed in the wind above a yawning cavern. Something drew me to step out upon the rope . . . pulled me toward the other side, hidden from view. I froze, unable to move, then started to fall away.

As the train rumbled on, I awoke, recalling the feeling which had possessed me while standing in the pulpit at Worms. The identical emotion that now hurled me toward Tübingen—the beginning of desperation.

Nestled on the southeastern edge of the Black Forest, Tübingen has a legacy of pride which preserves what is essential to its heritage while reflecting the vitality of its future. The reputation of Hans Küng is much like the city he calls home.

Following directions offered by a jovial attendant at the Bahnhof, I wandered along Williamstrasse, crossing a bridge built by Caesar's legions, and entered a rathskeller.

As I sipped espresso and picked at some rye, a mirror behind the counter assaulted me with my own reflection. Just what was I doing wandering around Germany like a gypsy in wrinkled khakis and a two-day growth of beard? How could I have been so presumptuous as to come in the first place? Küng probably wasn't even in the city. Even if he was, would he see me?

Though it was a shot in the dark, I started for the university. With each step taken along the winding sidewalk, the sense of folly in searching for Küng escalated. By the time I reached the ivy-covered walls of the Ecumenical Institute, I was ready to rush back to the Bahnhof and catch the first train to Munich. Just then, a bespectacled

German emerged from the institute in animated conversation, the athletic figure beside him, wearing a light blue suit, unmistakably Hans Küng. They walked across a parking lot, where the shorter man, still gesturing, climbed into a white BMW and drove off.

Hesitant, almost in spite of myself, I caught up with Küng. "Dr. Küng?" He turned, his blue, deep-set eyes not at all conveying the sense of intrusion I expected.

"You're either American or Canadian. Are you a student here?" His English was sharp. Precise.

I quickly explained my background. "Meeting you was an accident. Well, not really. I've come to Tübingen for only one reason." There was a desperation in my voice which immediately annoyed and embarrassed me. "There's something I've got to talk with you about. It's very important."

Apologizing graciously that he was late for a seminar, Küng invited me to sit in. I declined, admitting my German was terrible. So too, I thought, must be his impression of me.

Sensing my dejection, he reached into a vest pocket, withdrawing a calendar. "How long are you in Tübingen?"

"As long as it takes."

He would be leaving the city for the weekend, but we could have lunch on Monday. He would have an hour or so. Whereas I had hoped for a moment or two, he was offering part of an afternoon.

"I'll be anxious to know just what brings you here, and what you have to say."

"That makes two of us," I thought. While driven to speak to him, I suddenly wasn't at all certain myself just what to say.

Grateful for the time to prepare for Küng, I began Sunday with a morning stroll along the Neckar River. The worn footpath, first carved out by the Romans, paralleled the water, which spilled away from the city through a forest of emerald pine and lush fern. Scattered shafts of light penetrated the dense foliage, spreading over clusters of moss and mushrooms, as if cast through a window of stained glass. A rabbit, its fluffy tail bouncing, scampered beneath a hollow stump. I turned to whisper of its presence to Joan before experiencing once again the weight of her absence. For a moment, even the marigolds turned gray. We hadn't seen one another for nearly three months.

Then I heard her. The laughter skipping off the water downstream, splitting the stillness. At once I knew. No one else had that particular ripple to her joy. The woman giggled again as I raced down the path through the timber. How did she find me? How could she possibly know? No matter. She was here! The sounds were getting closer. There was muffled conversation. My heart pounding, I waited at the river's edge as the small boat drifted into view, the sun glistening off the woman's dark hair that spilled over her shoulders and down to her slender waist. I nearly called out, but then the gentle current drew the boat nearer, carrying the sounds of the young man facing her. He was speaking German. She laughed again, replied, also in German, as the boat passed by. Embarrassed, I turned away into the shadows.

By midafternoon, I reached an abandoned sixteenth-century monastery sandwiched among the rolling hills; paid a frail caretaker two marks to wander its cobwebbed corridors and stare into the silence from empty choir stalls.

In the damp must of the refectory, carved faces of monks long dead bordered the ceiling, their frozen lips unable to tell of what they had once prayed for . . . hoped for . . . their vacant eyes refusing to reveal whether or not they had looked upon the face of God.

Along an outside wall, I found their graves. Tried to pray over men closer to God than I. Words would not come. Were there periods, I wondered, when they too, caught up in a much different time and place, couldn't speak to the divine? When they, too, turned an ear toward the heavens and heard nothing at all?

Clearing away the weeds covering a bleached tombstone, I knelt to read its timeworn inscription. *"In te speravi, non confundar in aeternum.* I have hoped in you, O Lord, and will not be troubled forever."* I repeated it out loud, and for the first time in weeks the silence spoke back.

The following day, as the bells of the university tower announced the noon hour, I crossed the grass, still moist from an early rain, and ascended the steps to Küng's chalet-style home on Waldhäuerstrasse. I decided to bring up the document which had catapulted me into my journey in the first place. Our conversation would be formal. Academic. There would be no mention of Joan, or of our dilemma. After all, Küng was a theologian, not a counselor. Rather, we would focus on the world of ideas. Safe enough. I adjusted my tie and rang the bell.

An older woman, introducing herself in German as Frau Renemann, ushered me along a book-lined corridor. "Doctor Küng is waiting for you." She led me through an airy living room and out onto a sun-draped porch.

"Ah yes. Herr Miles." Casual slacks and a light sweater accentuated his handsome, rugged features. However, it was Küng's eyes, a misty blue, set beneath a crop of wavy blond hair, which took hold of me.

His handshake was firm. Warm. "Campari and soda?"

While Küng was responding to my question about his latest book, I struggled to relax.

"You were a *peritus* at the Vatican Council. My bishop was there for every session. You're about the same age."

"My age? Poor fellow! What's his name?"

"Hunthausen. As you probably know, it means 'doghouse' in the vernacular. He's German, too."

He twinkled. "Well, I'm not German. I'm Swiss. 'Doghouses', is it? He must have a time with that one!" He offered me some chips. "But enough of this. Our time is short. What can I do for you?"

As a diver testing the board, I hesitated, then plunged in. "The statement which you wrote . . . In English it's 'Against Discouragement Within the Church' . . . well, it had quite an impact on me and many in the States."

He sat quietly, sipping his Campari, as I recounted the statement's conclusion—whenever church authority acts in a way that clearly fails to correspond to the gospel, resistance is permitted. Even required.

"That's pretty strong. But the document's vague on how we are to apply it in the concrete. It's fuzzy."

He swirled the ice around in his glass, raising his eyebrows. "That document was translated into dozens of languages. We merely tried to offer general principles on how to proceed in the difficult situation which faces us all. We didn't intend to offer pat solutions, just encourage those who are tempted to give up, to hang on."

He rubbed his forehead, sighed, as if repeating an old story. "People in all walks of life are being denied the fruits of the Council. It's that simple. Human rights and Christian love are preached for the public, but disregarded internally. Those in power tend to forget that the church is sinful, not just holy. That all of us fall short and have to be converted again and again. But then, what can we expect? A profound struggle is taking shape. Unfortunately, Catholicism has a lack of spiritual leadership comparable to the time of the Reformation."

Frau Renemann called us to lunch. Over stewed vegetables and veal, I launched into a discussion of his latest book, when Küng suddenly pushed back his chair, holding up a hand. "Enough. Please.

Enough!'' His eyes locked onto mine. There was an edge of impatience in his voice. "You didn't come here to discuss theology. You've been avoiding something ever since you arrived. Please? Our time is short."

I looked away, fumbling with the napkin, knowing full well why I had come. What I desperately needed to say.

"All right. It's, well, frustrating to hear theologians issue benedictions from ivory towers. We're supposed to stick with it. When the powers that be fail to act in ways that correspond to the gospel, we're supposed to hang in there and help turn things around. Great! Just great!"

My arm caught the lip of a waterglass, nearly sent it crashing to the floor. I struggled to rein in my emotions.

"It's all fine, so long as we don't put such lofty ideas to the test. If we do, we risk coming up against the whole system. In the end, we'll get crushed, like so many others."

I had overreacted. Knew it, but couldn't back away from my own momentum. The phone rang. Frau Renemann summoned Küng. Politely, he waved her off.

"You're an angry young man. Well, maybe not so much angry as frustrated. Surely there's more. Please go on. Take your time."

Before long, I was pouring out the story of what it was like to discover that the priesthood meant everything to me and then to fall in love and discover that Joan meant everything also. What's more, that neither love would let go. When it was over, I sat back, utterly spent, regretting that I had even bothered him. Certain that Küng had heard such stories all too many times before. Looking out over the tiled rooftops below, he hadn't said a word. When he did, his response was measured. Cautious.

"If you're asking me what you should do, I can be of little help. Only you and Joan can answer that." He smiled broadly. "You care for her very much. From the sounds of it, you are a lucky man. But . . ."—he motioned me into the living room, where he poured coffee and settled back into a worn leather chair—"it's also obvious that you enjoy what you do. You love being a priest."

Küng went on to discuss the celibacy law, a law which the church seemed willing to sacrifice its own mission to preserve. He shook his head, referring to a catastrophe descending upon the church as fewer candidates expressed interest in ordination and more in the ministry were departing each day.

"Those in the hierarchy who resist this change are wrong. Most are well intentioned, but to demand celibacy is short-sighted. Freely chosen, yes, of course. But demanded? No. Not even Jesus himself asked that much.''

I nodded, but my heart wasn't in it. We had heard it all before. Both of us.

"But the church won't change the law. It's wrong. So what?" I asked.

"The denial of an option is more than wrong. It's more than unjust. It's *immoralisch*"—he frowned—"excuse my English—immoral, and flies in the face of human dignity. Anytime a person's freedom to grow in love is curtailed, it's immoral. Period."

Startled, I leaned forward, waited as he served more coffee.

"Michael, anytime we refuse to allow persons to live a married life, which the church admits is a basic human right, well, that too is immoral."

"All right," I said. "Say the law is immoral. What can we do? Just marry and refuse to leave? The Vatican would come down on us with full force. We'd fold like a house of cards."

He poured cream from a porcelain pitcher, stirring it slowly. "True. Still I cannot imagine that our communities will continue to sit by and lose their priests because certain people beyond marriageable age refused to abolish a law which is against the gospel itself. In the years ahead, we'll have priests who will refuse to disappear silently in shame because they are in love, and who will speak out and say they want to stay. And we'll have communities that will insist, 'If this man is going but would like to stay, we'd rather have him remain than no one or maybe someone worse!' "

Smiling, he looked directly at me, anticipating the question on the tip of my tongue.

"That's all for the future. No one suggests that priests should marry and press the issue now. That would just produce sacrificial lambs."

"Well then, what's left? Marry and leave?"

For several moments he was silent. "Like I said, I can't give you the answer. Only you can do that. But if you want my impression . . ."

"Yes, please."

"How did you put it? Being a priest is your life? That was it. Then, the way you speak of the parish, it sounds as though the people are responding to your work. Both are obvious signs of the Spirit."

I could feel it coming, braced myself. He would be no different than Upshaw had been, than they all were.

"With such signs, I'm troubled that you would consider leaving. It would seem that resignation would be the worst thing you could do. You don't want to, for that matter. Besides, it would just give pleasure to those who oppose renewal, and grief to those who don't."

Maybe I expected him to say something else. Somehow make leaving either the priesthood or Joan easier. My spirits sagged. He noticed.

"If you stay, then there is Joan. You make it sound like you must leave her if you remain a priest. You can be in love and not marry. Why not go on living out your lives despite the law?"

"You mean go on pretending we aren't in love?"

"That's nothing to feel guilty about. You don't have to expose your personal lives to anyone unless you want to." His voice rose with emphasis. "What would be shameful is for you and Joan to permit your love to die. To deny such a gift from God would involve a destruction of sorts for both of you. If we want to talk about sin, well, that's sin."

Küng rose, stood before the window in silence. Finally he spoke, his voice laced with sadness. "There is a terrible loneliness out there. Priests, God knows, who labor day in and day out with no one close to them. No one who truly understands or cares about them. Except, of course, the Lord. That is enough sometimes." He drummed his fingers against the pane. "But his love comes to us with a human face. A human touch. That's why you are blessed with your Fräulein. If she is what you say she is, she will be strong and supportive of you in the work our Lord calls you to do. That can be beautiful, too, you know."

I rushed to agree, but sounded a protest instead. "These past two years have been a mess. Love can't be hidden. It goes against the grain. The strain is like a cloud, always hanging over us."

He seemed weary, slightly impatient. "So you suffer? We all do. There can be no genuine renewal without it. If you choose to remain a priest, and Joan supports you in the decision, it will not be for yourself alone . . . cannot be, but also for the people you serve. After all, God's will is that we live for the sake of others."

For the first time, I recognized the seasoned suffering lying just behind his twinkly and ready smile.

A long shadow traced its way across the living room floor. I had overstayed the visit and rose to leave.

"It would be academic if the pope would just allow priests who want to, to marry. Little chance. Especially if you see yourself as infallible.''

''In this case, infallibly wrong. So don't expect it to happen under Paul the Sixth, but in five or ten years—who knows?'' He pointed toward my tie. ''Look how you are dressed. A few years ago a priest without a collar would have presented a problem. Now we are debating celibacy. Maybe someday we will get beyond such nonsense and focus on the true work before us.''

He opened the door. ''In the meantime, you have an excellent bishop, a fine parish. All the ingredients are there. You and Joan will find a way. Who knows? Courage is the first virtue. It makes all others possible. You might surprise us all.''

His smile reminded me of a column I had read in the American press.

''Apparently someone suggested that if you didn't like the church the way it is, you should just get out. You were quoted as responding, 'Why should I leave? It's my church, too. Let the pope leave.' ''

He started to laugh. ''Maybe I did say that. Oh yes. Now I remember. Life's too serious at times! My point was that the pope exists for the church, not the church for the pope.''

He retreated to the study, emerging with a copy of one of his books. As he wrote inside the cover, I asked, ''Where do you get the strength to go on? It's obvious you care about the church, but the misunderstanding you get, even from friends, must take its toll.''

His answer was immediate. Unpretentious. ''Where? From the Lord himself, of course. Oh yes, the Lord himself.''

I reached out to shake hands good-bye. He held mine firmly for a long moment, then went inside. Descending the hill, I turned to look back just as the light in Küng's study flickered on. An odd mixture of feelings cascaded through me. Something had happened to move me off dead center. Whatever it meant, I didn't understand. Not yet, at least.

That night, I opened the book he had given me, read there the inscription scribbled in Latin.

> *In te speravi, non confundar in aeternum*!
> Always confidence,
> Hans Küng

Cool breezes rustling through aspen leaves, pushing pedestrians along Max-Josef-Strasse, seemed to breathe fresh life into Munich, a city already vigorous with preparations for the Olympic Games. My own spirits had soared, awakening a dormant energy. The visit with Küng touched me deeply, giving birth to the mild assurance that there was a way out of our dark tunnel if Joan and I were willing to take the risks necessary to discover it.

Nevertheless, while wandering through the shadow cast upon mankind called Dachau, a gnawing loneliness caught up with me. The desolation of the site where Hitler sought to destroy the hopes and dreams of some two million human beings, underlined just how precious the fragments of life truly are. Impulsively, from a booth adjacent to the gateway of the camp, I called Joan. It was still morning in Montana.

"I'm not even out of my bathrobe. Where are you?"

When I began to respond, a heavyset woman carrying a small dog, started pounding on the booth, impatient for the phone.

"Can you come over?"

"You mean Europe?" Joan asked, with a whistle. She didn't hesitate. She would leave immediately.

The dog began to yap. The hefty woman was now hammering incessantly.

"I'm due in Vienna this weekend. Meet me on Monday. At the airport. I'll check the flights."

The woman began to push her way into the booth; I hung up, just as her terrier took a snap at me.

Upon arriving in Vienna, I arranged to stay in a convent run by Austrian nuns who provided accommodations for traveling clergy. The sisters were also quick to offer a room to convenience the unexpected arrival of "my relative."

The 727 with its bright gold and blue Lufthansa logo taxied over the apron at Schwechat International. Even though she had flown all night, Joan emerged beaming, her skirt tossing in the warm summer wind. Then, just as she passed through customs, I saw him—an American priest I had met only the night before at the convent. My stomach tightened as Joan skipped by him across the passageway. Seizing her arms, I stopped an embrace and, within earshot of the priest, blurted, "Hello, cousin," while whispering that he was an American. Whatever glow Joan had had evaporated in the face of the twisted logic of avoidance. Following an awkward night in Stephanhaus Convent, we departed Vienna and headed west.

The ensuing weeks in Austria and Switzerland sprang from a fairy tale. Insulated by language, culture, and distance, we basked in a freedom all but impossible at home. The days passed quickly. As our train rumbled north toward the Netherlands, we were more convinced than ever of the destructive implications of concealing our love. By the time we arrived in the Netherlands, we were more anxious than ever to discover whether the seeds of our own future lay buried somewhere deep within the heart of the Dutch Church.

Accidents, or so Grandma used to claim, are often the most telling signs of the divine. If she was right—and, growing up, none of us doubted she was—then a happenstance in central Holland might have persuaded even her that God didn't necessarily turn His face away from priests who fall in love.

Joan left the train in Amsterdam, resenting a return to the games of concealment, but determined to avoid questions which her presence would surely occasion. In turn, I went on to Leiden for a symposium, where the directors had arranged lodgings for me with a priest attached to the university parish.

Slender, with middle-aged furrows slicing beneath high cheekbones, the face of Huub van Doorn might have sprung directly from a Rembrandt canvas. Racing through the narrow cobblestone streets in his Fiat, we screeched to a halt before a large shuttered home just off Stationsplein. I asked how many other priests lived with him.

"You mean no one said it to you?" he asked, a hint of surprise showing through his fractured English. "Oh well, it matters nothing."

At the door, an attractive woman with turquoise eyes set beneath straw-colored bangs introduced herself. No doubt the housekeeper, I thought, and the three-year-old playing on the steps, her daughter. Erna was Tine's daughter all right, but not until she crawled into Huub's arms did it dawn on me that she was also his. Obviously mistaken in assuming Huub was an active priest, I mentioned that several of my seminary classmates were married, pursuing any number of careers. Inquired about his own.

"Oh no," he corrected me gently. "I am not . . . how do you say in English? A priest of no standing?"

"An ex-priest?" I responded.

"Thank you. No. I am still remaining as a pastor at the Ekklesia. The university parish."

Noting the quizzical expression on my face, he set his daughter down, wrapping an arm about Tine. "I'm sorry. We thought you knew. Does it offend you?"

"Oh no, not at all." I shook my head, baffled, as Tine led us into a spacious living room looking out upon a backyard ringed with flowers. While Huub descended to the cellar, returning with a bottle of Bordeaux, La Mule du Pape, 1972, she set out pâté, fruit, and cheese. After I confessed to being startled, they spent the next hour tracing an equally startling scenario.

Following their marriage, and in compliance with the bishop's request, they left the city for a year. Upon their return, Huub took a position as a social worker, carving out a new career as so many inactive priests had before him. What followed evolved slowly. Initially the Ekklesia invited him to assume a few minor responsibilities. Eventually the community asked him to preach; on occasion preside over the Sunday service.

Tine smiled softly. "The people in the community did not want to have Huub's *gaven* lost. How do you say 'gifts'?"

I nodded, anxious to hear the rest.

"They would not accept that as God's will. Before we knew what was happening, Huub was the first priest in our country who was married and able to . . ."

"Get back in the saddle again," I laughed lightly. "At least, that's how we'd say it at home."

Tine hastened to add that the parish was different from most others in Holland, in that the congregation was a heterogeneous mixture of Dutch Reformed and Catholic Christians, staffed by both Protestant and Roman clergy.

"You see, Michael," Huub emphasized, intent that I not misunderstand, "at first the Ekklesia used the same medieval cathedral but separate worship services. By the time we married there was but one Sunday celebration for all. Sometimes our own Catholic liturgy. Other times that of the Reformed. Of course, that bothered the bishop very much. He needn't have worried, though. To his credit, he wanted to keep the . . . strings?" He glanced at Tine for assistance.

"Lines," she replied, more skilled in the use of the language.

"Yes, he wanted to keep the lines of communication open, so not to lose his influence." He paused, fingering his pointed chin. "It has been easier for him to look away from me than have so much fuss."

"Are you laicized?" I asked, regretting the word Rome used in reference to priests dispensed from celibacy and subsequently forced to resign.

"Oh yes." He smiled, waving his hand as if shooing a fly. "But none of that matters, except to the big church." He shrugged. "But the bishop becomes very nervous, so we oblige him.''

A stream of questions rolled through my mind. Where was Rome in all of it? Perhaps part of the reason Huub survived was the Curia's perception of the parish as an aberration, more Reformed than Catholic.

"But I still can't imagine why someone hasn't forced the issue," I interjected. "You're married and for Rome that means you can't function as a priest.''

"You mean a disappeared person. Ah, Michael,'' he responded, smiling broadly. "You must remember—the Achilles' heel of the big church is publicity. The Vatican is cautious of any public discussions but that they might mention clerical virginity.''

"A debate Paul the Sixth declared to be officially over," I added, still incredulous but gradually getting the picture.

"So they wait in the quiet.'' He frowned. "Someday maybe we must go, but so far they can't do it.''

Tine moved over to the couch next to Huub, her voice cracking. "There have been many fights and too much of sadness. Too bad for everyone. It is not over and seems so pointless.'' She drew Erna onto her lap while speaking of her own life as she was growing up.

"All of us knew the local priests. Even some of the bishops. At dinner our talk was often about the faith.'' Her eyes darkened as she smoothed Erna's skirt. "Now things are so odd. Today most young people care very little for the big church. They see so many problems in the world. Whenever there is such fuss over little matters like whether we are married, they just throw up their hands and walk away from the Vatican's foolishness. Oftentimes they do not return.''

The Bordeaux, along with the emotional jarring, left me fatigued. Huub noticed and, promising we would talk more throughout the week, led me upstairs to the guest room. Once alone, I called Joan.

"You won't believe it! Remember that needle? The one in the church's haystack? Well, I'm sitting on it right now!'' I rushed on, only to remember Joan's vulnerability and shattered hopes following the Synod. I checked myself.

"But it's much different here than at home. The Ekklesia has only loose ties with the bishop, and is ecumenical, to boot. Resurrection is your everyday Catholic parish, so we can't get too excited.''

Nevertheless we were.

By the time I left Leiden, the enthusiasm hadn't waned. As our Aer Lingus flight lifted off from Schiphol, I regretted not telling the van Doorns about Joan, resolving to write instead.

Crossing the Channel toward the Irish coast, Joan admitted to the first inkling that the impossible might indeed be possible. And why not reach for what we dare not to, I thought. We had stumbled upon a distant star. If the Dutch could do it, maybe we could too. In any event, we were out of options, with little choice but to try.

In Ireland, the smell of the bogs, the sudden swell of the wind, or the distant roll of the sea, keeps the earth forever close. Ireland, a land which has endured enough to remind the world of its own mortality and which, despite its many moods, never surrenders a clean innocence. The land complemented Joan. At times they seemed one and the same.

Jostling along in a hay wagon between Killarney and Tralee, or sipping tea and munching scones in a wayside cottage, we were happy in the little things. Content to be in a land which framed everything in slow motion.

Our final day before flying home, we hiked along a narrow pathway inching its way toward the Cliffs of Moher. We passed through a cemetery where scattered crosses poked their Celtic heads through the high grass, as if to search for others toppled askew by the shifting land. Each stone a mute testament that life and death kiss one another at every moment of existence. We pored over the faded names of the dead, wondering if their own dreams had come true or sunk with them into the bosom of the land.

We rested next to a mortarless wall, both bleached and blackened by salt spray; our voices rose and fell with the waves skipping and crashing against the stones. Like the sea, my emotions were in flux, for days privately approaching, then backing off from the seemingly preposterous notion of marrying and remaining a priest. Now, staring over the wild waters, I thought again of the Fisherman. Of how Peter might have felt during the storm off Galilee. How he trembled, then coaxed his reluctant body over the boatside to step into the slashing depths. A step fraught with peril. A risk perhaps made easier by what he thought to be the call of his Christ.

How could I be sure if my decision would be born of faith and love, not simply selfishness? After all, in countless little ways I compromised the gospel. Besides, we were no match for the church with its lightning rods of power, which could unleash the war horses and with them, crush our dreams.

I stood, then walked alone beyond the wall to a limestone reef—

there, against a salty spray, to pray for direction, for some assurance that whatever step we took, we would not drift, abandoned and lost. In response there was nothing. Nothing but the roar of a thousand seashells. Nothing but fragments from Genesis rolling over the azure blue.

"In the beginning God created the heavens and the earth, the earth was without form and void . . . darkness hung over the face of the abyss, and an awesome wind swept over the surface of the waters. God said, 'Let there be light.' "

Nothing. *Ex nihilo*. Creation out of nothing. Stars, suns, offspring of nothingness. Nothing but light . . . Nothing but fire! In the beginning God created with fire!

Though the comfort I sought was not forthcoming, at long last something cracked within me. We would lay hold of love's fire and from nothing else forge a new way.

The path wound upward. Eventually we crested the ridge, emerging atop the cliffs whose sheer walls dropped six hundred feet into the pounding surf below. The wind tossed and swirled Joan's hair, playing with it as a lover might, unable though to disturb the still center within her which the land of her ancestors restored.

Two gulls, translucent against the naked sky, drifted by.

"They ride the wind," Joan said, "rather than fight it. That way they're free. Utterly free."

The gulls turned, dropped, settling on a shelf along the craggy cliff wall. With our time together coming to an end, we both felt perched on the edge of our own destiny.

Somewhere between the gentle wisdom of Schillebeeckx and Küng and the stunning discovery in Leiden, the shroud covering our future started to fall away. Still, it wasn't until Kerry that I picked out the ring; not until the frozen moment in the cemetery below that the decision broke through with full force.

Taking her hand, I placed the ring into her palm. "This looks like something out of a Cracker Jack box. Someday we'll get the real thing."

She stroked the band, her lips full, the way they always were when she was about to cry. "Does this mean what I think it does?"

"Yes. Sure. After this summer—being with you day after day— well, there's no going back despite the fear of what might be ahead of us. No longer are you second to my work, the law, even to the church."

Although we had talked around the subject many times over the years, this time I was actually proposing we get married. Once home, we would approach the bishop. Seek his support in my efforts to remain as a priest. If he couldn't accept our suggestion—and most likely he could not—then we would face the consequences. I would leave. If, however, against all odds he approved, then we would go from there. Either way we would marry, and soon.

"We have a chance. Look, Dutch is a human, open bishop. There's a fantastic parish which seems fond of us and . . ." I pointed out into the dusk. "Montana is out there somewhere, about as far from the Vatican as we can possibly get!"

When Joan shook her head, my knees buckled.

"It won't work. You said it yourself. Huub and Tine are in totally different circumstances," she said, her voice flat. "You'll end up outside the priesthood like the rest."

Squatting down for a handful of pebbles, I tossed them against the mossy ground like dice across a felt table. How could I have been so presumptuous, never imagining for a moment she would say no? Never dreaming she would refuse to take on what was at best an uncertain future; forgetting it wasn't my decision only. After all, why should she let the church play dice with her life any longer?

The sun began to sink beneath the horizon, casting a shimmer of velvet and gold across the ocean.

"I'm afraid. It's like we're inside an eggshell which could crack under too much pressure. Sometimes I don't know if we can go on," she said, slightly melancholic. "If we lost and you weren't a priest any longer, you might blame me. I could live with most anything but not that."

"Blame? Don't be silly. Anyway, maybe the shell has to crack so what's inside can be born."

"Maybe," she said quietly. "I love you, always have. Never could I say no to that." Suddenly she stopped, her eyes splashed with an orange hue.

As the evening faded, so too did all doubt. In the silence we knew that for her also there could be no choice, no other way.

I reached for her hand. "But we have to try. Sometimes I feel pulled, as if we're called to this. Not just for ourselves, but maybe it's for the sake of the church, too. If need be in spite of the church."

Just as the two gulls perched below us lifted off the jagged wall, I slipped the ring over her finger. We stood, holding one another as the sun settled into the ebony sea.

Before long we were sauntering through a field ripe with the aroma of fresh clover, only to stumble into a patch of thistles, which tore at our legs. A poignant reminder of a land, fiercely beautiful but quick with its cruelty. We were about to discover, too, that all life was Ireland.

❧ PART II

I am being driven forward
Into an unknown land.
The pass grows steeper,
The air colder and sharper.
A wind from my unknown goal
Stirs the strings
Of expectation.
Still the question:
Shall I ever get there?

—DAG HAMMARSKJOLD,
Markings

It was one thing to romanticize over our prospects atop the Cliffs of Moher, quite another to face the sobering facts of our circumstances. The closer we got to home, the less certain we were that our dream would ever become a reality. Still, I wanted to tell Tim of our decision at once. As my associate at Resurrection, he had a right to know. As a friend, I needed him to know.

To understand Tim O'Mera one has to understand Butte, the city of his birth. Grandpa used to say that in the early days, whenever he drove the iron horse out of state, most folks had never heard of Montana. But of Butte, the mining city, dubbed the "richest hill on earth"? Well, that was a different matter altogether!

Butte—Irish and Catholic to the core. Where if a young man truly wanted to be a success, truly wanted to make his family proud, then the way did not lie in the things of this world, but with the one vocation which surpassed all others. The one life wherein a man from the most humble of origins could emerge head and shoulders above even the executives of the Anaconda Mining Company. The one vocation for which mothers prayed and fathers took fierce pride—the priesthood of Jesus Christ!

Butte, a city heavy with machismo but tender of soul. A city which gave to the world its copper and to the church in western Montana, most of its clergy.

Tim O'Mera was one of them. With his tousle of red hair and

ready laugh, one might think he had just stepped out of the bogs himself. Word had it he might have played for the Fighting Irish of Notre Dame—a grand calling in itself—had he not decided to surrender his life to the cloth.

Much like his hometown, which straddles the continental divide, Tim was caught between two eras of the church. Raised in an atmosphere wherein a priest was a man set apart, distant, even aloof, he was in ways the epitome of the pre-Vatican Council cleric, but one surprisingly resilient in the wake of its changes. Like Butte, he was anchored in the past, nourished on the milk of clericalism, while struggling to lay hold of the future.

Settling back in an overstuffed chair, Tim popped a can of beer. It was the first opportunity for us to talk since my return from Europe.

"Place looks nice. You've always had a flair for interior decorating," I said, feigning inspection while easing into the sofa alongside him. "Where's the tires?"

Tim's laughter was unique. It came out of him in layers.

"How long'd you have those things in your room at Carroll?"

Rolling his eyes toward the ceiling, he thought for a moment. "Ever since I sold the Chevy and found out the snow tires wouldn't fit the Olds . . . Let's see . . . two, maybe three years."

"All that time propped against the bookcase in your living room. Not even whitewalls! Geez, the razzing you took!"

"You guys just didn't appreciate my *au-courant* style. Besides, we philosophers can't be concerned with such trivia. We have the larger issues to ponder." He chuckled, reminded of our time together on the Carroll faculty.

"Speaking of trivia, remember when you heard the men's dorm was planning that panty raid? I'll never forget you standing outside St. Charles Hall with a bullhorn. What would Thomas Aquinas have thought? There you were, the chairman of the philosophy department, toe to toe with the Mongol hordes. I can repeat your words verbatim," I said, visualizing the moment. " 'Listen, you guys! First student who heads toward the women's dorm is campused indefinitely!' "

Pretending to scowl, Tim picked at a bowl of peanuts. "The ultimate sanction. Only trouble was, as I was threatening 'em, the thundering herds were streaming by on the raid, damn near trampling me in the process!"

"That's the night you told me you were going to get a law degree and become a DA. Then, instead of campusing, you could sentence them to the electric chair!"

He shook with laughter, dropping a few peanuts in his lap. "Oh Lord, I'd forgotten that . . ."

"Well, I ended up with egg on my face more than once, too. Remember when . . ." I hesitated, then backed away from the temptation to continue beating around the bush of memory. "Ah, maybe we shouldn't be talking about yesterday but today instead. There's something we've got to get ironed out."

He blinked as I abruptly changed the subject and plunged in.

"Over the summer I've become convinced that those who say it's impossible for most people to grow without intimacy are right on the money. You know, without a deep relationship with someone."

He nodded, waiting for me to continue.

"There are lots of advantages to the way priests live. I enjoy the freedom. We can do what we want, usually when we want," I said hesitantly. "We don't have to worry about where the next meal is coming from. How to pay the bills. How our children will do in school. In ways we're so bloody insulated!"

"That furrow between your eyes is showing." He smiled. "It does whenever you get serious. What are you getting at?"

"Well, it's so easy to get caught up in ourselves and close up as human beings. Geez"—I winced—"sounds like I'm reading from a textbook."

"Yeah. I'm having a hard time tracking you."

"I'm talking about love. It's as vital as water to a flower. A priest is no different from anyone else. At least I'm not."

He took another handful of peanuts, shaking them like a craps player before popping them into his mouth. "You won't get an argument from me. There was a day when you might have, but since meeting Christine, going through all that hassle with her last year and then breaking it off . . . well . . ." His eyes clouded over. "What the hell. It's water under the bridge."

"Anyway"—I paused—"you remember Joan Doyle? I introduced you at the picnic just before leaving for Europe."

"No, can't say . . . Oh wait. Yes! Dark eyes, long hair? A physician?"

"Psychologist."

"Yeah, right. Got it now."

Since undergraduate days, Tim's memory impressed me. As dean of men, he had kept tabs on us, rarely forgot the slightest infraction. That, too, was water under the bridge. I went on, struggling against feelings of a truant confessing to the dean.

He sat quietly, interrupting only once to ask how long we had been in love. When I finished, a slight sadness occupied the space between us. While we were close, things would never be quite the same. Not that he was unaccepting. To the contrary. Just that things were different and we both knew it.

"You're firm about getting married?"

I nodded. "She embodies the best of all I believe about life, even the church. When with her, I'm more myself than at any other time."

Somewhat awkwardly, he expressed his happiness for us, adding that if the contemporary church had taught him anything, it was not to be surprised at anything.

"But I have to admit to being bowled over by this. Not that you want to get married—though it comes as a jolt. Just that you are about the last person I'd have guessed would leave the priesthood!"

"Who's leaving?" I replied, spilling out the rest of the story. We would marry with the hope of my remaining as a priest in the parish. Hearing myself say it for the first time to someone other than Joan, it sounded utterly unrealistic.

Tim swung off the chair. "Holy shit! David and Goliath! I need another beer on that one!"

He returned shaking his head, slumping down with an audible sigh.

"God, but I wish you could do it, but it's sheer fantasy. The odds are way against you. Worse than that, there aren't any! It's a pipe dream, Mike. There's no way!" He went on, clicking off on his fingers the hurdles before us. There were the laity, people like his mother, who were adamant that priests shouldn't marry. Then, too, the church itself, an institution prepared for change in some areas but not to the point of abandoning its eight-hundred-year-old insistence on celibacy.

While he reacted, I struggled with a rising sense of irritation. He'd been around over a decade more than I. Knew the ropes well. But his caution was frustrating.

"Why couldn't your mother accept it? Does she know that the apostles were married? That the church had married priests for its first thousand years? Maybe she'd understand if given a chance."

Tim held up his hand, as if quieting a class. "Hey, easy. Don't get me wrong. I'm just trying to help. The people could probably be educated. For the most part, they'd be okay, especially in this parish. But we both know damn well who runs the show. The Vatican won't budge on this one. Nope. You've got to have your ducks in a row, but there aren't any ducks. You'll never pull it off."

"I'm not trying to pull anything off," I said angrily.

"Poor choice of words. I'm just trying to be honest with you. God, what about the priests? Even if some of them would go along with the idea, like me, they won't see how you can get around the law. But most of them will have trouble regardless. They'd raise up on their hind legs and . . ."

"But why?"

"Hell, who knows! Just don't underestimate them."

"What good is a church which doesn't speak to the heart? Anyway, someone has to try. Besides, I don't have any choice. I want to remain a priest."

"That I know," he said quietly. "But good intentions aren't enough. There's no precedent. No path for you to follow."

"We'll just have to find one. With the Holy Spirit's help, maybe chart our own."

"Better get it down. Otherwise you're just hurling yourself at the system. It'd be suicide. You'll go down like a Kamikaze."

Folding his hands behind his head, lost in thought, Tim let out a deep breath. "I hate to sound so pessimistic, but have to be honest with you. Then again, you know me. I'm not one to take risks, but if you're really serious about this, just know I'm there and will support you in whatever way. If there's one."

Although unnerving in its candor, the conversation with Tim ushered me through another door of inhibition. Despite his frankness, there wasn't a clue of rejection. The next door, however, led to Bishop Hunthausen and proved far more difficult for me to approach, let alone open.

Whenever I started to write him, the pen lay dead on the page. Whenever I picked up the phone, my fingers froze on the dial. Each time I imagined our encounter, the scenario buckled, invariably collapsing through the sheer weight of my own audacity. Despite resolute moments, I was unable to go the last mile and run the risk of being turned away.

Before long, Tim quit asking me about it. When Joan, just once, reminded me to make an appointment at the chancery, I snapped back at her. By the time the leaves turned, I still hadn't approached the bishop. Finally, frustrated by my inertia, I tossed a few things in a suitcase and set out for an isolated cabin on Seeley Lake, uncertain whether it was flight from fear or a dash headlong into it.

The isolation spawned a comfortable routine. Each morning on the porch overlooking the lake, I leafed through the New Testament, straining an ear toward God. Midway through the week, I stumbled across a small episode sandwiched between the more pronounced adventures in the large life of Peter.

As a fisherman, he respected the storm's fury which tossed the boat like a cork over the waters; if anything, his love for the sea was exceeded only by his respect for its savage power. Peter also knew the tales of the careless, caught in the wrong time and place. Their lungs bursting, their breath strangled, then claimed by leviathan. Oh yes, he knew, as did the others out with him that black night when the water's rage turned dread to panic and their world to chaos.

At the fourth watch of the night, off in the distance, they saw what some feared was a spirit. Perchance one of the dead given up from the bottom of the deep. Then again, maybe a mere figment of their terror. Only one among them claimed to hear the cry. "Courage! It is I! Do not be afraid!" Peter, a bull of a man who always seemed to say the wrong thing at the wrong time, appeared to snap inside and go mad, shouting, "Lord, if it is you, tell me to come to you across the water." Poor man. Couldn't he see it was but a dream? That wishing didn't make it so?

"Come!"

Did he hear it again, or didn't he? Certainly the others, cringing against the ribs of the vessel, saw only the look of madness as the aging fisherman rushed aft, before backing away in panic again toward the stern.

"Come!"

Seaspray obscuring his view, Peter abruptly bolted out into the churning water only to experience a failure of nerve. He had gambled too much. This time folly would cost him his life. Sinking into the blackness, his lungs on fire, he managed to cry out in bloody terror, "Lord, save me!" as the lights flickered out on his dream.

Suddenly, a hand! The firm grasp of Jesus drawing him from the waters, holding him close. Not until he risked everything had the foolish fisherman at long last become an apostle.

Uneasy, I set aside the Scriptures, putting Peter out of mind, unaware he would return full force that very evening.

At first, it sounded like drifting logs bumping against one another. Only after the naked moon slipped out between the clouds could I see that the winds had torn the boat from its tether, slamming it against the dock. I rushed to the water's edge just as the battered craft was about to slip away, managing to anchor it once again.

Moonlight slithered across the whitecaps, then disappeared. It was pitch dark but for a random burst of lightning far down the lake. The jagged bolts cracked closer, and out of one the ghost of Peter emerged.

Clearly I'd been avoiding the bishop all along, unable to summon up the nerve. What was there to fear? Disappointing him? Letting him down? Woul he think less of me? No longer trust me? Time and again, like Peter I'd gather a few strands of courage and rush to the boat's edge only to retreat to the security of the stern. I was paralyzed.

Pellets of rain lashed out, stinging my face. Not only would the bishop be disappointed, but the decision to marry Joan would force me out of the priesthood! Hunthausen would have no choice. How could we have been so foolish as to think the fate of others wouldn't also be ours? I'd seen the sword raised over the heads of priests who married. Like theirs, our heads, too, would roll.

The lightning cracked, skipping across the lake, so close that the thunder and fire were simultaneous.

On the other hand, what if the voice of the Living One was calling me to lay it all on the line as Peter had done? With no guarantees? Maybe it wasn't a dream, and like the Fisherman, we might not drown in the process after all.

The storm passed. A quiet calm settled over the lake as I prayed for the courage to talk with the bishop. Turning, I walked across the dock and up the hillside to the cabin.

Though haunted by the memory of Peter's ghost, several weeks would pass without my making an effort to see Hunthausen. Time and again, I sought excuses for delay; I avoided Joan, unwilling to admit that the slender threads of confidence were coming unraveled. Something had to give and finally did.

Tourists regularly evacuate the gateway to Yellowstone Park at the first sound of school bells. Consequently, the area around Castle Rock, enveloped in a crisp bubble of cloudless sky, was abandoned. Normally the ascent up her rocky spine took two hours; anxiety now propelled me to the summit in half the time. A light blanket of snow covered the peak, muffling all sound save for the faint roar of the Gallatin River, a ribbon of blue far below.

Jesus had his desert; Alice, her looking glass; I, the needle's eye, a slight window carved by erosion into the cliff's face. Slipping inside, pulling my knees beneath my chin, I gazed directly down the thousand-foot drop to the canyon floor.

A blank hour or more passed until, through the heavy silence, a voice seemed to whisper—that of the Tempter who, two thousand seasons earlier, had visited another pinnacle.

Why risk your career? The status you have? Why walk away from the promise of success? Suffer the rejection of your friends and family? Deny this love or all will be taken from you!

Melting snow, as so many teardrops, slipped down the needle's eye.

Where is your God? Who are you to expect bread from stones? Dare to put the Lord God to test? It's futile. Turn back, lest all hell swallow you up!

An abrupt movement startled me as a majestic eagle swept by, settling an arm's length away. In the stillness he hadn't noticed the intrusion. When his eye caught me, its golden lens flickered, opening up on a black pool, holding me, then drawing me inside. In an instant he was gone, plummeting like a stone, before soaring back upward toward the window, where he floated by in a soft, sweeping arc, caressing the sky with his wings.

My gaze rested on the eagle's sleek back. For a moment it was though we were one. Rising higher and higher we flew, wondrously free, before entering the blazing sun. As quickly as he came, he was gone. Catching my breath, I clung to the needle's shelf. Though I had nearly fallen, an onrush of ecstasy tingled through me.

The descent from the needle's eye was an exhilarating blur. My voice ricocheted off the canyon walls. "Joan! I love you! We can fly. Honest to God, we can fly!"

Reaching the river, I knelt to drink, the face of Peter's ghost swimming back and forth in the reflection. Cradling the water in my hands and splashing away the perspiration, I prayed for a new baptism.

The next day I arranged to see the bishop.

Alongside the highway on the drive to Helena, telephone lines, draped heavily with dew, whisked by, sparkling like strands of diamonds. Hunthausen had agreed to see me as soon as he got in from

skiing. As a flock of birds flitted in front of us in a swirl against the
fading light, I told Joan of my first attempt on skis. Never one for
moderation, the bishop had encouraged me to take the chairlift to the
top of Sun Valley, starting out on a long but gentle run.

"I was petrified! What seemed easy to him was mountain goat
country to me. But he sent the others ahead and rode it out with me
until I got down. It took the whole morning!"

"Well, let's hope he rides tonight out with you, too," she said,
laughing, somehow more alive just knowing that the threat of failure
which had shackled me for so long was shattered.

She shifted in the seat, running a finger over the back of my neck.
"Hon? You really love him, don't you? Just remember, he loves you,
too." She bit her lip. "Hey? Sure about tonight? No second thoughts?"

No answer was necessary. I was sure. We both were.

It was nearly dark when I dropped Joan at the Carroll College
library. She would wait, by now seasoned in such waiting.

Winding along the dimly lit streets of Helena's upper west side, I
passed stately mansions, monuments to Montana's gold rush. Approaching the episcopal residence, I wheeled into the carriage way.
An imposing edifice, occupied by Hunthausen's predecessor during an
era noted for lavish parties and distinguished guests, its massive stone
walls now housed a community of nuns. An illuminated window, above
the adjacent chancery office, indicated the bishop was home.

The glistening tile floor of the chancery smelled of antiseptic. At
the far end of the narrow hallway a door was ajar, opening onto the
stairway to Hunthausen's small apartment. In the semidarkness a flickering vigil light sent amber shafts along portraits of former bishops
and popes lining the walls. For the first time since descending Castle
Rock, I trembled inside, imagining the prelates shouting at me in a
ringing chorus. Accusing me of betraying the church. Of setting down
an apostle's torch. Of denying a sacred call. The twin dogs of failure
and guilt hounded my every step. Passing through the gauntlet of faces,
I took the stairway and knocked on the bishop's door.

"Mike? Come on in!" The familiar, mellow voice of Hunthausen
set me somewhat at ease. Dutch remained in his chair.

"I'm just finishing compline. Sit down."

Grateful for the time to compose myself, I glanced at a photo on
his desk. It had been taken the summer before the opening session of
the Second Vatican Council. The two weeks on horseback seemed
somehow so long ago.

Captured in Kodacolor, the bishop, along with two others of the hierarchy, surrounded a makeshift altar deep within the Bob Marshall Wilderness. Momentarily exchanging chaps and felt hats for fiddleback vestments complete with maniples, they posed in a meadow before morning mass. A chalice, covered with a pall, rested on a communion cloth, alongside two crystal cruets, a Latin missal, and matching candelabra.

The camera's eye drew me closer, as through a zoom lens, into the memory of that sparkling day, of crisp and snappy air. Next to the bishops, their hands folded in matching spires, my own face peered out through the tunnel of time. Clad in Levi's and a saddle jacket, I stared back at myself. I drew closer as if I might see through that same face into my mind. Whatever it may have contained, there were more answers then and far fewer questions.

In the foreground there was another seminarian with close-clipped hair. A sheathed fishing knife hung from his belt. Both of us were destined to become priests, unsuspecting that within a decade one would be married, the other about to be.

Surrounding all of us, the wilderness and its thousand hills. Unquestioning. Sure of itself. Everything held together in fragile balance.

I picked up the photo, lost for a moment in its faces. Surely we made a peculiar sight, yet it spoke of another enduring balance. Hinted of a church sure of itself. Unquestioning, with everything in its place.

"There!" The bishop made the sign of the cross and closed his breviary, twinkling. "Don't ask me how it was up there today. Fresh snow. Sunshine. You wouldn't have liked it. No way."

"Come on. Rub it in! Some of us had to work today."

"Let me just say one thing." He whistled. "Powder river! Yes, sir. Powder river all the way! Talk about dynamite!" His hands slapped together with a pop.

Years earlier I had awaited those same hands. Shortly before the evening ordination ceremony, a TV commentator, bemoaning our tumultuous times, announced that Robert Kennedy had been shot.

Later, as I lay face down on the sanctuary floor awaiting the moment, the picture of Kennedy lying in a pool of blood intruded. I shuddered, then rose in a rush of joy to feel Hunthausen's thick hands settling over my head, calling me at last to the priesthood of Jesus Christ.

Now he recognized the preoccupation spreading like dye over my face.

"Mike?"

"Huh?"

"You're somewhere else. What's up?"

"Dutch, remember when you told me how surprised you were to be named bishop? You asked the apostolic delegate for time to think it over?"

His mood shifted. The bishop removed his glasses, rubbing his forehead as he habitually did when anticipating something heavy.

"It was the last thing you ever expected—thought it was a mistake they'd asked you. All you wanted to be was a parish priest. Finally you said yes because it felt like God's will?"

Hunthausen remembered, drumming his fingers on the armchair. Waiting.

Once I tugged at the first thread, the whole tapestry of Joan and our decision to marry unraveled completely. The bishop sat quietly throughout.

"I've wanted to tell you about it for ages. Now I wonder why it took so long." His flat eyes and sagging face answered why.

"Golly, Mike. Well, ah, frankly, I didn't have the foggiest idea. How long have you been thinking about this?"

"More than two years."

He winced. "I'm sure it hasn't been easy. You've lost weight."

"Yes. Twenty pounds."

"Do I know Joan?"

"You met her a couple of times. She's head of our parish liturgical commission."

He didn't remember. "Two years? Well then, you've thought it through. Gosh, you could have knocked me over!"

He was hurting. We both were. I hastened on, explaining I'd had close friendships with women before. Was once even a bit smug in my ability to maintain distance and detached control. Falling in love came as a surprise.

"It's so natural, Dutch. If anything, loving Joan complements the work I'm called to do. It feels right. If only it weren't for the church stepping on stage, repeating those worn lines about celibacy. It's all from a different world, and a stupid one at that!"

Hunthausen bristled. "Hey, hang on. I have to disagree! Celibacy has real value. In my own life it's been meaningful. Besides, at least for me, it wouldn't be fair to a woman and family. For one thing, I'm never home."

"I'm sorry. I didn't mean it the way it sounded. Sure, it's good for some. Maybe more so for a bishop, but not for everyone. Anyway, being a priest is about ministry, not celibacy. Or should be."

He leaned out on the edge of the chair. "But when I was ordained, I knew the cost. You knew what you were getting into. It's not like we didn't give you time to choose."

"True, and I intend to toe the line. It's just that things have changed. I don't believe God binds us to impossible standards."

"I have to admit"—he smiled softly—"that celibacy has always been the most difficult part for me. In the seminary they said we were to be victims. Like Christ, the victim dies."

Throughout the diocese, Hunthausen had a reputation of doting over children. Not until that moment did it strike me that their absence in his own life was perhaps his harshest cross.

He went into the kitchenette and returned with coffee, recounting the stories of other men who talked with him of marriage. Shared his frustration at seeing them lost to the work of the church.

"It hurt me to see them go, believe me. Like Vance Mudd. So many lately. But you, Mike." He cradled his forehead in his hands, sparse silver strands protruding between his fingers, and thought a moment before glancing up. "I feel the Lord truly wants you to be a priest. Always have. Seeing you leave, it's tragic. I'd almost see my own vocation lost."

Moisture rushed to my eyes at the prospect of losing it all. Losing what filled the soul of every day. I swallowed hard. Any thought of being cast out of a life so focused and utterly right was shattering. Still, for her, I would do it.

"It's all because of getting trapped in the spider's web of celibacy. We call her 'Mother,' but the church is really male. Even when I was a kid, the nuns were scurrying about in 'Father's' wake. Everywhere you look it's men. Men at the altar. Men in their robes. Men in Rome. No wonder celibacy is everything. It keeps women out!" I snapped, struggling to stay on top of my feelings.

He waved me off. "Let's pray you don't grow bitter with the church."

For several minutes we sat in silence, the bishop sensing there was more. In a way, it didn't seem fair to put him on the spot and force him to reject me when he didn't really have a choice. Then again, neither did I. As a gambler risking deuces against a stacked deck, I spilled out my desire to marry and remain at Resurrection. Throughout, he barely moved, an incredulous expression inching over his face.

"The church is willing to waste priests despite the needs of the people. All in the name of a law which doesn't make sense," I said, pausing to catch my breath. "But, I'm getting off the track. No way do I want to make a cause out of this. It's too personal. Dutch? Please. I just don't want to have to leave, but I love her."

When he did respond, it was anything but what I expected.

"You know, you're not by any means the first priest to sit in that chair and tell me he wanted to get married. You are the first one to suggest staying. That's great. Really it is!"

I leaned back, relieved that at least he hadn't suspended me on the spot, which many bishops might have done. Nor had he rejected me along with my suggestion, which he most certainly would now have to dismiss outright.

"It would delight me if you could stay, Mike. There's no way. You know the law of the church as well as I do. The Holy Father is especially adamant on this point."

"For sure. He's recently been calling priests who get married, 'Judases'."

"So I've heard," he said sadly. "I just don't believe he really said it. Whatever he is, Paul the Sixth is kind. Though I do know many of those in high places feel betrayed by priests who've left to marry."

"They were kicked out," I corrected him, knowing at once it was unnecessary. "Judas betrayed Christ. Those guys fell in love, that's all."

Regardless, the bishop was stressing what we both knew. There was no way Rome would tolerate my suggestion. With little to lose, I switched the focus, rushing on about Huub and Tine. Midway through, Dutch went over to a desk, returned with a pad, and began taking notes.

"Does this priest celebrate mass?"

"All but the words of institution. He whispers them under his breath while the priest next to him says them out loud."

"Gad, that's absurd!"

"Not really. It's what we all do at concelebration. Besides, that way, if the Curia checks around, it's technically the other priest saying the mass."

"Does he do everything else?"

I nodded, then corrected myself. "His situation is so different from ours. I wasn't there long enough to know for sure."

Hunthausen asked a few more questions, mostly about Joan. Her background and relationship with the parish. He emphasized that America wasn't Holland; that Resurrection was much different from the Ekklesia. More ordinary. Not at all on the fringe. "Still, I think a bishop is sometimes obliged to overlook concerns which occupy the Curia for the sake of larger issues."

I don't know when it dawned on me that the tide had shifted. That the bishop was actually considering my remaining at Resurrection after our marriage.

He sat back, lifting his feet onto the ottoman. "Even if we agreed on your remaining, I can't for the life of me think how we'd do it. I'm not so sure the people are ready for it. For Catholics, a priest isn't married and that's that. No. It would be too tough on them. It'd blow up in your face."

I disagreed. Willing to admit he might be wrong, the bishop insisted that even if the parish accepted us, some priests would offer firm resistance.

"I can't understand that!" I flushed. "You'd think it would be in their best interests, if nothing else."

"It's too intimidating. Throws into question what they've devoted their whole lives to. Besides . . ."

Frustrated, I interrupted. "The same guys you're talking about look the other way at a buddy who's playing around or one drinking up the parish funds! But if any of us want to marry, they'll throw a party so long as we get the hell out!"

"Come on, Mike. They deserve more than that."

The fact was, neither of us knew how anyone would react, though for the next hour we tried to guess. It was nearly ten o'clock when the bishop removed his glasses and massaged a deep furrow above his nose.

"Okay. I'm weary of seeing the church lose dedicated talent this way! Caston Broderick is the best canonist around. I'll talk with him in the morning. If there's a way through the law, he'll know."

He was willing to give it a try. I couldn't believe it.

"It's pretty risky for you, Dutch," I stammered. "It's just that . . . well, I don't want you to get into any trouble."

He stood, stretched, then touched me gently on the shoulder.

"Quit worrying about me. We both know any serious attempt at renewal is bound to have its critics. Besides, it's the right thing to do and someone has to take the first step." His eyes brightened. "All they could do is retire me early to a country parish somewhere. That's all I've wanted ever since becoming a priest anyway!''

I smiled, still stunned by his willingness to test the waters.

"Now don't get your hopes up too much," he added. "We'll take it a step at a time and see how it goes. Just so you understand, you may have to bail out somewhere along the line if we hit a snag.''

So we agreed to search for a way. Before leaving, we knelt together. It didn't make sense. There was no way he should have said yes. Then again, perhaps the Holy Spirit we prayed to was involved in the ancient game of writing straight with crooked lines. For Dutch's sake and our own, I hoped so.

When I returned to the car, Joan, who'd been waiting at the door of the darkened library, slid into the seat next to me, kissed me quickly. "Well, hon?''

"He bowled me over! It was beautiful. If only I could be half so good! He didn't lash out—assumed the best of us from the start. He wants to talk with the chancellor first, but he's willing to give it a shot.''

"I know," she said as we pulled onto the highway.

"What do you mean, you know?''

"The first hour in the library was crazy. I kept worrying about you. So''—she clenched her fist, shaking it in front of her—"I thought, 'Lady, what are you doing just sitting here?' I went over to the grotto, thinking a little prayer wouldn't hurt. No one was there, and, well, somewhere along the line my stomach settled down. It felt like you were okay. Don't ask me how, but I knew.''

"Well, we're not there yet," I cautioned. "It's going to take lots of time and more patience. We might fumble the ball, yet—in fact, probably will.''

"Hey, hon.'' She punched me playfully. "I know. But doesn't it feel fantastic just knowing there's a chance?''

Indeed it did.

I scurried about the rectory, dusting furniture, emptying waste-baskets, straightening bookshelves. Due to arrive at any moment, the bishop's chancellor always triggered within me a compulsion for order and precision.

Following his ordination in Rome, which necessitated special per-mission from the pope because of his youth, Caston Broderick emerged as the whiz kid of the diocese of Helena. With a doctorate in church law from the Vatican's Gregorian University, at thirty-two he was blazing a name for himself as president of the American Canon Law Society. Although the ranks of the episcopate were normally reserved for those who earned their stripes by going-along-to-get-along, the consensus among the clergy was that Broderick was born with a crosier in hand and would someday be elevated to the hierarchy. While Caston may have suspected he would end up at the top of the clerical heap, I wondered if deep down he was uncertain it was where he wanted to be or for his own good, where he should be.

He arrived precisely on the hour, brushed the ever-present dandruff from his overcoat while accepting a cup of coffee. His penetrating eyes, set deeply beneath bushy eyebrows, struck me as belonging to someone much older and out of place on his boyish face. Not one for small talk, he got right to the point.

"The bishop spoke with me about your decision to marry. Congratulations," he blurted out in full baritone, his smile suggesting polite reserve. "But, good grief, this business about you wanting to stay on as pastor here! You can't be serious."

"Absolutely—serious, that is."

He cleared his throat, set the coffee down carefully. "I was afraid so. To tell you the truth, I'm not at all hot on it."

I hadn't expected him to be, and sat quietly while he unsnapped a thick leather briefcase.

"Here's a memorandum I worked up for Dutch."

I glanced over it, understood enough, and pushed it aside coolly. "I can read it later. You tell me."

"Look, Mike," he said, stroking back a shock of coarse black hair that fell over his forehead. "The people here are enthusiastic about your ministry. No one doubts that. In fact, it makes the bishop's decision that much harder. He knows Resurrection's one of the most alive parishes we've got. However, that doesn't give you license to come bouncing into his office and ask him to take on the entire Roman Catholic Church!"

"For godsakes, Caston. Who's asking that? I just don't want to quit being a priest. You're a good one. You ought to understand that," I replied, trying to make it easier on both of us.

"Well, working in the chancery I sometimes wonder if it's possible to stay in touch with the real church, but I try. Anyway, back to you. I've advised the bishop not to go along with this whole thing. It's preposterous."

In a plaintive voice, as if tiptoeing around a minefield, Broderick repeated what he said to Hunthausen. The most sensible approach would be for me to resign immediately and leave the city. Perhaps go to school. Find a meaningful career. Once a dispensation arrived, we could marry.

"You're saying to leave the priesthood. That's just the point. I don't want to," I said flatly.

"Look. Lots of guys don't want to, but they do it for the good of the church."

"Don't give me that crap about the good of the church! Losing all the training and commitment—that's good for the church?"

Caston sipped at his coffee, his ears crimson. "You know what I mean. It's just not healthy for the church to get pushed like this."

"Pushed! I suppose it's healthy for me, for Joan, for God knows how many others to live this way!"

"Look. It's not my decision," he replied, steadier. "The night you two talked, Dutch responded from his heart. You know how he is. But he's also a bishop. He's had second thoughts."

"He's backing off?"

"No, no." Broderick's arm shot out as if to push the words back into me. "Don't get me wrong! He's still willing to give it a try, but he's a bit more realistic about the obstacles."

"No doubt after listening to you!" I said, regretting the tenor of our conversation.

Caston sat back, to disengage. "I understand your cause. It's a noble one."

"There's no cause. We're caught between a rock and a hard place. It's wrong to leave Joan or the priesthood. Call it a question of conscience."

"So's my obligation as chancellor. All hell could break loose over this if the bishop buys into it," he said more firmly.

"All hell is breaking loose, Caston," I countered. "Dammit, how many more priests is the church willing to toss away for a tradition with a weaker theological base than indulgences?"

"Mike, the law is clear and . . ."

"A law that says Joan is a problem because she is a woman! It denigrates her and all women, and devalues marriage, to boot!"

He laughed, still tense. "I thought you said this wasn't a cause."

"Touché! But look at it. Fewer priests. Parishes closing. We're like lemmings rushing into the sea. Somewhere people have to stand up to this institutional suicide and say no!"

Broderick acknowledged that the price the church was paying for a celibate priesthood was too high. Agreed that there should be a change, an option. Yet he spoke with a Roman collar wrapped tightly around his soul. I wondered whether or not such an option would threaten his own adjustment to a world he measured in right angles.

"The Vatican is paranoid over celibacy," he was saying. "Just the other day Pope Paul called it the most beautiful stone in the Blessed Mother's crown." We both winced as he continued. "There'll be a change but probably not in our lifetime."

"Another lifetime's too late. Besides, if it's a gift, why demand it of everyone? If being celibate makes you a better person, a better priest, great! Have at it! Loving Joan has done the same for me."

"Whoa," he said, holding up both hands. "No argument. But the bureaucracy at the Vatican is unreal. Last time I was there it took me six weeks to recover. About a third of them are sincerely trying to foster the gospel. Another third mostly direct the machinery of the church. The final third make you realize that original sin is alive and thriving. They can be brutal. You've got to be realistic."

"Realistic? Jesus wasn't realistic with the Pharisees. He had harsh words for those who place heavy burdens on others and make rules as if they were from God!" I sat back, stretched to shake off the tension, unsure whether we were arguing about celibacy, the church, or each other.

"Just remember that putting the bishop on the spot like this . . . well, he could get creamed if the Curia gets wind of it. Cardinal Wright is heading up the Congregation of the Clergy. He already thinks Dutch is a radical and would love to find a reason to put him on a shelf."

Like two wrestlers seeking to elude each other's grasp, we continued to maneuver for the better part of an hour. In the end Caston took back the memo, his voice weary.

"All right. It was important to try. I didn't think you'd agree." Tearing the memo in half, he rose and limped from the room—a permanent reminder of the time he let loose with reckless abandon on the ski hill, only to pay the price. In his absence I lamented the tension between us; longed for the day we would quit competing and come closer together. The toilet flushed and he returned.

"Okay. Let's get on with it," he sighed, removing his suit coat, and proceeded expeditiously to outline the problems we would have to confront from the outset. In a nutshell, there were three—church law, the people of Resurrection, and the priests of the diocese.

While at first glance the law appeared clear, the bishop had asked

Broderick to seek a way around its quicksand. Never one to take a challenge lightly, he had dusted off a few books, discovering a footnote buried in the regulations.

"When the pope grants a dispensation to marry, the priest is laicized. Problem is, no one knows what that really means. Even Wright himself admits it's a legal fiction. No one denies the basic dogma, once ordained a man is always a priest, and that is definitely on your side."

It was basic enough, nothing new. The Vatican admitted as much by permitting married priests to hear confessions and grant the last rites during emergencies, as with death at hand and a celibate unavailable.

Caston continued; he might have been lecturing to an entire class. "For the bishop to do this, he'll have to be convinced the law is contrary to the spirit of the gospel. Even then, he'll want to be somehow within it."

"That's where its vagueness comes in?" I asked.

"Exactly. The law's vague and leaves it up to the local bishop as to when a dispensed priest can be used. You know, what constitutes an emergency. That's our loophole. If we stretch the law to its furthest point. After all, we're getting short on priests. The people have a right to the services of the church . . . well, it's possible."

The whole point was to be low-profile and keep the Curia off us. However, if they did catch wind after the marriage, at least there would be something in the law to fall back on.

It was my turn to smile. "In other words, if they want to count the number of angels on the head of a pin, we at least should get a few of the critters on our side!"

Caston flipped a note pad on the coffee table, leaned forward over his knees. "Dutch is right that someone has to go out on a limb first—just wish it wasn't him. The Vatican keeps grinding out the line that the people aren't ready to accept a married priest. It's a Catch Twenty-two because there aren't any precedents." At last he lightened up. "You can imagine the response if we cited the example of the Protestants!"

For the first time, it struck me that Caston, too, was running a risk. Any identification with efforts to keep me in the ministry after marriage could pull the hierarchical ladder out from under him.

"The bishop won't go ahead if there is firm resistance by his priests or your parish."

"All the bases covered beforehand?"

"It'll take time, Mike. Lots of time."

It was my turn to slip into the bathroom; in the mirror my bloodshot eyes stared back at me. The prospect of still more delay felt dreadful. After waiting this long, Joan and I were just beginning. Maybe Caston was right all along—just get out and take up another career. I threw cold water on my face and, remembering the eagle on Castle Rock, returned to the room as the chancellor was saying the parish was unlikely to accept a married priest.

"Caston, come on now," I said impatiently. "The church has a big thing but the people could care less."

"Some will say the law is the law and you should leave like everyone else."

I pointed to the shelf containing a copy of Paul VI's encyclicals. "Well, if they do, then we can ask them when was the last time they practiced birth control. That's against the rules, too."

Whether or not they would accept us was something we could only guess at. However, like Hunthausen, Caston felt the major opposition would arise among the priests.

"Geez, it's unreal," I blurted, pointing toward a picture of my seminary classmates on the wall. "I can't imagine it from any of them."

"It's not them, although the younger ones might surprise us. Mostly it's the older guys. You know, they've paid their dues and would resent you, at gut level."

I wondered about Caston. Would he too have a tough time at that level? Then again, he seemed content with celibacy; appeared to find comfort in its style, its distance.

Never one to waste time, he glanced at his watch, declining an invitation to lunch. Trudging through the snow to his car, he turned abruptly. "Just so you understand. I've got to be the devil's advocate on this, but will do whatever I can." He hesitated. "Maybe the Holy Spirit is in this more than we think."

I thanked him, wanting to say more, to get beyond our defenses somehow, but I didn't know how. Seconds later, he was driving away, already dictating into a tape recorder.

It was my turn to wait. Feigning interest in a magazine, I repeatedly glanced through the glass door behind which Joan and the bishop were in animated conversation, like characters on a silent screen. In that opaque interlude the drama of what was happening hit me full force.

It had taken two years of groping our way inch by inch to arrive at the juncture now before us. I wondered what expression would cross the stern face of Joan's childhood pastor were he to witness the scene before me. Wondered, too, about her family, raised at a respectful distance from the hierarchy, within a tradition forever obliging Catholic women to stay in their proper place. Despite myself, I began to question what was coming. The bishop had wanted to visit with Joan. Had he succumbed to the temptation to fall in line? Were her expectations about to be hurled against the glass, shattered in pieces once again?

I flipped through another couple of pages, just as Joan reached over to touch the sleeve of his sweater. He laughed, slapping his knee. If there was any reservation or tension between his instincts and the miter he was obliged to wear, it didn't show. All my concern over his possible second thoughts evaporated when the doors swung open.

"Not only are you fortunate to have her in your life," he said, "but so is the church."

Joan blushed. We sat down to discuss the task ahead. It would be necessary for the Personnel Board—a group of priests responsible for clergy assigments—to affirm their support of the bishop's decision to keep me. If they turned thumbs down, then we would abandon the effort. If they agreed, we would proceed with the next step. While the bishop would do his part, it would be up to me to talk confidentially with the board and later with as many priests in the diocese as possible. Only then would Joan and I consult with the parish.

"We have a morale problem with priests everywhere in the country; our diocese is no exception. We've lost so many good men to the celibacy rule. It really hurts," Dutch said, speaking to Joan.

Indeed it did. For a second, I thought of those men and the women they loved. Of their loss. Knowing it was they who gave us the chance, their often-broken hearts, like so many cobblestones, had paved the way now open before us.

Hunthausen was still talking.

"Now we have an opportunity to hang on to one. After we see if it works out with Mike for a few years, there may be others. In the meantime, it should boost the troops' morale."

"There will be some who aren't going to like it," I said.

"Yes, but most of the guys will be okay. They'll want what's best for the church. If there's a problem, they can always talk it over with me."

So the plan was set in motion. If the Personnel Board went along—if there was no major opposition from the clergy or the leadership of Resurrection—I would apply for a dispensation from the Vatican to be released from the law of celibacy. In the meantime, with the exception of those we talked with in confidence, we would continue concealing our love.

"I trust you two to handle it well," Hunthausen said gently. "You'll have a real balancing act, what with this and the demands of a large parish. It'll take patience. The entire process will take a while."

Joan took a breath. "How long?"

When the bishop said a year or more, she turned white, started to say something, then bit at her lower lip and fell into silence. We paused. There was nothing more to say, except to pray aloud at that moment—each for the other.

At the car the bishop hugged Joan, startling us by thanking her for what she was willing to endure for the sake of the church. Over his shoulder, I noticed a stiff movement. The vicar-general of the diocese was watching us from behind the curtains of the chancery window.

Within a few weeks, I managed to see all seven members of the board. One suggested our venture was preposterous and could seriously disturb "the flock." Another drilled me repeatedly about Joan, making no attempt to conceal an underlying hostility. Among those remaining, the pattern was the same. Stunned silence, followed by curiosity and a willingness to think things over.

The board scheduled a meeting for the first Monday in March. That same morning, I sat across the breakfast table from Tim, who was starting still another round in his battle with the waistline. Since the bishop was lending support to our efforts, Tim was beginning to feel we might just succeed, though confessing he got tired just thinking about the energy it would require of us all. This morning, staring into the sports page, he tactfully didn't raise the subject at all.

Throughout the day I kept turning the possibilities over in my mind. Hunthausen needed a clear majority. It was all but certain that two, probably more, from the board would reject us outright. What if the vote split too close? Then again, the tide might run decidedly against us. If so, could he really blame them? Acceptance was risky business for the diocese, the bishop.

Though crammed with appointments, a weekly conference with Protestant clergy and a seminar for divorced Catholics, the day dragged on forever. By late evening, with still no word, the dull ache of failure set in. However reluctantly, I would have to leave. The only solace, we had done all we could. Then the phone rang.

Hearing Larry Haefield's voice, I knew at once. As a member of the board, and a close friend, it fell on him to break the news. We had first met as students in college while I was selling magazines. With little change to spare, but not wanting to turn me away, he bought a subscription. It was the only one I managed to sell. This time, too, it would be hard to turn me away. He would be nervous. Hurt. My heart went out to him.

For several minutes I rambled on about the parish, deliberately avoiding the blow he called to deliver. Eventually he prevailed.

"Sorry we're so late getting to you. We met through dinner. Just broke up."

"And you drew the short straw."

"Huh?"

"Hey, Larry, you sound so serious. Lighten up."

"Pot calling the kettle black, I'd say. By the way, Stenzel's here. He's sprawled out on the couch behind me."

Ernie Stenzel was also a board member. For a moment the picture flashed by of him leaning out the Jeep whispering about "Mother's" nice-looking legs.

"What do you think of that?" Larry asked. "Mike? Did you hear what I said?"

I hadn't, but knew anyway.

"Oh yeah. Well, that's the breaks. Sometimes I sink my teeth into things like a bulldog and have a tough time letting go. Well, we tried. It was up to the Spirit," I replied, suddenly empty.

"What are you talking about? It was a clean sweep. They gave you and Joan the green light."

"You're kidding. Come on." But he wasn't joking. I let out a low whistle, wanting to reach out through the wire and rumple the thin wisp of hair concealing his baldness.

"A hundred percent for? How'd Dutch take it?"

Larry reconstructed the day's events. To avoid pressuring the group one way or the other, Hunthausen hadn't attended the meeting. Still, there was little question but that his backing was a decisive factor in the decision.

"All day long, I've felt like Zacchaeus perched up in his sycamore. It's a helpless and lonely spot to be in. You guys just called me down from that tree and it feels damn good!"

Stenzel heard me and took the phone. Ernie was normally casual to the point where we often teased him about not having a pulse rate, but this time it was racing.

"Listen, Miles, just to keep your ego in check. Larry knows Joan and so do I. Both of us voted more for her than for you! Sometimes I have a nightmare that I'll end up the only priest left in the diocese except for Black Bart."

He was referring to an older pastor notorious for his treatment of assistant priests, and nearly everyone else for that matter.

"In all seriousness, you know what did it? Deep down, most of us for the first time admitted to feelings of anger and loss when guys leave to marry. It hurts. The fact that you want to stay and are willing to put up with all the crap that it could involve . . . well, it means a lot."

"Okay," Larry said, taking back the phone. "That's the good news. Now for the bad." Most of them were concerned about church law. Doubted whether even the broadest interpretation would be acceptable to the Vatican.

"We'll be low-profile. Rome won't know, at least for a while," I said, feeling Larry squirm a bit on the other end of the line.

"Yeah. As far as I'm concerned, what the Curia doesn't know won't hurt them, but we can't expect the rest of the board to feel that way. Plus the fact that a couple of them are adamant that after the marriage there be definite distinctions between you and us celibates." His voice was tight, protective. I could picture him tugging at his beard.

"To tell you the truth, Mike, I think a couple of the guys are still resentful. See you as trying to crash a men's club with Joan. They may have gone along because they don't believe it will ever happen. They think you'll run into too much flak down the line. They just don't want to be saddled with the responsibility of saying no, especially to the bishop."

Just as we were about to break off, Stenzel added a word of caution. "Metzner there at Rosary could be a real stumbling block. It's no secret he's miffed at you. Seems to blame you—in part—whenever people leave his place for Resurrection. You have to get to him soon. My guess is he'll oppose it as a way of getting rid of you."

I thanked them, hung up, putting Metzner out of mind. Outside, I raced the few blocks to Joan's house. The lights were out. I wanted to walk in, kiss her softly, and whisper that the vote was unanimous. The door was locked. Scrawling "Thumbs up!" on a frosted bedroom window, I let her be, knowing we would both need rest for the way now open before us.

I knelt in the chapel of Borromeo Hall before going upstairs to see Father Gregory Kohl. Of all the places on the Carroll College campus, the chapel contained the most memories for me. It was there, surrounded by stained glass and silence, that I ultimately decided to enter the seminary. They were different days, when Catholics prided themselves in offering sons to the church. Days when ordination provided an entrée into an exclusive clerical world where institutional loyalty and sense of fraternity were of paramount value. A world where everyone knew his place, and one which the Second Vatican Council was about to turn upside down.

Since the Personnel Board's decision, I started out the New Year determined to talk with as many priests in the diocese as possible. Initially I gravitated toward those most likely to be open to our plans. With rare exception, the response was incredulous but positive. There were always questions, ranging from the nature of my involvement with the sacraments once married, to such minor concerns as the use of clerical garb. My reply was always the same. The experiment needed time to evolve. Nothing would be carved in stone. As time wore on, and I worked down the list of more than a hundred priests, the going started to get rougher.

I rose from the pew, genuflected and went up to Kohl's room. So many times as a student I had knocked on that same door to be welcomed by the stern but pious man, once considered the finest spiritual director available.

"Yes?" Gregory whisked open the door, poking his bald head around the corner, a slight smile behind his shy demeanor indicating he was pleased to see me. I hadn't worn a cassock in nearly a decade, yet there he was looking much the same as he had years earlier. He pulled the cassock around his wiry frame, settling back into the same corduroy chair I had knelt against whenever he heard my confession. Nearby, a crucifix—no larger than a man's hand—which he held while granting absolution.

"Father"—I never called him Gregory—"it's been a couple of years, but you haven't changed." He hadn't on the outside, though he was rumored to be growing increasingly conservative on the inside.

"Teaching the classics preserves me, gives one perspective. Remember, *Domine—sic transit gloria mundi.*"

He waited for me to translate.

"Thus passes the glory of the world," I said dutifully.

He smiled approvingly, pointing to the streaks of gray running through my hair. "Look what the world's doing to you! I told the bishop he shouldn't have sent a young man into such a secular environment. You're still a bit wet behind the ears."

I wondered how to tell him. How to break the news to the one man who more than any other had encouraged me along the many years to the priesthood. Unable to think about it any longer, I inched in.

"Ah, the reason I called was . . . well . . ." I faltered, feeling stifled, remembering the days in the dead of winter when Kohl would toss open the window to spur our early morning Latin class to life. Removing his rimless glasses, he began to polish them with a white handkerchief, waiting for me to continue. Unable to sit any longer, I walked over to the window, turned, and looked up at the crucifix.

"I just wanted to tell you before you heard it from someone else." Easing into the topic, I told him how much he and the priesthood meant to me. He sat silently, still polishing the lenses.

"I stopped in the chapel and prayed this would all come out okay. Well, here goes—I've met a wonderful woman. We're going to get married." Though somewhat apologetically, it was out.

"Oh Lord. No!" Kohl tossed the handkerchief to the floor.

Before he could say anything, I rushed on, underlining that there was no rejection of the priesthood we both treasured, explaining the bishop's intentions to permit me to stay. At first, he didn't react, just kept sitting there, staring at the floor. Finally he spoke, nearly inaudible.

"You're dead set on this?"

I nodded.

"All this business about you staying as pastor. It's so much foolishness. Who do you think you are? Rome will never tolerate it. She's far too wise."

It was my turn to remain silent. I leaned against the wall, folding my arms as if to protect something deep within me, while he dismissed any and all reasons for carrying out my intention to marry and remain at Resurrection.

"Now, listen to me, please! It's not too late. Get out of Bozeman. Go to a monastery and get on your knees until they bleed," he pleaded.

"I've been on my knees, Father. It's too late. You don't know what it's like to fall in love."

"Hogwash!" he said, repeatedly clenching his fist as if to break each word in two. "It's only too late if you decide to go on with this foolishness. Why didn't you come to me when this affair started? When you first met this . . . this . . . whatever she is! The church canons specifically warn against associating with suspect women."

The crown on the top of his head was crimson, a vein protruding along his right temple. The more I sought to explain, the angrier he became. I started to feel sick, not wanting to lose this man who meant so much, yet feeling him slip away.

"Well, go ahead. You and the bishop do whatever you want. That seems to be his pattern anyway. It's tragic, but the church will survive. She always does. Just don't expect me to go along. Not that it makes any difference to you anyway," he muttered.

I reached over and touched him on the shoulder. He pushed my hand away.

"Go on! You're in Sacred Orders. I just don't see how you can betray the church this way," he stammered.

"Betray?" I fumbled for words. There were none.

He sat back in the chair, the vein along his temple throbbing. "Why in God's name did you get tied up with the floozy in the first place?"

"Floozy! How can you call her that? It's outrageous! You don't even know her. She's Catholic. The best person in my . . .' '

"Some Catholic. It's your soul, Michael. If you want to throw it away on some woman who has nothing better to do than chase a priest, then have at it!" he shouted, looking more injured than angry.

Kohl yanked open the door, pointing to the hallway. Casting a final look back, I wanted to ask him about the ordinary clay he so often reminded us that priests were made of. It was no use, his mind was set, and my distress too tearing. All I could muster was a whispered "Good-bye." He didn't answer. I went downstairs to the chapel, kneeling before the tabernacle, fighting off tears of anger and loss.

Although I was unable to see all the priests in the diocese, for the most part those whom I did see appeared supportive. Even those who greeted the news with stony silence or open hostility were content to sit back and see what developed, confident that what sounded like a pipe dream would never materialize. By the end of spring, it was time to turn our focus to a sampling of Resurrection Parish itself.

Whenever I brought up the repeated warnings echoed by some clergy that the laity constituted a minefield on the celibacy issue—

Joan tossed the gospel back at me. "Martha, Martha, you worry and fret about so many things!" It was that same capriciousness which one afternoon led her to jump the gun.

She was strolling across campus with Kirby Walsh, a prematurely gray psychologist who had come to know us over the years as well as anyone in Bozeman. Recognized as bright and articulate among his peers, Kirby was known best through his unbridled wit.

"You know, Kirby, from the back your walk resembles Charlie Chaplin," I ribbed, catching up with them. "What are you up to?"

"Just chatting," she said, moving alongside me. "But now that you're here, well, this is right out of the blue, but maybe we ought to tell Kirby?"

I stopped short, my stern glance a reminder that we hadn't told anyone in the parish.

She ignored me. "As a friend, we want you to be the first in Resurrection to know."

"Also, since you're co-chair of the parish council," I added, realizing she was not about to back off.

"It involves you, doesn't it?" Walsh prodded, taken by the broad smile spreading over her face.

"Yes, it . . ."

"Whoa!," he said, cupping his hand over his mouth. "Don't tell me. Let me guess. The ol' sleuth here has been watching you birds lately. Every time I'm at the church, no matter what day of the week, Joan's there. Oh, I know—you're helping with retreats, liturgy and all. But there's got to be more to it than that."

Joan's eyes danced along with each word, like notes across a musical score. Suddenly there wasn't a doubt in my mind he had figured us out long ago. After all, he had the training, the perception, and had been close to us for years.

Playfully Joan continued to egg him on. "So you've got it all worked out. What's that crystal ball say, doctor?"

"The woman doubts my perception," he said, lifting both hands in resignation. "All right . . . When the most eligible female on the faculty doesn't date—and the only man who seems to have her attentions is a priest . . . Well?"

The muscles along my back tightened. Since he knew, maybe others did, too. Despite our seasoned caution, our names had no doubt been drifting in waves of chatter above coffee cups all along.

"Well, what? Come on, shorty," she said, tugging at his sleeve.

Spinning around to face us, he snapped his fingers. "Okay, if I must display gifts of insight second only to Sherlock Holmes himself . . . Joan's entering the convent!"

Giving him a quick hug, Joan started to giggle. "Oh, Kirby. I love you. What in the world ever made you think . . . ? Come on, you're teasing."

His ears turned crimson. He wasn't joking.

"Well, when a woman shows precious little interest in marriage. Is all caught up in the church . . . what else is a good Catholic like myself supposed to think of but the nunnery?"

"Who's not interested in marriage?" she jibed.

Stopping at a courtyard fountain, we sat and told him of our plans. Throughout he kept repeating, "That's fine. Yes, sir. Oh damn, but it is!"

When we finished, he mentioned that his wife once suggested we were a good match for each other. He had half-admonished her, refusing even to consider the possibility of a union which could never be.

"My Catholic upbringing and all. Still, I've always wondered why Protestant ministers and rabbis could do a perfectly good job, yet if I decided tomorrow to become a priest . . . no dice. Just because of Maxine and the kids. That's a bit of an insult when you think about it." He leaned back against the fountain, speaking softly. "Then, again, I can see where it's hard for popes and bishops. Unless they're in love, it's hard to understand."

When I started to apologize for not mentioning our relationship earlier, Kirby sent a scolding look right through me.

"No one has a right to know. Anyone you choose to tell is purely and simply your guest."

He cautioned against telling too many in the parish until we were certain there were no stumbling blocks.

"There are going to be some who think they should have known earlier," I said.

"Well, that's their problem, isn't it? They don't own you, for crying out loud! You have a right to your own lives." He stood, mimicking being in the pulpit. "Maybe all you out there should tell us how many times you've had intercourse in the last month so we can put it in the parish bulletin."

Our seriousness gave way to laughter. A joy as much at finally being ourselves in front of him as anything else. He excused himself for an appointment, but not before reassuring us that the response in the parish would be positive.

"Most everyone will be great. Believe me. The only thing they won't like are the restrictions you mentioned."

"We don't even know what they'll be yet." I shrugged. "They won't jeopardize anything essential to my work. Rather than tie us down, the bishop wants to leave enough elbow room for the whole thing to evolve."

"A smoke screen?"

"Not really. It's just that we don't want to smother the Spirit."

"Well, no big deal. My guess is most folks will see any restrictions as a punishment for being married and they won't like it. But as far as you two getting married. No sweat." Standing, he wrapped an arm about Joan's shoulder. "You've got to remind this character that it's his preaching—the way he gets to people—which keeps packing them in. They won't want to lose him, or you. When they hear you won't be packing your bags, it'll blow them away. All this crap about celibacy is small potatoes to that."

Noting he was late, he started across the campus to his office. Joan threw him a kiss, but he didn't notice as, shuffling like Chaplin, he rounded a corner out of sight.

From the outset, we agreed with Bishop Hunthausen that unless the community of Resurrection was willing to assume part of the responsibility for a married priest, it would be unfair to them and to us to proceed. In late spring we confided in a portion of the parish leadership. Unlike the previous exchanges with the clergy, Joan accompanied me to each household. Though protective and anxious to shield her from possible rejection, I needn't have been. Without exception the reaction was enthusiastic, though there were some who were initially upset with the news of our pending marriage.

On one such occasion, an attorney stood abruptly and, turning away from us, blurted out to his embarrassed wife, "Oh shit! They've got to be kidding! That's awful. Simply awful!"

When we explained that my position in the parish would be preserved, he relaxed and sat down.

"This thing about us poor innocents in the pew not being able to take it when a priest marries is baloney. No one gives a damn about the marriage. It's just that we don't like it when a guy leaves. It's like jumping ship and abandoning the rest of us. You know, it kind of shakes a person's faith to think that the padre has quit the church.''

By the time Joan suggested that marriage forced such men to leave, often against their will, his mood was altogether transformed.

Then there was the young mother who admitted that throughout her life she had been taught that a love like ours was wrong, even sinful. "But I never could figure out why. If you ask me, a few of the fellas at the Vatican have a hang-up with sex. They probably see it as something to be tolerated for the sake of the race but off-limits for real Christians. You know what I mean—the priests and nuns.'' When she added that only a married priest could really understand those with marital problems, I disagreed, ironically spending the remainder of the conversation defending the values of authentic celibacy.

Now and then someone wondered about my backing away from a permanent commitment.

I acknowledged that in making the promise of celibacy, I intended to keep it. However, it now came into direct conflict with my deepest instincts and values. Besides, my central commitment to the priesthood itself remained unchanged.

Those with such questions listened patiently, their queries tempered by an appreciation of the unpredictability and power of human love. Yet what inevitably cleared the air was a common feeling that the law of celibacy, mandated by Pope Boniface VIII in the thirteenth century, collided head on with a higher one: God's call to love.

The acceptance continued regardless of age or circumstance; with it, the straitjacket cinched tightly around us began to unbind. The impact of such affirmation followed me even into the confessional. There, listening to muffled voices whispering in the darkness, I felt somehow more tolerant, less sure of life's complexities. More than before, confession became a time to listen, console, reach out, and try to heal.

Our confidence grew. Stress lines faded from Joan's face. Years seemed to fall away, leaving her more beautiful than ever before. Whatever the future held, she was worth it, and more.

Though the Frankenstein's monster which supposedly lurked in the closet of the average Catholic failed to show its face, a major hurdle still stood between us and my application for dispensation to the Vatican: Father Paul Metzner, the pastor of Holy Rosary.

I stopped inside Holy Rosary Church for a brief prayer. Immediately the fragrance of incense and candle wax, hovering over oaken pews worn smooth from a century of Sunday suits, ruffled dresses, and children's shoes, gave comfort and centered me.

Metzner was crucial. His opposition could divide the city's two Catholic parishes. The bishop would have to intervene, perhaps abandon the course before us. I prayed that the fears expressed by Ernie Stenzel were unfounded. Then again, maybe he was right. If Paul was upset over the loss of his parishioners to Resurrection, then what better way to solve the problem than raise an uproar over my remaining in ministry after marriage.

Crossing through the dim sanctuary and along a narrow walkway, I entered the rectory. It smelled of mothballs. Characteristically high-strung, Paul seemed more electric than normal. I wondered if he already knew. As one who kept his ear close to the clerical rail, it would be out of character if he didn't.

Fidgeting back and forth in a frayed recliner, he launched into the prospects of keeping the sole parochial school in the area solvent. I couldn't listen, wondering instead about the figure with small darting eyes behind the thick glasses. Though well read, he remained cautious of renewal, suspicious of change, as demonstrated in the recent tension over the half-dozen nuns attached to Holy Rosary.

It had begun with an invitation from the sisters to lead an evening discussion on contemporary theology. Before long, we were meeting weekly in the convent. When Metzner found out, he cautioned that the older nuns would get confused, while the younger ones would have difficulty applying new ideas to their lives. Some things were better left alone. Though he seemed to agree that religious women had been kept from attaining their rightful place in the church for far too long, nevertheless he requested a halt to our seminar. We complied.

"Paul," I said nervously, cutting into his diatribe of rising costs and shrinking income.

He stopped. Waited politely.

"I've never forgotten your story about escaping from Eastern Europe during the war. The refugee camps. How you suffered to become a priest. Well, in a tiny way, I've been suffering, too—thought you might understand." Without pausing for a reply, I plowed into the story, which was by now wearing thin in its repetition. Throughout, he listened attentively, now and then cutting in with a couple of quick coughs, a habit of his ever since I'd known him. In the end he appeared visibly moved, setting me at ease.

"I'm sure you have prayed about this," he said, more of a statement than a question. "Your girlfriend came to church here when she first moved to town. She helped me with a few counseling cases." He shuffled in the chair, bumping against a tarnished brass lamp, leaving the lace shade swaying overhead. "Has she told her parents?"

It was the first time anyone had asked the question. I replied that, until things looked more definite, we didn't want to say anything to our families.

"Right. Because it might never happen. You should make other plans just in case."

"What're you getting at?"

"Well, you know. Things could fall between the cracks," he said, crossing his legs, recrossing them. Fidgeting again. "The people up there at your place may not be able to understand if you go off and marry your girlfriend, no matter how much you try to justify it."

I let it pass.

Paul laughed uneasily. "Don't get me wrong. I don't have a problem, though I can't see how you can be faithful to the Vatican and still stay at the helm."

"Faithful? To Christ maybe."

"You sound so sanctimonious. Take it from someone who's lived longer than you, Mike. None of us are holier than the church." He coughed again. "Anyway, what you're asking for will take a small miracle. Some of the priests aren't going to like this one bit. They think Bishop Hunthausen is too liberal as it is. Oh well, it's his neck."

Tempted to ask him if he felt the same way, I didn't because he abruptly returned to the subject of parish finances. There was something left unsaid between us. Something neither of us felt inclined to pursue. Still, to my relief, though skeptical about our success, Metzner didn't appear opposed. The way was open to see the chancellor and prepare to petition Rome.

The chancellor struck us as more receptive to our intentions than he had earlier on. Seated stiffly in a high-backed rocker Joan had received on her thirtieth birthday, Caston Broderick reviewed the next step in our journey. Whenever a man sought release from the law of celibacy, it was necessary for him to petition the Vatican. Such release, if granted, invariably carried with it immediate removal from the priesthood. Now it was my turn to seek the dispensation. Only this time there would be no such banishment.

"As you know," Caston explained to Joan, in the smothering tone he frequently used with women, "it's important to the bishop and I presume just as imperative for you that your marriage is sacramental. Therefore, we have to get Mike released from his promise."

She understood. Both of us had been over the procedure several times. Hunthausen and I would channel petitions to the pope through the Sacred Congregation of the Faith.

"Just so you know. We're playing Vatican roulette. Many who apply for dispensation get turned down," Broderick said.

When Joan asked why, he frowned. "They probably don't give the right reasons, or at least the ones Rome wants."

"Mike will just tell them he's in love."

Broderick shook his head. "There's no way I'd lay those cards on the table. They won't grant a dispensation if the only reason—as they put it—is 'merely to marry.' Even though the guy will be out of the priesthood anyway."

"You're kidding me."

"Nope. We have to play by their rules. In Rome, do as the Romans do!"

"Or?"

"No dispensation." The chancellor turned in my direction, his tone more familiar. "If they accepted love as a reason for people taking back their commitment to celibacy, it would leave open the possibility that they might still be good priests."

Confused, I asked what the Vatican wanted.

"A hint that you were unsuited for the priesthood all along."

Broderick waited, his dark eyes fixed upon me.

"In other words, lie?"

"No. Tell the truth but not all of it." He let out a slow sigh. "Look, Mike, any suggestion that the sentiment between you two might complement the priesthood is anathema over there. It would throw the whole system into question. You just can't be totally candid or you won't get to square one. They need to believe that falling in love was the result of a character flaw which the church overlooked or you wouldn't have been ordained in the first place."

"Then?"

"Then, presto!" he said, snapping his fingers with a loud crack. "They permit the marriage to avoid your infliction of even further scandal."

Abruptly Joan went over to the window, her back to us. Placing her elbows on the sill, she spoke to the last traces of a sunset. Her words laced with anger.

"Dispensation! Laicization! Leave it to the Holy Roman Catholic Church to come up with terms like that. Can you imagine them on the lips of Jesus Christ? Imagine any of this! Would he laugh or cry?"

Broderick glanced at me, giving me the first opportunity at response. I had none. He turned back to Joan.

"Nonetheless, the Vatican's obsessed with celibacy. The institutional church maintains a delicate balance in the world as it is. Men like Mike give it a feeling of being knocked off-balance. You've got to understand the curial mind."

"Some mind! Rome has to be right all the time," she replied, still staring into the fading sky. Then she returned to the couch. "Sorry, it's just that it's so frustrating. Maybe they ought to just divide up the church's property, sell it off, and close the whole thing down." She waved a hand, as though brushing her words from the air, and fell into silence.

Convinced that I would never say the priesthood was a personal mistake, Broderick suggested an alternative.

"Hunthausen's letter to the pope will contain something which he sees as a plus, but which will wave a red flag in front of the Curia." He smiled somewhat sheepishly. "I was looking through your file the other day and noticed where the seminary rector once cautioned us that you were an independent thinker."

"The fly in the ointment?"

He nodded.

"That doesn't mean that the bishop won't praise your work in the ministry. But in mentioning this independent thinking, it permits an opening for why, in their minds at least, a man would deviate from the pattern."

Throughout the rest of our strategizing, Joan remained somber. Eventually Broderick spoke to her mood.

"It's a bit weird, if not sick, but it's the system we have to live with. We should count our blessings. Technically Mike should be suspended even now. From the moment he told the bishop he intended to marry, he was supposed to have been put on ice. If that's not bad enough, some in the Curia want Paul the Sixth to forbid dispensations altogether. To his credit, he hasn't. Lord knows what the next Bishop of Rome might do!"

Joan seemed not to hear.

In the end we settled on compromise. I agreed to write the pope, seeking the dispensation, at the same time stressing my fondness for the priesthood and the hope that someday celibacy might be optional.

As for sharing my deepest feelings with the pontiff? No. They would remain crumpled in the wastebasket of reality.

For his part, the bishop could not mention that once the dispensation was received, I would continue. Even the hint of such a precedent-shattering move would bring the game of Vatican roulette to an immediate and explosive end.

I accompanied Caston to the hallway closet as he got his coat, inquiring how long it would take to receive Rome's response.

"Who knows? A year or so maybe. If at all. They deliberately drag their feet sometimes just to give the petitioner a chance to back off. It's also a way of making him pay." He brushed dandruff from his coat, draping it over his shoulders, suddenly more serious than before. "Just remember. You might not get it—that's a real possibility, too."

When we returned to the living room, Joan was holding a copy of the New Testament. She began reading aloud.

" 'Jesus replied . . . "I came into the world for this: to bear witness to the truth; and all who are on the side of truth listen to my voice." "Truth?" said Pilate. "What is that?" ' " She slapped the pages closed, reaching over to squeeze Broderick's hand gently. Without a word, he opened the door onto the night.

Inch by inch the gentle brush of spring spread a swath of color across the earth, with clouds swelling like geysers before rolling over and sweeping the land with a fine carpet of rain. The Gallatin Valley—a canvas where newborn calves danced across fields heavy with seed. Where tulips, impatient with waiting, lifted their heads open-mouthed toward the sun, there to sway in a breeze smelling of topsoil and honeysuckle.

It was the fourth springtime of our love and like the earth, we put the frozen times behind us, looking to a future of promise. Our work assumed a new texture. As the parish continued to burst into life, we seemed to find energy in the prospect that the end to our journey was in sight. Sunday after Sunday, I looked out upon the congregation, wondering how they would take the news, which we still concealed in case the Vatican denied our petition. A haunting possibility we refused to consider.

Seated on the corner of Joan's desk, looking out over the flow of university students scurrying between classes, I took her hand and began toying with the ring she had accepted on the Cliffs of Moher.

"We've got to get you something nicer."

"I like this one," she replied, drawing back her hand and holding it up against the light. "It may be from the five-and-dime, but it's not for sale."

"It turns your finger the forty shades of Irish green."

She smiled. "It would be nice for both of us to have something a bit more permanent. But Bozeman's a small town. You can't just bounce into a jeweler's and say, 'Hi. I'm Father Miles and this is my fiancée!' Though I'd love it."

For an instant she seemed lost in the prospect. I wondered how often she fantasized over the little things which accompany engagement, only to wrap them as fine china, storing them away within the tiny drawers of her heart. Knowing full well what was natural to others was impossible for her. I wondered, too, whether we would be permitted to drink together from the small cup of time our lives were allotted or see it spilled away.

Occasionally it all felt like make-believe. Despite our talk of dreams coming true; despite all the conversations, the acceptance and rejection, was it all simply noise? A type of Gregorian chant, droning in a theater where nothing changed. Nothing, that is, but the seasons, blending one into another.

Her eyes widened before the nakedness of my thoughts. There was no way I deserved her; merited an attachment which continued to transform a distant God's love into flesh and blood. We would go on reaching for what we dared not, for at that instant I knew that though nothing was happening, everything was.

After see-sawing back and forth, we decided that Joan would stop by a local jeweler and have the rings made. They would contain symbols once sketched upon the crumbling walls of Caesar's empire. Signs fixed over the tombs of the nameless who embodied the hope, faith, and love of another time but one stretching into our own. Their symbols, now ours: the ichthys—a fish, sketched around the first letters of the primitive creed "Jesus Christ Lord and Savior"; the Alpha and Omega—proclaiming the Messiah as the beginning and end; the cross—the pledge of life over death.

In a city where everyone seems to know everyone else, I parked the car down the block from R. Evans Jewelry, waiting for Joan to emerge. No sooner had she slipped into the seat next to me than she placed her hands over her face, fighting back the tears.

"What's this thing doing to us?" she cried, shaking her head.

"What's the matter?"

"We've been hiding for three years. That's a purgatory of time. We can't even get our wedding rings without sneaking around!" She pointed up the street toward the jewelry store. "That man knew me. He was so nice, asking me about the wedding date and all. You know, just trying to be civil. I invented some dumb thing about my fiancé being out of state. Couldn't come in for a measurement . . . and . . ." She stopped, lifting a white-knuckled fist against her mouth.

I wanted to hold her, promise the hiding was nearly over, but couldn't, anxious despite myself to avoid being seen.

"Hey, honey. I'm sorry. It never dawned on me he'd ask you . . ."

"I'm okay," she sniffled. "It's just that this is getting so old. We can't go to a movie. To dinner. We can't even walk down the street together anymore. It's so unnatural. Gosh, but it goes so much against my grain, not to be up front with people. We can't even tell our families we're getting married. I wonder if we're any better off than that priest you told me about."

"Who?"

"The one your family knew years ago . . . had to disappear?"

Though before my time, the story had made the rounds. Following his marriage and subsequent excommunication during the reign of Pius XII, he vanished in shame. Embarrassed, and assured that her son's soul was plummeting straight into hell, his mother never spoke his name again. Never, that is, until she cried out for him on her deathbed. By the time they found her son, it was too late, though he did attend the funeral in careful disguise.

"Times have changed," I said.

"The church had hold of him. It has hold of us. It lacked compassion then and sometimes I think it still does," she said, more composed.

Whenever she talked that way, I remembered her earlier innocence. Felt guilty about exposing her to a side of Catholicism she might otherwise never have seen. She sensed my tension.

"I don't want to feel this way, but don't be so protective of the darn church."

"I'm sorry. This thing is bound to be harming us enough without it eating into your feelings for it."

Her eyes flashed. "Sometimes I get so angry though. In the first place, we don't know when—if ever—those monsignors in Rome will push away from their plates of spaghetti long enough to read your letter to the pope. We don't even know if he'll say yes. We don't know anything!''

"Well, at least we know the rings will come if nothing else does," I said, feeling utterly helpless.

She stared blankly out the windshield, tears slipping down her cheeks. "Don't make light of it."

"I didn't mean it that way. Listen, lady. Regardless if we make it with the church or not, we'll still use those rings . . ." I reached over and pulled her close.

"No, not here. We're in the middle of Main Street."

"The hell with it," I said, kissing her softly.

At summer's end the rings arrived, and Joan rushed immediately to my office.

"If you'd do me the honor, sir," she said, handing me the unopened box.

I fumbled through the tissue paper and slipped the slender band over her finger.

"Perfect. Now if only we knew there was going to be a wedding." She reached for the other ring, started to place it over my outstretched finger, then frowned. "It fits like a Hula-Hoop! What'd you give me, your shoe size?"

Sheepishly, I removed it.

"Wait," Joan perked up. "I've got an idea. Remember when you broke your finger playing handball?" She took the ring and slid it onto my right hand, where it fit perfectly.

I kissed her on the tip of the nose. "Nothing we've done so far has been according to the book. No use starting now."

Moments later we removed the rings, neither of us saying what we were thinking; wondering when, if ever, we'd put them back on again.

From then on, every time I witnessed the wedding of still another young couple, enthralled at the prospect of life ahead of them, I saw those rings. Each time I clasped their hands together, pronouncing the church's blessing and belief in the dignity of love, I saw them. Whenever I looked into the sparkling eyes of a new bride, I glimpsed the image of a cross etched in burnt gold.

By early fall, the wildflowers vanished and baled hay stretched across the valley like so many biscuits in a bowl. We still hadn't heard from the Vatican, and our rings gathered dust on a cabinet shelf. Aware of our mounting anxiety, the chancellor agreed to contact a priest from the diocese living within the shadows of St. Peter's. As a student at Gregorian University during the Vatican Council, Brad Robesheau managed to secure a better seat for its sessions than most of the bishops themselves. In the ensuing years, his rugged good looks and quick mind earned him the reputation of the diocese's *bonhomme* and a sure shot for the hierarchy. If anyone could track our petition through the corridors of the Vatican and discover its fate, it was he.

In October, the Indians' "moon of changing seasons," his cable, though brief, was enough to send our spirits soaring.

SITUATION COMPLICATED BUT ENCOURAGING. SHOULD BE SOON.

Each day, as we waited for further word, Joan visited a nearby park, gathering a basketful of fallen leaves, preserving a fragment of her favored October. Delighting at the prospect of celebrating our wedding with its color, regardless of when the dispensation arrived.

It was 1:00 A.M. when the phone rang. At once I recognized Brad's voice.

"We're just sitting down to breakfast here, but I wanted you to know that a friend, a guy from New York who works in the Congregation of the Faith, ran your petition down." The line faded. He repeated through the static. "This is for sure. It'll be on the pope's desk any day now, with a recommendation that he grant it. We'll know by the end of the week—that's October thirty-first. I'll call unless something goes haywire. It shouldn't, though. It's *pro forma*. All pretty routine."

Halloween night, confident of the news from Rome, I picked up a bottle of champagne to share with Joan and Tim while we waited for Brad's call. Early in the evening, a group of students left a gigantic pumpkin glowing on the rectory steps. Joan set it on the dining room table in a basket of leaves as I popped the bottle in anticipation of the coming news.

Tim proposed a toast. "All good things come to those who wait and never give up hope. And . . . surprise the hell out of some of us!"

Smiling, while dabbing away a rivulet of minuscule bubbles from her upper lip, Joan added, "To the Great Pumpkin!"

We laughed; before long we were entertaining each other with stories of Halloweens past.

By the time the pumpkin's light had burned away, the call still hadn't come. With the pitch black of early morning upon us, a haunting unease seeped into our celebration. The champagne was drained by the time Tim awkwardly excused himself for bed. Joan began sweeping away the leaves from the dining room table, tossing them into the trash. Neither of us dared to express our fears. Suspicious that something had gone wrong; that perhaps a disgruntled priest, aware of our intentions, had tipped off the Curia, forcing the pope to back off at the last moment.

Passing by the phone, I felt a compulsion to tear it from the wall, to hurl it out into the trash with the leaves.

Joan asked for her coat, insisting over my protests on walking home alone. "It's nearly daylight. You should stay just in case Brad couldn't get through. Besides, I need to be by myself."

Limp as a rag doll, she came into my arms. Unable to think of anything to say, I prayed that closeness would give comfort when words could not. We kissed. Her lips were cold. Her eyes were flat. As she stepped out into a November morning, I saw her old for the first time. After so many seasons of waiting, she had once again lowered her defenses and become vulnerable. In the game of Vatican roulette, she had taken a shot full bore. Not only had October passed without word, but with it a part of her spirit—carried away as if on bat's wings.

I put on a pot of coffee and sat at the table. In the emptiness, witches seemed to shriek, stirring my thoughts about in a bubbling kettle.

Out of the kettle emerged the stories of those who had waited for the church. Waited to receive its blessings, its forgiveness. Waited in broken marriages, fractured lives. Always waiting. In his day Jesus never kept them waiting. As with the woman in despised Samaria who offered him a cool drink of water beneath the desert sun. Despite the criticism of the righteous, despite the failed marriages, ignoring her faults, he reached out across the well with a compassionate touch which at once healed and transformed. Now I prayed that out of our experience I might learn to be more sensitive to those who each day crossed my own life; those who waited, all too often in vain, for the church's soft touch.

Ah yes. Prayer. When we first met I was afraid of it. Fearful that by beseeching a hint of divine will, God might call me away from Joan. When at last I dared to lift up our lives, placing them before God as Isaac had done with his only son, the knife did not fall. Since then, all the signs—however opaque—pointed toward the path we now chose. Yet how much more could I ask of her? It was one thing to ask Joan to cling to frayed threads of hope, quite another to see her suffer so. Then, too, even if we got the dispensation, our journey would be far from certain. What kind of future awaited us down that road?

I looked up from the coffee cup to where across the table the jack-o'-lantern leered.

Days later, a terse cable arrived from Brad indicating only that my request was unaccountably detained. The weeks which followed were a Gethsemane as time continued to eat away at our expectations, encouraging our fears.

We were planning the parish Christmas celebration, the sound of driven sleet against the roof nearly drowning out Tim's words.

"Winter kills," I thought, the continued delay from Rome once again surfacing feelings that seemed to seep in shades of gray from my pores.

It had been a year since I first talked with the bishop; still nothing. The pelting on the rooftop continued as I thought back to Castle Rock, wondering if the river where I had seen the face of Peter's ghost still flowed beneath the ice.

A light knock on the door drew me back into the room. Our secretary stuck her head around the corner to say there was a call.

"Probably Santa saying he's not coming this year," I joked, at once regretting the forced humor and the strain our circumstance was placing on all of us.

"Hello. This is Father Miles."

"Mike."

The bishop's voice was somber.

"There's been a mail strike in Italy."

"Wouldn't you know!"

"The Congregations have been sending important documents in the diplomatic pouch. We got yours today."

I held my breath, afraid to hear more.

"You there?"

"Oh yeah. Sorry, Dutch. I was thinking of Joan. Wishing there was an easy way to tell her."

"It shouldn't be too hard. Just tell her you got the dispensation."

"What?"

"You got it. I'm sorry, I should have said it right off."

"Got it? Oh, thank God! Thank God!"

A tide of relief swept over me as the years of waiting fell away in seconds.

Hunthausen said he would get together with us to arrange the next few steps. "One of which is for you two to get married," he added.

"No sweat," I replied, unable to conceal the elation. "Maybe even before Christmas."

He whistled. "That's only three weeks. Is that enough time?"

"Time? Yeah, sure. We're going on four years of preparation. Believe me, we'll make it."

Sounding relieved, he sent greetings to Joan and hung up.

Forgetting about Tim and further discussion of Christmas, I bolted out the door, running through the swirling snow toward the university. Remembering the gentle flakes on Joan's eyelashes several winters before, when we had first kissed. I needed to hold her, tell her how much she had been then, how much more she was to me now.

Breathless, I knocked on the office door, pushing it open. Still warm, a half-cup of coffee sat next to a copy of the Scriptures on her desk.

"I'm fudging a bit," she said, startling me from behind. "Shouldn't be doing that up here, but the liturgy group meets tonight and the Advent readings aren't selected."

She closed the door, brushing her lips quickly against mine. "What brings you up here, hon?"

I wrapped an arm about her neck, covering her mouth while whispering into her ear. "We got it! Dutch called this morning. The paper came through!"

She let out a slight whimper. Her knees buckled. Releasing my hand, I held her close. Felt her heart beating against my own.

"Michael." Her voice shook. "I'm so happy for you. Oh, Lord, I don't know what we'd have done."

"For me? For us!"

Just then the bell for class rang.

"Want to get married, young lady?" I said, stepping back, resting my hands on her shoulders.

"Thought you'd never ask. You've got a deal!" Joan gathered up her notes, squeezed my hand, and dashed down the hallway to her second lecture of the day.

I lingered a moment at the door, then returned to slip the Scriptures containing two pressed October leaves into the desk.

A few days later, we convened the parish council to break the news and seek their support, without which we dared not proceed. No sooner had I started to outline the situation to its twenty or so members than Kirby Walsh interrupted.

"Way back . . . when you talked individually with most everyone here, you said you didn't want to cause a problem in the parish. Impose a burden upon us by asking to remain. Bur-den," he said, exaggerating each syllable. "Your term, not ours. Anyway, Tim leaked the word to us about the bishop's call. So we met last night, just to save you any hassle." His voice started to crack. "It was unanimous. We want you to stay as our priest. By damn, it's high time someone did this and we're delighted it's the two of you . . . and now us."

Instinctively I reached beneath the table to clasp Joan's hand before deciding to put an arm about her and, for the first time in front of any of them, give her a hug. With that simple gesture, we took hold of something within ourselves. A lump settled in my throat. I started to speak, but Walsh waved me off and someone produced a couple of decanters of wine.

Drake Shepler, the council president, shouted for attention over the buzzing conversation. He waited, stroking his white patriarchal beard until the room grew quiet.

"From what we hear, we'll be having a wedding in a couple of weeks," he said with utter seriousness while filling a wine goblet. "So we lift this to one of our priests, thankful you'll be staying to serve among us—and to Joan, whom we have grown to love more than she knows. To Tim, who's stood by you, and to Bishop Hunthausen for his faith and courage. But most of all, we praise God for an event none of us would have expected to see, much less be part of!"

He lifted the goblet to his lips before passing it around. Everyone drank in turn.

The following morning, Raymond Hunthausen joined Joan and me in a back booth of the Western Café. Throughout the next two hours together, he was far more than a bishop permitting us to walk an uncharted path. He was an intimate participant, confident that whatever the future held, the step we were taking was the correct one. Still, he remained apprehensive over how my announcement during the coming Sunday masses would be received by the entire parish.

"After all," he said, buttering a warm cinnamon roll, "the people on the council all know you well. The handful of others you've told are friends. The hierarchy maintains the public is as adamant against priests marrying as ever. This weekend you'd best be prepared for anything."

I was the first to admit that every time I thought of standing up before the community of Resurrection, my palms grew moist, my stomach churned.

"Come on, you guys," Joan quipped, stirring cream into her coffee. "Just because this thing is for real now, doesn't mean you have to get cold feet!" She then told Hunthausen we would like to have him witness our marriage on the Thursday before Christmas, but feared such a role would put him in an awkward position.

"I'm afraid you're right. I'd love to be there, but there are some in the diocese who . . ." He sighed, pushing back from the table. "Well, let's call a spade a spade. Some of the priests are going to be terribly troubled about this. If I preside at the wedding, it would just make things worse."

We understood. After all, he was already going farther out on a limb than we ever had a right to hope for.

"Speaking of problems." He reached into a worn leather case and withdrew a manila envelope, pushing it across the table. "These are what the Curia sent along with the dispensation. You aren't going to like them, but try to take it with a grain of salt."

Tracing my fingers across the envelope, I didn't open it as the bishop looked over at Joan.

"Every time I see what they demand of a priest who marries, it hurts. Golly sakes, if we played by their rules—not only is he supposed to abandon the ministry, the two of you are supposed to get out of the city entirely."

"Well, they've got the only game in town. They want to let us know who's in command," I replied.

"The list of demands and restrictions is extensive. Caston Broderick thinks we ought to put together a much smaller one to show to any of the priests who get upset." He frowned. "He's got a point, but it's still my inclination to hold off. Not to tie you down. It'll give your situation time to evolve. And it will, so long as you take it easy.''

I recalled a recent letter from Hans Küng cautioning us to be prudent, not to give those who were critical of Hunthausen's generally progressive policies in the church any unnecessary fuel. I agreed to be careful. As for Resurrection, if they accepted our decision they would look to me for guidance along an unmarked way. Whatever the pitfalls, we would have to be low-key in approaching them.

Outside the café, the bishop hugged us both. ''Thanks for being willing to wait. Mostly though, for being willing to share your gift with the church.'' He reached into the leather case, withdrawing a slender cross bearing a carved figure of the Crucified.

''Just a little something, for the wedding,'' he said a bit self-consciously. ''For the good times and the difficult ones.'' For the first time since I'd known him, his eyes filled and he said good-bye.

''His neck's out there a mile,'' I said as the bishop's Volkswagen rounded a corner and disappeared.

''But I think it's easy for him,'' Joan mused. ''The man's not ambitious. More than that, he lives the gospel. Wasn't it Paul who said the Word cuts through all the garbage like a double-edged sword?''

''Loosely translated,'' I answered, as we turned back to the café.

Back inside the Western, I unsealed the envelope embossed in red, *Sacra Congregatio Pro Doctrina Fidei*—formerly the Congregation of the Holy Inquisition. Glancing over the two pages of stiff Latin, I handed Joan the attached translation. ''Let's see what the good fathers have cooked up for us.''

Neither of us was prepared for what we saw.

Families know one another's vulnerable spots. Those in the Vatican knew well what most priests treasure. Stunned, I thought of the thousands of other priests in recent years who, like me, had received similar documents, and I wondered how they had felt before their directives. The three pages, milked dry of all compassion, stung like a bee. Like any priest dispensed from the law of celibacy, I was to be placed under wraps. Forbidden to exercise all priestly functions. By a pen's stroke, all that I was, and still knew myself to be, was stripped away. To avoid harm to the faithful, our marriage was to be private. The event itself recorded only in the secret archives of the chancery.

Only once did I look up at Joan, embarrassed that after a lifetime of putting the church on a pedestal she should now be exposed to this. She caught my eye.

''It's much worse than I expected. They make you sound like a leper. I'm surprised you aren't supposed to be burned at the stake! I feel dirty just reading the stuff." Frustrated, she thrust the papers aside. "They talk about scandal! How'd they get so far away from the spirit of Christ? There's the scandal! Some dispensation. It's not so much about you being free to marry, as the death of your priesthood."

"Dutch said take it with a grain of salt, remember? The bureaucrats in the Vatican are like parents who sense their loss of control and have to take their frustrations out on someone in the family."

She winced. "More like fratricide."

"They don't see all this as wrong. In their minds, holding the line on celibacy is God's will," I said, again regretting my instinctive rush to protect the church.

Joan shook her head incredulously. "They're willing to waste you. Waste your talent, commitment, and love of the church. For what? Just think of all the others they've tossed by the wayside. That's God's will? You must be kidding!"

A solitary figure seated at the counter turned at the sound of frustration in her voice. Looking out from beneath his Stetson, then satisfied that what appeared to be a marital spat was over, he returned to the newspaper.

"Hey, easy, honey. I'm not defending them. Just saying what's probably in their heads," I whispered, running my finger over the heavy seal of the documents. "There's nothing in here about the gospel, nor what our parish or any other might want for that matter. Küng's right. The whole mess is immoral."

"Lump the Vatican's priorities in that mess, while you're at it," she said, still angry. "Maybe I don't know as much as I should about the bureaucracy, but it doesn't take much to see that those papers have precious little to do with Christianity."

I lowered my voice further. "The church can be like any other institution, somewhere along the line it becomes hell-bent on self-preservation."

"At any cost."

"I admit, it's wrong."

"No, it's much worse than that," she replied, searching for a word. "Sinful, even evil."

A waitress began spreading silverware across the table next to us. Against a far wall, the hands of a pale yellow clock stood straight up at twelve noon. Sliding the papers back into the envelope, I noticed a statement each priest receiving a dispensation was required to sign and return, indicating acceptance of all provisions. Leaving it unsigned, I folded it slowly, never to look at it again.

Outside, we passed a schoolyard, and for the next hour we unwound, helping children roll together a snowman. Out of pinecones and apple cores, we eventually created a smiling face to watch over their world and our own.

For Thomas Aquinas time was the "measure of motion." Whereas the four years of seeking a way out of our dilemma seemed interminable, now time accelerated, one day colliding with the next, as we prepared to share the news first with our families, then with the entire parish.

Mother frequently repeated that my ordination was the happiest moment of her life. Proof positive that a string of novenas to the Blessed Virgin, praying that her son might become a priest, worked. Rather than the trauma I expected, her initial reaction upon hearing of Joan was to make still another novena, this time thanking our Lady of Perpetual Help that her son would not be forced from the priesthood.

Dad's reaction was as predictable as hers was not. Never one fully to understand my choice of the cloth over more worldly pursuits, he immediately admitted his bewilderment about all the huff over celibacy in the first place.

Yet, both Mom and Dad cautioned us about Grandma, who, sure enough, began to weep when we told her we would marry the week before her ninetieth Christmas. Growing up, I had always been one of her favorites; forever the object of overflowing affection. That attachment now came into conflict with her faith. It made little difference that Irish blood also flowed through Joan, even less that we were in love. Nothing mattered when weighed against my eternal salvation, which she was certain would be forfeited once we married.

None of my arguments penetrated her conviction that a favored grandson was knocking at Satan's door. None, that is, until I mentioned that priests in the first thousand years of the church were married. Settling back in the overstuffed chair she took over after Gramps died, she fixed her milk-gray eyes on me.

"Even the Lord's first holy priests?"

"The apostles, Gran?"

"'Tis them I'm asking you about, Father."

"Yes, even them. Saint James, Saint Matthew. Probably all of them."

"Married men, you say?"

I let out a long breath. Nodded.

"You mean, Father, 'tis like us not having meat on Fridays and all? 'Tis a law from the monsignors and not from the Blessed Lord?"

I smiled, assuring her it was so.

All at once she began to laugh, her brogue crackling. "'Tis from the monsignors, is it now? Oh, the good monsignors, they are forever telling us what they want as if it's what the Savior wants! If 'tis good enough for Jesus that his very own followers were married, sure but 'tis good enough for someone as low as me—that you do!"

If Grandma's reaction went smoothly, that of Joan's parents did not.

One of ten children, she had captured her father's heart from the beginning. In her early years, Joan could always be seen at dawn tagging behind her dad toward the milk barn, or bouncing atop his shoulders as he came in late from the fields. It was to this curly-haired three-year-old that he wrote the first of many songs he scratched out next to a kerosene lamp long after the children were tucked into bed.

> Pretty little songbird, busy as can be.
> Pretty your song that I've heard.
> Many are the hours I've watched . . .
> What I wouldn't do just to be like you,
> So I too could sing the whole day through.
>
> Pretty little songbird, don't go away.
> Just keep on singing as you are today.
>
> Please don't leave me, my pretty little songbird.

She never had. Never would.

As she grew up, Joan would kneel on the hard tile of the kitchen floor each evening as her father led the rosary. Now she did so alone, praying he'd understand.

"Mom'll be okay, as long as she knows we're not excommunicated or something," she said, obviously troubled. "It's Dad I'm worried about. He's cut from the old cloth."

After swinging back and forth between options, she decided upon a letter as the best way to break the news. Excited, yet still apprehensive, she waited a week for it to arrive, then called. The phone rang dead. She tried repeatedly until advised by a rural operator that the line was off the hook.

"For me to marry a priest is probably too much for him," she said, shuddering, a lone tear slipping down her cheek. "The church did a good job on Dad. He bought the whole package."

She never mentioned it again, but looking into her eyes, I could almost see the little songbird who once walked hand in hand with a proud father melt away.

The Sunday morning for the announcement to Resurrection finally arrived. Just the thought that each of the four masses would remove part of the shadow which had so long eclipsed our lives left me off-balance. Even though the parish council had reacted to our impending marriage with tenderness, a pronounced disquiet now seeped through me. After all, who were we to imagine that two thousand people, many of whom we barely knew, would tolerate such a departure from tradition? While my head and heart told me to push on, my runaway emotions began to question both.

Rosy-cheeked, stamping snow from boots and wiping children's noses, the crowd streamed into the auditorium, unsuspecting. I envied their innocence. Fumbling with the vestments, I prayed to be clothed with an assurance and calm that wouldn't come.

Standing alongside me, Tim tightened his cincture.

"Make it brief. If they have any questions, we can deal with them later. Whatever you do, don't make it out to be a big deal. If you're calm, everyone else will be." He smiled. "Okay, so I'm a bit edgy. Damn right. This isn't your everyday happening in Mother Church, now is it?"

All the seats were taken; people were lining up in the aisles along the walls.

"Feels like a New York subway in here. Stuffy, elbow to elbow," I said to no one in particular. Around us, the usual small talk continued. "No, it isn't supposed to warm up. . . . Yes, hard to believe, only twelve more days until Christmas."

Nervously, I glanced around for Joan amid the growing din. Where was she? The edge of panic dampened my palms—drummed against my temples. I felt short of breath, as though I were in an elevator plummeting out of control. What if the shock was too much for them? What if some . . . maybe most . . . simply walked out at the news? Perhaps the hierarchy was right. They weren't ready for a married priest—least of all for us!

Too late. The opening song of the mass was over. Turning to face
the crowd, I heard a voice far away, beyond me. It was my own.
"Lord have mercy. Christ have mercy. Lord have mercy."

The room began to spin. Suddenly it was as though everyone in
the congregation wore miters. Held episcopal crosiers. Waited in
judgment.

For Forrest Ullman the morning was no different from a lifetime
of Sundays, stretching back to when his pioneer family helped settle
the valley. Though thwarted by a recent hip operation, his rough
cattleman's hands knotted with arthritis, Forrest saw himself as becoming an altogether new man. Not until his eightieth year did he
discover that his faith had everything to do with a compassionate,
accepting God, and precious little to do with the fear of hell which
had plagued him throughout his life. Each Thursday evening he now
made the drive from his ranch home to the parish center, where he'd
sit for two hours with a group of a hundred or more university students
to discuss the Scriptures. Our gatherings were informal, permitting
anyone at any time to reflect on a section under discussion, and attempt
to apply the message to their own circumstances and lives. At first
reticent to speak up, Forrest in no time became a focal point of the
group, confessing excitement at the discovery of the New Testament,
the centerpiece of his and the church's faith. It was largely because
of his influence that a ministry to shut-ins and the elderly, spearheaded
by many of those same students, took hold in Resurrection.

Alongside him this morning, as she had almost every morning for
some fifty years, was his wife, Ann. Not quite as short or as gray as
Forrest, she carried her age well but for her ears and teeth. More often
than not, her hearing aid gave off a high-pitched squeal, intruding
upon conversations. Whenever she smiled, her teeth would click. But
smile a lot she did, and click a lot they did.

This day, the Ullmans would not understand. Could not. Regret-
tably, our worlds were about to collide.

I proclaimed the gospel: Jesus telling the crowds not to hide their
lamps under the tables but to place them on lampstands for the whole
world to see.

For a moment I was certain the congregation already knew. Then
again, they couldn't know. Maybe the timing wasn't right. Far better
to hold off, wait yet another week. Another season. Where was Joan?
I needed her. Wanted to flee to her—bolt for the door.

I paused in the sermon, the stillness, leaden. There would be no turning back. The years of waiting, of searching, now pushed me to the edge. Again, my voice seemed distant.

"Sometimes we must quit hiding our own lamp. Take a chance that others will look kindly on its light. So . . ." I stammered, "I want to share something personal. Something which has been and is a light for me . . . ah . . . I'm going to get married."

Nothing. No reaction at all. The words hung there. The silence a slap in the face. A naked bead of sweat slipped down my back. Suddenly there were no familiar faces. Strangers all. I wanted to scream, "Damn it! Are you all made of stone?" Then among the field of eyes, I found Joan's, held on, was lifted up, and continued.

"You see, it won't be necessary for me to leave here. We'll be married in the parish. I'll be able to remain as your priest . . . if you want me. Ah, us."

The stillness shuddered, then relaxed and softened. "I'm in love with Joan Doyle. Many of you know her. The wedding is here in the parish next . . ."

Then from somewhere in the back it began. At first, a ripple, then a roar. They were on their feet, including Forrest, grinning from ear to ear, and Ann, her teeth probably clicking. The applause washed away all shackles of doubt. Unable to continue, I stepped behind the altar. The applause vibrated for several minutes before we could proceed with mass.

Throughout the day the spontaneous acceptance continued. As always after each mass, I stood at the exit of the auditorium, which this day was a hopeless bottleneck. While the words of support were uplifting, it was the hands, hundreds upon hundreds of hands, which touched the deepest part of me.

Hands, reaching out through my numbness. Hands for embracing. Innocent hands of children, pulling at the chasuble, hugging my legs in an attempt to share what they didn't comprehend, but which they felt a need to be part of. Hands . . . of students, soft and untested. Hands . . . shy, squeezing against mine when words wouldn't come. Hands . . . patting, punching, pumping, enfolding. Gnarled, arthritic hands. Forrest's hands.

Joan's attempt to remain inconspicuous was an utter failure. She seemed at once embarrassed with the attention, yet aglow with the affection all around. Whether engulfed by adolescents happy at the thought of romance, or couples anxious to share her joy, she sparkled.

Watching her, I never felt more thankful to be in love, or more grateful to be a priest.

Following evening liturgy, Tim wheeled the bleached horse skeleton back onto the stage for morning classes.

"Whew," he whistled. "What a day! Even this guy's grinning."

"I'm not sure which of you looks worse. You look shot."

"I'm wrung out. Who in the hell wouldn't be, going through a day like this. What an experience. It was unreal."

We sat, dangling our legs over the stage, peering out over the now vacant auditorium.

"At times I see," I said.

"What?"

"It's like I know a little of what Saint Paul meant. That we only see a part of things now—as through a mirror darkly. The church is changing faster than we think. But we're so close to things it's hard to see. Except for days like this one. I just can't get over today. It sends goosebumps all over me just thinking about it."

Tim turned, raising his bushy eyebrows. "The whole thing blew me away. They don't give one good damn if you get married. They just don't want to lose you. Or Joan, for that matter."

"I've never wanted to be a priest more than right now. They were happy for us. Honest to God, happy! I'm constantly surprised by the goodness of people, but this—wow."

"Well, you're going to stay on if they have anything to say about it," he said, peering out among the darkened rows. "I watched them. At every mass their faces fell the moment you mentioned getting married, then lit up when you said you wouldn't be leaving. That's when the applause always began. And you," he said, tapping me on the knee. "You seemed so strong. So sure."

"Sure? Yeah, but strong? Not on the inside. At least not until the first mass. After that—for the other three—I was more at ease. Even felt a . . . well, a certain power or something . . . deep inside."

"Say that again."

"It sounds presumptuous. I don't mean it to, but, well, like someone bigger than me was providing the strength."

"The Lord?"

"Yeah . . . like that."

For an instant the auditorium came alive with the memory.

"Well, whatever," Tim said, easing off the stage. "I just wish the bishop had been here today. Just to see it!"

                              * * *

Much as an old movie at accelerated speed, the week passed by
in a comic blur. Not until we gathered for the evening wedding were
we able to step back and view the world through the lens of slow
motion.

Outside, the campus chapel was ringed with cedar trees. Covered
with mounds of fresh snow, they appeared like so many giant mushrooms. Inside, earth-tone candles of all shapes and sizes flickered atop
a thin wooden altar, casting an illumination across an adjacent wall of
glass. Leaving the impression that the chapel, now hopelessly crowded,
was engulfed in fire.

While Tim chatted with a group of priests, Joan and I welcomed
the last-minute guests. Over the din, Drake Shepler motioned me over,
his beard and twinkle reminders of simpler days—of children's toys
and Santa Claus.

"Didn't someone say you're supposed to save the best wine until
last?" he shouted into my ear. "People are usually this way after the
ceremony, not before. I think the celebration began the day you told
the parish! Too bad there wasn't enough room here for all of them."

Danforth Chapel had its limitations. When we explained the situation, everyone seemed to understand. The two hundred people we
had invited to squeeze in reflected the spirit of all the others in an
opening song that left the chapel walls vibrating.

When Joan approached the lectern, she seemed as unpretentious
and delicate as her dress, hastily sewn by friends in the parish. Brushing
back her hair, which spilled down across her breast, she read aloud
from the Scriptures, her voice soft yet sure.

        I am going to show you a way that is better than any. . . .
        If I have all the eloquence of men or of angels, but speak
        without love, I am simply a gong booming or a cymbal clashing.
        If I have the gift of prophecy, understanding all the mysteries
        . . . and if I have faith in all its fullness, to move mountains,
        but without love, then I am nothing at all.
            Love is always patient and kind; it is never jealous; . . . it
        does not take offense . . . but delights in the truth; it is always
        ready to excuse, to trust, to hope, and to endure whatever comes.
        . . . In short, there are three things that last: faith, hope and
        love; and the greatest of these is love.

The room smelled of Advent wreaths. From somewhere in the back the wistful melody of a flute recalled the song of the wind that crisp afternoon in the needle's eye. I saw once again the eagle arcing away before disappearing into the sun. Looking out over the faces circling us—friends, including Larry Haefield, Vance Mudd in from California, Brad Robesheau just back from Rome, children, members of the parish council—I wondered if they, too, had ever dreamed of being lifted up on eagles' wings. I opened the Scriptures to the Gospel of John.

> I give you a new commandment:
> love one another;
> Just as I have loved you,
> you also must love one another.
> By this love you have for one another
> everyone will know that you are my disciples.

I reached for Joan's hands, knowing that without her little made sense, but that with her everything did. We faced one another to speak our vows, and the room faded away.

> God, our Father, has blessed me with you. You have been ever loving in our joys and our tears. You have always given your love freely; for this I am thankful. Tonight, before our Father, confident of His blessing, and before our friends, I give my heart to you. Please take it, for this time, our lifetime, for eternal time.

Then her turn, each word sealing what for years she already lived.

> Michael, you know what is in my heart. I accept your love and give you my heart in return. Throughout our lives together, I will be faithful and loving; supporting you in life and in the gospel ministry entrusted to you. Relying always on our Father's strength between us, for this time, our lifetime, for eternal time.

We exchanged the rings, no longer covered with dust. Pronouncing us husband and wife, Tim joined our hands together with a rainbow-colored stole presented to me at ordination.

Moments later, Joan stepped to the altar with an hourglass, my gift to her our first Christmas, unturned since then. Now she rolled it over, setting it firmly next to my chalice. With the past behind us, we prayed for tomorrow as the sand began to flow, grain by grain, along a new way.

PART III

I wonder what I should become if I resigned myself to the part which many . . . would have me play—those that are so preoccupied with social preservation, which really means their own preservation.

So many of us, supposedly standing for law and order, are merely clinging to old habits, sometimes to a mere parrot vocabulary, its formulae worn so smooth by constant use that they justify everything and question none.

—GEORGES BERNANOS, *The Diary of a Country Priest*

Nothing changed, and yet everything did following our marriage. Nothing—in that even though we crossed a seemingly insurmountable hurdle, we were the same people with the same work. Life went on much as it had before. Everything—in that the little things, those fractions of life which make up its whole, were forever changed.

Normally waking before dawn, I would wait for the first shimmers of light to draw Joan into the day. In that warm buffer zone to the outside world, just feeling her breath against me was reminder enough of how far we'd come.

The freedom not to conceal our love any longer was the most telling sign that we were set free of the straitjacket of the past. Whether it was just driving into town from our small rental, or lingering over a cup of coffee in the student lounge, it was from the simple everyday affairs that life took on a new texture. However, it was not until Christmas night, with the festivity of parish celebration behind us, that we were able at last to feel how transformed our lives truly were.

Sprawled on the carpet next to a tiny fir tree which we had taken from the surrounding hills the day before, Joan rested her head in my lap while reaching up to adjust a few bulbs.

"When you spoke at mass this morning about people waiting for centuries for the birth of a promise even when all the signs were there that nothing would happen—it struck me how most people, in some ways, go through the same thing we have, waiting for their own miracle to happen. Sometimes it does. Usually it doesn't. We were lucky.''

Perhaps, but it also had something to do with our choice not to accept a narrowly defined future. Undeniably, however, there was still precious little room for us within most sectors of Catholicism's inn. Would the eggshell-thin protection around us someday be shattered, or would we indeed survive?

Catching me staring out at the twinkling lights of the city ten miles in the distance, she tapped me on the chest. ''Hey, penny for your thoughts.''

''Oh, nothing really. Just thinking about how it was at the parish today. People seemed genuinely happy for us.''

''Well, Christmas is all about the impossible coming true. Love becoming flesh. That's what you said. Maybe they sense that's what's happened with us.''

I pinched at her nose. ''You're sounding pretty philosophical, lady.''

Joan laughed. ''It just hit me today how happy I am to be with you.''

Leaning down to touch my lips against hers, I felt her yield, knowing at last it was no longer a dream.

In the weeks following the New Year, it became clear that our marriage and my remaining as a priest would escape the attention of the media. Whether it was the holidays, our low-key approach, the remoteness of Bozeman, or sheer luck, it didn't matter. Only once did a reporter call. We were out. He never called back.

By the time we were midway into winter quarter, it was obvious that while one of their priests being married was of undeniable interest to the people of Resurrection, by and large, life went on in the parish much as before, with the exception of a few slight but telling changes.

Whereas couples experiencing difficulties within their marriages still sought out either priest, there was an increase in requests for the ''one who's married.'' Paradoxically, there was a greater understanding of Tim's celibacy. More startling was the response of students within the parish. In the months immediately following our marriage, more young men ventured forth to inquire about becoming priests than had done so in all the prior years combined. Cautioning them against any illusion that the church was likely to change the law of celibacy, both Tim and I stressed that mine was an unusual situation. All the while we both knew that few, if any, from the core of the church's future would leap the required hurdles to ordination.

The most notable change unfolded within me, within Joan. Just the fact that we had come up from underground, that what was hidden for so long was now revealed to the light of day, unleashed a surprising font of energy.

Joan's involvement in my work deepened. Her activities ranged from helping prepare young couples for marriage, to emergency counseling. Still, it was in the personal area of preaching where the subtle impact of our marriage manifested itself. Gradually I began to draw on the little everyday events in our own relationship, those common to couples living intimately day in and day out with one another. Weaving them into the homilies, I attempted to draw out the meaning of the Scriptures themselves. Through the example of a lover's quarrel, the acceptance of each other's idiosyncracies, or shared housecleaning, I sought through the ordinary to touch the sacred.

In all of it, I seemed more myself, more able to give. Living with Joan, I felt more effective as a priest and wondered if someday because of her, I might even become the good one I so desperately wanted to be.

The reaction Joan and I received outside the church was equally telling. Among her colleagues at the university there was a noticeable increase in respect for a changing church that permitted such freedom. Even former Catholics, long disgruntled with what appeared an intransigent institution, expressed interest once again in their faith. Meanwhile, the number of invitations increased for both Joan and me to guest-lecture or participate in university functions.

One such invitation, to a banquet honoring fiftieth-year alumni, provided the arena for a poignant lesson.

Through the clinking of glasses, the university president stepped before the microphone to welcome the distinguished guests assembled from throughout the country. Few appeared to be listening as he introduced the head table. Few, that is, until he came to us.

"To my right is Father Mike Miles, Catholic pastor to Montana State University—and his wife, Doctor Joan Miles."

For a second, I thought no one noticed, until a white-haired woman toward the far back of the ballroom straightened up, peering above the crowd like a long-necked crane. Throughout the entire meal and speeches, she kept an irritated eye trained upon us.

"Well, what can we expect?" Joan smiled. "She's probably a Catholic and it's not every day the priest and his wife come to dinner.

Come on, it'll be something for her to talk about when she gets home.''

By the time I offered the prayer following dinner, we'd nearly forgotten about her. Yet the woman was not to be deterred. Darting through the crowd, she literally pulled me to a stop by the exit. Her cheeks were flushed, jaw set; a slight trace of perspiration glistened on her upper lip.

"Young man, hold on there! Are you a priest?" she asked curtly.

"Yes."

"A Roman Catholic priest?" she persisted.

I glanced at Joan. We could see it coming. There was little choice but to ride it out.

"Well, listen to me," she said, thrusting a finger into my chest, her voice rising. "I've been a Catholic all my life and am mighty proud of it. I live in Virginia now. Believe me, the church I come from is mighty different from yours out here. Thank God!"

A few people stopped, curious about why the slight, seemingly proper lady was so obviously irritated.

Joan tapped me on the shoulder. "Maybe we should be going."

Undaunted, the woman turned, just inches from her. "Are you his wife?"

Joan nodded.

"Well, excuse me, but I just want to ask this . . . this . . ." She looked at me, lost for words. Nervously, I buttoned my sports coat. Waited.

"I've been a Catholic for seventy-five years. Before even the parents of young whippersnappers like you were born. Unfortunately, there are a few priests hell-bent on ruining the church. When the president introduced you, I was appalled. Never have I . . ."

"Really, ma'am, I have to go," I said, as much embarrassed as irritated.

"Well, not before you answer my question," she said, icily fingering my tie.

"Okay, but just one."

"Young man, where in heaven's name is your collar?"

Next to me, Joan started to giggle. I didn't dare look at her for fear of losing my own composure. Not until I explained the reason why many priests no longer wore collars—an explanation she refused to accept—were we able to break off and leave.

"Here you are the first married priest she's ever run into and she doesn't bat an eye," Joan exclaimed on the way home.

"Yeah. No kidding. I could have told her the pope just announced that Jesus didn't rise from the dead and it might not have upset her nearly so much as the damn tie. After all, first things first!"

Just then I thought of Joan's father. Of her family's pained account of his inability to accept our marriage; one which a lifetime in the church taught him was grievously wrong. I could see Joan's tear-streaked face, desperate to explain the truth of our lives, but to no avail.

"I wish it was as easy as taking off my tie," I said under my breath, unwilling to impinge upon Joan's playful mood.

When the letter arrived, I was surprised it had gone out to several priests in the diocese; equally so that Andrew Sexton had bothered to send me a copy. Between the lines, jammed closely on a single sheet of yellow paper, I could hear Andy's high-pitched voice, see his ruddy, chinless face.

Addressed to the bishop, the letter sounded a strong protest on behalf of its author and unnamed others among the clergy.

> The things I'm going to say are the thoughts of many priests with whom I have discussed them . . . I take strong exception to his remaining . . . The arrangement is bound to do harm to the morale of the priests and seminarians of the Diocese. Either we all now have the option of marriage after ordination, or Mike's is a specially privileged case not meant for the rest of us . . . I have no doubt that to most of those in Bozeman, Mike's laicization is a technicality and he is still the priest who served them before but with a new and radically changed commitment in which neither they nor the Church come first.

Not reading any further, I walked across the hall, pushing open the door to Tim's office.

"See this yet?" I said, flipping it over his shoulder onto the desk.

When he spun around, the crimson spot just above his forehead was answer enough.

"Yeah. Got it in the mail today. What a cheap shot! It's one thing to disagree with you staying on, but something else again to go after you like he does at the end. Then again, he might have said worse."

"Worse than this?" I held out the crumpled sheet.

He looked away.

"Tim?"

"Well, I'd heard he was saying you're nothing more than a guy with a case of hot pants. It's pathetic."

"Also adolescent," I said, more hurt than angry. "Maybe I should have talked with him first. I've always gotten along with him . . . his sense of humor and all. But his parish is almost three hundred miles away. Still, he might have listened."

Both of us knew now it wouldn't have done any good.

"You're not going to show that to Joan, are you?" The spot above Tim's eyes was fading.

"Why not? She'll see it's empty." I turned down the hall, weary at the prospect of further tension, whose sharp teeth might well grind up our souls.

Tim shouted, "Try to ignore him. He just turned fifty. Maybe it's a mid-life crisis. Besides, who's he to be questioning your commitment, much less calling for your resignation?"

If we chose to ignore it, the chancellor could not. There was a steely edge to his voice when he called to inform me that more letters expressing similar resentment among priests were on Bishop Hunt-hausen's desk. I expected Broderick to say he told me so, but he refrained. Still, he made little effort to conceal his concern that those who were protesting might stir up a kettle of trouble. He returned to an earlier conviction that the bishop had to spell out conditions on my ministry, not only to satiate those protesting, but also to protect himself. Fearing he was right, I promised to discuss the matter during Hunt-hausen's upcoming visit to Resurrection, and broke off the conversation.

It was the first visit to the parish for the bishop since our marriage. As he unbuttoned his collar, settling into a worn leather chair in my office, all apprehension that I would find him upset over the rumbles of protest vanished. He inquired about Joan.

"She's now the rabbi's wife."

I went on to recount an incident from the day before. Each morning near the university, we passed a tot on her way to kindergarten. It was always the same. Following our best hello, she would look shyly at the sidewalk, passing without a word. Always the same, that is, until yesterday. Accompanied by another child, she looked directly at us, receiving our greeting with familiar silence. Once we passed, however, she blurted out to her small friend, "There goes the rabbi with his new wife."

Hunthausen laughed along with me but only slightly.

"If she were, it'd probably be lots easier." He paused. "Father Sexton's letter must have hurt her."

"Yeah. Sure. She doesn't want to be a source of division. Neither of us does."

"Christ was."

"And look what it got him," I quipped.

He frowned, returning to Sexton. "Golly, I can't imagine what got into him."

Typically, the possibility of malice, guile, or any of the cardinal sins never entered his mind.

"Andy and I got together right after that," he continued. "You know what he said? If I let you marry, why not him! I told him to go ahead, if he could find a woman to marry him, and his parish would accept it. Providing, of course, he was willing to go through all you have."

"What'd he say?"

"Nothing!" Hunthausen slapped his fist into his hand. "He just sat there glaring. He made me so mad I nearly walked out!"

We talked for a while about what Sexton and the others really wanted. The bishop had assured them that, while still a priest, by marrying I was no longer a cleric but a layman—a distinction that had more to do with trappings than substance. No longer was the church responsible for my room and board, my life insurance or clergy retirement. Furthermore, I had agreed to remain for a minimal salary.

"But that's not enough?"

"Definitely not," Hunthausen replied, elevating his palms as if beseeching help from on high. "They're upset because you get to do the same work they do. These men gave up a wife and family long ago. There's no arguing with them about shortage of priests. About the good job you and Tim are doing. Their minds are made up. They can't tolerate people seeing you as a priest."

"But I am. They ought to recheck their dogma!"

"I know you are. You know it. Resurrection does. Even Sexton. But to put it mildly, he has a hard time with you functioning as one."

"Well, that's the whole point of my staying. Otherwise I might as well have got the hell out in the first place!" I replied, struggling to calm down.

"Out, I'm afraid, is what they'd prefer."

Remembering Broderick's warning months earlier—that those opposed to the bishop's style of renewal might get at him through us—I wondered just how far we could expect Hunthausen to go. He didn't wait for me to ask the question.

"They're in the minority and are going to have to live with this one. It's right and we're going to see it through, but . . ." He paused, fingering through a folder next to his chair. "Caston worked up a list of restrictions I can send to the troops. They might go a long way toward clearing the air. We've talked about most of them before. Here, look them over."

Taking the single page, I scanned the list. No longer could I claim insurance or clergy retirement. Or employ the titles "Father" or "Reverend." Nor could I preside during mass itself, or at the sacraments. A knot of tension spread along the back of my neck.

Hunthausen didn't wait for me to reply.

"Look. I know the titles don't make a difference to you, but to some of these fellas, they mean everything. Besides, people will go right along calling you whatever they please. They know who you are."

"It's not a big deal. But the mass and all . . . well, it's at the very heart. All this," I said, snapping the back of my hand against the list, "well, it would gut my priesthood. What's the point of staying? Dutch, I thought you trusted us."

Assuring me he still did, he asked me to review the arrangement Tim and I had worked out with the parish.

Conscious of the tightrope we were walking, we agreed to concelebrate each Sunday. During the consecration, Tim would say the words of institution out loud while I repeated them silently. In all other parts of the mass, I would continue exactly as before.

"No problem then," the bishop said. "Caston Broderick tells me the key word in the Vatican's restrictions is *preside*. Technically it's accurate to say Tim's the one presiding."

"Though de facto so am I. Rome's lexicon just doesn't include someone like me at the altar. So, technically, yes. We can say that."

As long as another priest was in the room with me, and therefore presiding, the same would hold true for baptisms and weddings. When it came to confessions—of their nature more private and thus sensitive—Hunthausen was firm. It would be far safer to let Tim handle all of them. I balked. The sacrament was a highly personal one. What of those people who already saw me as their confessor and needed to continue? Besides, even church law permitted a dispensed priest to grant absolution in time of dire need. Hunthausen didn't waver, but agreed that in the end my conscience should determine what constituted such need.

Indeed, conscience was the question. My conscience. In wandering through this virgin terrain in Catholicism, it was one thing to let the process unfold, perhaps to reveal opportunities for generations beyond our own. But what of the man next to me? How much more could I ask of him? At what point would he risk too much, jeopardizing his own position beyond all reason? Together we were feeling our way through the darkness. Was it fair to cling to his hand every step of the way? Was it even realistic?

The bishop sighed while buttoning his collar and preparing to leave.

"There shouldn't be any problem. Just stick with what you and Tim agreed to and things will work out fine."

I stood with him, focusing upon his dilated right pupil. While president of Carroll College, he had crawled beneath a jammed lawn sprinkler, attempting to free it. He succeeded, only to be struck by its whirling blade in an eye, which was left permanently damaged.

I didn't want him damaged again, certain the church needed his vision far more than it did mine. In that fraction of time between us, I knew there would be decisions surrounding my role which would have to be made with but, in another sense, without him. Still, of one thing I was certain. If we ever went too far at Resurrection, he would tell us.

Hunthausen asked for the chancellor's letter.

"It's almost like a game," I said, half-smiling.

"Maybe, but one on behalf of the gospel and human dignity. Oh, I suppose there will be some who will say it's all a violation of church law, but I don't think it's outside its spirit."

"Well, even if it's a violation," I said, handing him back the sheet of paper, "someone's got to do it. Hell's bells! Blacks would still be in the back of buses in the South if no one took the first step across the line."

He nodded.

"Anyway, we'll just keep on doing what we can and leave the rest up to God."

"Better reverse it," he said, putting both hands on my shoulders. "Please?"

"Let God do all He can and you folks do the rest."

"Touché."

So we agreed, the bishop would provide only a broad outline of the restrictions in a letter to the priests. Meanwhile, we would allow the experience at Resurrection to continue unfolding. We would forge ahead essentially uninhibited, searching along an uncertain path for what seemed to us, at least, the elusive will of God.

At that moment, Tim knocked, poking his head inside the doorway to remind us that the parish council was waiting. Going down the stairway, I pushed aside all thought of Sexton and the others.

Throughout the meeting, Hunthausen appeared as moved by the council's enthusiasm as they were, in turn, by his support. Not until he brought up the matter of Sexton's complaint and the possibility of still further opposition, did the group sense that there might be a serpent slithering along the borders of our joy.

Joan reached over, stroking the top of my hand. "Kirby has that look on his face. You know the one he gets when his dander is up. Something's coming."

She called it. Just before we broke up, Walsh stood, clasping the back of his chair, his knuckles white.

"It took a lot of faith and, well, just plain guts on your part, Bishop, to do what you have. You heard it again tonight, how appreciative we are in holding on to Mike and Joan and—forgive me—in moving beyond a law which strikes me as embodying the worst kind of moral coercion. If someplace had to jump the gun on a change that's too long in coming, we're glad it was here. But . . ." he said, pointing across the room at Joan and me, "with all due respect, I can't leave here without getting a few things off my chest about them. Granted, their marriage may have changed a few things as far as some of the pious fathers are concerned, but not for us. I was raised in a traditional family. Graduated from a Catholic college. The whole nine yards. This thing's got me questioning what a priest is in the first place. Someone who we only see on the altar? Mike came here and over the years emerged as a leader for us in things of the Spirit. Both he and Tim put things to us in ways which hit our lives. For the first time in years, I actually look forward to going to church."

He hesitated, his voice steadier.

"Around here we may not be nearly Christian enough, but we're trying. Maybe the church ought to try, too, and start by listening to its own people. It didn't with birth control, and look at the mess! What's happening in this town has nothing to do with whether or not

Mike is married. What makes a difference is that he's a person who touches people. He helps us believe we can be more than we are and makes believing in the gospel so much easier because he so obviously does himself.'' He took a deep breath, as if to swallow the trace of nervousness in his voice.

"What I'm trying to say is, he's a damn good priest. Just because he's living with an equally good woman doesn't change that fact one iota. He's the same person as before, though maybe a little better. So please,'' he concluded, a smile as thin and tight as a rubber band stretching across his lips, "tell whoever is complaining that we have a priest who puts himself out there on the line for us twenty-four hours a day and we intend to do the same for him. We're going to keep him—and Joan, too.''

A distant look covered Dutch's face. Clearly moved, he promised to stand by us. In the silence that followed, there was a sense in the room that all of us were on the edge of something far bigger than we had bargained for.

Later, when the rectory was empty, Tim inquired of Hunthausen whether or not the apostolic delegate to the United States knew what was taking place at Resurrection.

The bishop shrugged his shoulders. "He'll be at the meeting of all the hierarchy in Chicago next month. If he asks me, I'll tell him. He's pretty well informed. With something like this, he probably knows.''

Asked whether the delegate would approve—or, indeed, whether he might pass the word on to Rome—Hunthausen said he couldn't guess, then he went upstairs to the guest room, where he spent some time alone kneeling on the *prie-dieu*.

The following morning was the second Sunday after Epiphany— the Feast of the Holy Family. When Joan and I arrived, the auditorium, though full, was hushed. Everyone was holding their breath as Raymond Hunthausen, balancing on the top rung of a ladder, stretched toward an upper rafter.

"It's a bird, trapped in here when we came in,'' Tim said, coming up to us. "Dutch took off his coat, rolled up his sleeves, and has been up there ever since. Half of them think he's the janitor.'' He looked around the room as the tiny finch fluttered off the rafter, zigzagging through the auditorium. "He's determined to do something,'' Tim wheezed, looking at his watch. "We're going to be late, but no one seems to mind.''

By the time the center of attraction settled back on its perch,

Hunthausen had managed to inch over to a dusty window above the rafters. Stretching out, he popped it open, sending a gust of fresh air swirling through the curtains. With a gentle nudge, he flushed the exhausted finch toward the opening, where it escaped to freedom, amid a scattering of applause.

The bishop scurried down the ladder to join us in vesting for mass. As she hurriedly adjusted a flaming red stole over his shoulders, Joan's touch reflected just how much she had come to love the man who had opened the window of fresh air onto our lives and set us free.

Throughout the liturgy, I experienced a cascade of emotions. Delivering the homily, I was all but swept up by an awareness that the man who had ordained me—called me to speak God's Word—had not moved to stifle that Word, but had in fact unleashed it even more.

When together we elevated the Host and cup, a part of his strength seemed to wash through me. Not only was I convinced that what we were doing was right, but for the first time I realized even more that what we opposed was terribly wrong.

The breeze from the still-open window above us fluttered through a long banner as we distributed the Eucharist. Until then I hadn't noticed the bright inscription etched against the burlap: "I am the Alpha and Omega. The First and the Last. Behold—I make all things new!"

Between masses, Tim drew me aside from a sea of parishioners surrounding Hunthausen.

"Look at them. They love the guy!"

"Who doesn't?" I asked lightly.

Tim wiped the perspiration from his forehead, the closeness of the auditorium forever assaulting his pores. "A year ago I wouldn't have given you a snowball's chance in hell. It's still hard to believe. Rome would have his head if they saw you up there at the altar with him. There's just no guile in the man. He goes on doing what he feels is right."

"So do they," I replied, pointing at the expanding circle around the bishop.

Just then, a boy no more than three scooted by, and Hunthausen swept him up in his arms. Though the future was uncertain, with no way to see through the mist around us, I wondered whether someday that same child might tell a story. By then it might be a quite common and ordinary one. Then, too, maybe completely unbelievable. Perhaps he would tell of the time when the veil of absurdity fell away from the institutional priesthood. A time when there was a priest and his lady . . .

I started to say something to Tim, but he had disappeared, leaving me to savor the moment alone.

"Let the little children alone and do not stop them . . . for it is to such as these that the kingdom of heaven belongs."

The lone fluorescent bulb buzzed overhead, casting an icy glare over the conference room. The Personnel Board's invitation sounded more like a summons. Despite the bishop's efforts, complaints among the clergy continued to trickle in. Much like water dripping in a sink, each drop small in itself but, taken together, threatening an overflow if left unheeded.

One by one, the chairman listed the grievances, his booming baritone slapping against the walls. The litany was becoming all too familiar. People can't see any distinction at the altar between you and any other priest. Why do newspapers continue to list you as officiating at weddings? Aren't vestments reserved for clergy only? Parishioners still call you "Father." Why should you have your cake and eat it too?

Whenever I requested the identity of those who were upset, the chairman would toy with his slickened hair, pasted flat against his forehead, and repeat that while the priests must remain anonymous, their woes would not.

Once during my response, Ernie Stenzel interrupted.

"It doesn't make any difference what you say. These guys doing the bitching have their minds made up. They aren't about to accept a married priest—period! They won't be satisfied until you're in the last seat of the last pew of Catholicism. Pure and simple!"

"Well, what's the use?" I asked, my eyes burning from the stale cigarette smoke. "Maybe they'll listen to the people of Resurrection. They have a right to have a word on this. It's their church, too."

The chairman cut in. "But it isn't just the priests who are having trouble, as you seem to suggest. Father Metzner was telling us . . ." Recognizing he had let slip one of the names, he fell silent, looking apologetically around the room.

"You were saying?"

No reply.

Larry Haefield, who until that moment had slouched quietly in the corner, straightened up.

"We have to lay the cards on the table," he said reluctantly. "The reports we get are that people in Bozeman are in fact not taking all this nearly as well as you and Tim imply. They're pretty upset that you got married in the first place. Even more so that you're still in the parish.''

"You've got to be kidding!''

"There's more,'' he continued, taking a quick gulp of coffee. "Not only are we informed that since your marriage there's been an ongoing exodus from the parish, but that some are leaving the church altogether.''

"Metzner said that?''

Silence.

"I can't believe he feels that way. If he does, it's not true. Moreover, it's an outright distortion. If anything, Resurrection's still growing. Besides, neither Tim nor I have heard one complaint.'' I took a long breath.

"You know, Mike, it's possible your perceptions might be a little clouded.'' I turned to face the board's youngest member, who exhaled a stream of smoke, then slowly ground his cigarette into a polished ashtray.

"What I'm saying is that Paul's well respected and he carries weight with lots of the guys.''

"He's also pretty upset. Lots of people are leaving Rosary for Resurrection.''

"That's not what Metzner says.''

Exasperated, I turned back to the chairman.

"It's so damn frustrating! It would help to talk to these . . . these . . . bearers of the Lord's Good News. But they're nameless. Faceless. If only they'd come to the parish and see what we see. Hear what we hear. I'll lay odds they've never set foot in the place.''

"And probably never will,'' he replied.

For the next hour we batted the issues back and forth, getting nowhere. Apparently willing to let matters stand, the chairman finally called the discussion to an end, but not before warning me of mounting pressure.

Walking from the room, Haefield echoed my own ambivalence. "Metzner probably knows that things are going well at Resurrection. In fact, too well. That's the problem.''

"But he was so gracious. Even came to the wedding!''

"He's crafty. Just be careful. Whatever you do, don't underestimate him.''

"Come on." I chuckled, determined not to dump my feelings of disappointment on him. "This isn't the Mafia, it's the church."

For the first time all day, a smile spread over Haefield's face. "You've always been too damn idealistic. It's also the big leagues."

"And you know what?" I added, wrapping an arm about his shoulders. "As the poem says, 'There are some men too gentle to live among wolves.' Thank God you're one of them."

Children love to play in sandboxes. However, there is a price exacted, a tax levied against their tender skin. The protesting clergy struck Joan as being like children, limited by the confines of a narrow sandbox world. As far as she was concerned, the only way to avoid the gritty emotional grains which threatened to work their way into the most tender area of our lives was to resist crawling into the sandbox in the first place. An opportunity for avoidance presented itself midway into the summer when a friend offered her Hawaiian home and we broke away for a belated honeymoon.

In the ensuing weeks, time was measured by the rolling waves spilling across Kona's coast. Our lives were wrapped in simple ritual. Each morning, just before dawn, we celebrated mass on a porch over-looking rows of pineapple plants. From there it was a comfortable two-mile jog to Albert's Donut House, where, seated in a room smell-ing of cooking oil and yeast, we shared coffee and buttermilk dough-nuts. Whether the remainder of the day included a stroll along a secluded beach or an afternoon tour of the shaded markets, the world seemed as gentle as the palm leaves swaying overhead.

Kilauea was none too gentle. The air surrounding the volcano reeked of sulfur, rising from its crater on dozens of steaming plumes. Edging across the jagged rim, we were mindful of a recent eruption.

"You sure it's okay to be up here?" I shouted over a hot wind.

Unable to hear, Joan stopped ahead of me, waiting. Sugar-colored clouds billowed behind her in the distance, contrasting with her full tan. Approaching, I wrapped my arms about her, feeling the warmth of her skin against my own.

"You asked the rangers? They said it's safe enough?"

She nodded, running her hand across my chest before stepping away to peer into the crater.

"The natives say Pele lives down in there."

"Pele?"

"The goddess of fire."

"You believe in her?"

"Sure . . . in a way."

"You know, the Old Testament pictured Yahweh as fire. Moses saw God on Sinai. Poor guy came down with his eyebrows smoking and his hair singed off."

"Why fire?"

"The strongest force they knew."

"That's what I mean about Pele . . . down there, at the earth's very heart she's all fire . . ."

As the easy Pacific light fell across her shoulders, I recognized the feeling smoldering, then heating up, within me since first arriving at the Islands. The feeling of falling in love all over again.

"Well, if there's a Pele, I'm looking at her right now."

As she turned, her eyes widened in a quiet smile.

"Hon, just hold it right there," I said. "I could look at you all day."

She blushed, pressing her hands along her shorts, then came into my arms.

The church's concerns seemed far away. Not until we picked up a West Coast newspaper while switching planes on the way home did the world once again shrink to sandbox size. Sandwiched between the sports page and the classifieds, it was by now a familiar story, the only difference the players and the stage upon which it was performed. Still, it struck a nerve.

After underlining the point that he was not resigning but being kicked out after more than a quarter century in the ministry, the priest acknowledged he was finished. Washed up, as he put it, without any concern for his welfare. He and his future wife would leave the area, seek something new. Perhaps someday Rome would tolerate such intimacy and permit similar couples to remain. Perhaps, but not yet.

As the public address system called our flight, Joan wondered if the pain would have been less had they and their devastated parish known that what they longed for had already taken place. Her question raised yet another. How were we destined to fare in a church which everywhere around us continued to punish its own for the fault of love?

Anything extraordinary about our particular circumstances was all but overshadowed as the hectic routine in Bozeman took hold once again. It was only when we were able to back away, stand outside the parameters of our everyday lives, that the force of what was taking place would strike home. Such was the case in Missoula.

Early in the fall, I accepted an invitation to celebrate Sunday services in Christ the King Parish. The opportunity to be within a parish other than Resurrection dovetailed nicely with the annual assembly of priests scheduled there for the following day.

The church was empty. Entering the vestibule, I knelt at the outer ring of mahogany pews which encircled a stone altar like ripples on a pond.

Such moments, alone before the naked eye of God, were always hard to come by. With a recognizable hunger, I swallowed the solitude, once again reminded that without prayer—without a stillness stripped even of words—the deepest part of me would be as empty as the building itself.

Within minutes, the front lights were flicked on. Blake Robins entered and began busily arranging the sanctuary. Unnoticed, I drifted back to an earlier time.

Just admitted to Sacred Orders myself, I had helped Robins move into his first parish assignment. Clad in a pressed cassock, his hair cropped close, he struck me then, as now, as meticulously well groomed. That day we had unloaded mainly books in his room at St. Anthony's. I could still see their dust jackets, trumpeting biblical themes and Vatican II promises.

Robins switched on the main chandeliers, illuminating the graceful lines and heavy beams overhead. Forever bursting with nervous energy, the short, wiry figure spotted me and came over. In our handshake there was a bond we both recognized but rarely referred to. Since the musicians and ushers were just arriving, he had only a moment to say he had previously informed the parish of my marital status. It came as no surprise to most, since they had already heard.

"How'd you do that?" I asked, tugging at the sleeve of his tweed sports coat just as he started to turn away.

"Last Sunday. In the homily. Lots of them already know you. You've been here a half-dozen times over the years."

"Yeah, but what'd you say?"

His pale blue eyes danced just a bit.

"That you leap tall buildings in a single bound."

It felt good to laugh.

The first mass contained a heterogeneous mixture of families, students, employees from a local lumber mill, and residents of a nearby nursing home. From the outset, the atmosphere was warm. Yet there was more, something pronounced and undefined. Robins recognized it, too. As we prepared the bread and wine during the offertory, he leaned over, suggesting in a whisper that the place was on a high.

It was only after the service that the collective feelings came into focus as time and again perfect strangers, as well as individuals I barely knew, made it a point to stop, expressing their support and encouragement for what the events at Resurrection might someday mean for all of Catholicism. Although I was surprised and embarrassed by it all, my spirits soared.

Having underestimated the atmosphere of Christ the King Parish, I was even less prepared for what took place the following morning at the assembly of priests.

Descending the stairway into the parish social center, Robins threw open the doors, peering into the noisy throng.

"Where else could you get a room full of males all wearing the same suit?" he teased, stepping back to let me pass.

Approaching a small group of priests clustered around one of the coffee bars scattered throughout the room, it dawned on me that I hadn't seen many of them since our marriage. Blake scooted by while I paused to say hello. At first, I presumed my voice had been drowned out in the din of a hundred others vibrating throughout the center. It was only after a second greeting, which again received no response, that I turned away just as one of them raised his voice. "What's that son of a bitch doing here? Maybe someone ought to tell him to crawl back into the sack with his little darling! I hear they have mirrors on the bedroom ceiling!"

I felt the wind sucked out of me, as if I'd been struck by a sharp blow. Struggling against a gush of rage and shock, but trying to pretend nothing had happened, I turned away, nearly stumbling into a middle-aged priest talking with Paul Metzner. We had known one another since I was a teenager. Still shaken, I held out my hand. Looking right through me, both men brushed by as though I wasn't there.

Robins brought me up short. "Pardon me for saying so, Father, but you look shitty. What'd you do, get salt in your coffee?"

I told him what happened.

His forehead furrowed, the muscles in his lower jaw beginning to twitch. "What'd you expect, a marching band? You're no longer in the club. If they accept you, it might be the unraveling of the first thread. The whole spool of their world could come unwound."

"Yeah, maybe." Struck by the intensity spreading across his sharp features, I feigned a laugh. "Look at me! I don't have two heads, do I? Dammit anyway. It's like I've got the plague or something."

He looked away, his small agate eyes darting about the room. "Some of the brothers out there think Dutch is hell-bent on destroying the church. You're the ultimate insult." He stroked a hand through his thinning hair, then laid it on my shoulder. "Don't let it get to you. They're insecure and afraid. You still have more friends in here than not."

Perhaps, I thought, as I recognized that some of my closest friends were in the crowd—knowing, too, that the majority were fine men, the best in many ways. Later on, several went out of their way to be friendly. Still, whenever an occasional back was turned or a hand once extended was withdrawn, it stung. The gnawing sense of being tolerated, of being isolated from those whose company I had felt a part of for years, was inescapable.

After a series of conferences which barely penetrated my discouragement, we concluded the day with common compline. It was not until then, during the evening prayer of the church, that the scales of despondency covering my eyes fell away, and I saw. For a split second, as we uniformly recited the Breviary, I caught a glimpse of what had been right in front of me all along. Despite the resentment and rejection from some, I remained among them still. Among them, happily married and having survived as a priest.

Though there was no denying the sense of toleration that emanated from all too many who were chanting psalms around me, in that frozen instant I also knew again that the church was indeed changing and that miracles were possible after all.

In the following months, we strove to close the shutters on all thoughts of clerical opposition. By the time we turned the first spade of earth signaling the construction of a house of worship for the mushrooming community of Resurrection, we had nearly succeeded. Then Hans Küng's note arrived.

In stiff German he informed us that Hunthausen's statement to the clergy regarding my ministry had been immediately forwarded to "very dangerous and conservative quarters within the Vatican." He urged extreme caution, while advising with characteristic humor that "Mafia ears" within the Curia were now turned in our direction.

Seeing the painful surprise in his eyes, I regretted showing Hunthausen the note from Küng. Still, he had to know that some of his dissenting priests had contacted Rome. My own reaction was similar to Tim's. We weren't at all surprised.

"We haven't any idea what those 'dangerous quarters' really know," O'Mera said. "Besides, if Rome's going to do anything, it's a little late. It's been over a year since the wedding. With Dutch so supportive and the parish behind us, all hell would break loose if they came storming in here. That's the kind of publicity they don't want or need."

In writing to thank Küng, I was more concerned about the Curia's investigation of his recent books than our own situation, assuring him we would continue our low profile, confident our position was secure.

Yellowstone Park is more than an icy wilderness in wintertime. With its percolating mud pots and geysers spouting translucently against the sky, it is a land of unapproachable grandeur. Yet it was the sheer expanse of its silence which captivated us as we whisked over the trail, the only noise the gentle swoosh of our skis. In part because of the quiet, the old bull startled us. Trudging shoulder-deep through mounds of snow, the massive buffalo crossed in front of us with barely a sound.

Joan spun around, her breath a soft puff hanging in the air.

"Shh . . ." she whispered, just as a herd of cows and yearling calves pushed by so close we could hear their snorting and see the slender icicles clinging to their manes.

"Oh Lord, but they're so . . . so very beautiful and primitive," she said, watching a straggling calf bound out of sight.

"So are you," I replied, inching alongside her.

"Don't be so corny." She giggled as I slid over and kissed the tip of her nose, only to collide and send us both sprawling into a drift, which tumbled away from us in tiny avalanches.

Her laughter slid across the snowfield, which in the bright sun sparkled as if strewn with precious gems. The struggle which so smothered our lives appeared to be behind us. We were happy and knew it.

We decided to pass the night within a cavelike overhang used centuries earlier by tribal inhabitants of the Yellowstone. By the time we found it, the sun, descending behind a canyon wall, bathed the surrounding spruce trees in a purple hue.

As Joan scraped the wax from our skis, I gathered a mound of twigs and struck a match. Protected by the rock walls from the stinging breeze outside, the fire burst into life.

"The Indians who stopped here knew what they were doing." I whistled, warming my hands as Joan hung a kettle of soup above the blaze. While she moved about, I wondered about other women who had done the same hundreds, perhaps thousands, of years before. Wondered, too, about how much of their spirit lived within her, their strength complementing hers.

In the winter, darkness comes quickly to the Yellowstone and with it, a numbing cold. Following steaming mugs of soup and chunks of French bread, we slipped into our sleeping bag, Joan's head resting on my shoulder as we watched the flames' shadows dance across the ceiling. They seemed to speak of our past, one in which she had waited alone—waited for me; for the church; enduring long days and seasons; paying the price—never had I felt so close to her, so thankful for the gift of her life.

Leaning up on an elbow, I brushed a strand of hair back from her forehead. In the flickering light her dark eyes seemed to float between us.

"I'm sorry."

"Sorry?"

"For all the crap. All the pain. For what it cost to get where we are."

"Hey, enough of that. Don't break the spell. Listen, you've given me more than you know. As for the price? It was worth it."

"I need to believe that, but it's just . . ." I shook my head, groping to get at what was digging at me. "Your faith was strong and the church held things together for you. Then you ran into me. I don't know. It's just that I worry about what's happened to, well, you know, your faith and all."

She sat up, scooted closer to the heat, speaking into the fire.

"Faith? Maybe. Yet I didn't know anything. No kidding. Oh, I know, the Irish washerwoman's belief is probably the strongest going, but not for me. Before I met you, holy water was as important to me as the gospel. I knew more about the Blessed Virgin than Jesus." She waved an arm toward a slight opening in the roof where smoke spewed out into a star-clustered sky. "Everything that's happened has merely separated the wheat from the chaff."

"But dragging you through so much, just so I could stay a priest. Well, sometimes it seems pretty damn selfish."

"Hey, hon. Do you have any idea of the impact you have as a priest? Every time you preach, it thrills me to watch the people. You have no inkling of the lives you touch. Mine included. Remember the Fat Lady? It wasn't just you who wanted to stay."

We settled back, the only sound the wind whipping at a tarp over the cave's entrance. I was nearly asleep when Joan reached over to stroke my cheek.

"Michael Miles? I think we should have a child."

We had spoken often of having children but because of the stress and uncertainty of our lot, decided to delay it indefinitely.

We talked until the fire faded into smoldering embers, enveloping the cave in inky darkness. Certainly our lives would never be secure. Then again, neither were those of any couple we knew. Our marriage was in its second year. The parish was firmly established. The bishop remained solidly behind us. Moreover, the tension which for so long had permeated our lives was on the wane.

Joan snuggled close, the heat of her body against mine.

"Whoever the little one might be, I know one thing. He'll have a whale of a woman for his mother!"

Her lips came to mine, full and warm as the fire. Suddenly I felt a passion of such intensity that it startled me. As I pulled away, Joan came on with a gentleness which soon gave way to such strength that I nearly lost my own.

The morning was perfectly still as we skied toward home. In a playful mood, Joan criss-crossed Specimen Creek, imitating the murmur of flowing water echoing up through the frozen layers of ice.

Curious, a young moose bounded through the powdery snow behind us. When I tossed a snowball, the animal bolted by close enough to send me telemarking down an incline. Through the stillness, Joan's glee echoed another time. A season of innocence.

Reaching the car, we uncorked a thermos of lukewarm cider stashed beneath the seat.

"To little Michael!" Joan said. "Or whoever it might be, if we're lucky."

I sipped the sweet liquid, savoring the spicy smell, thinking back to our first kiss amid Luther's snow.

While we waited for the heater to remove the frost from the windshield, I switched on the radio in search of a road report. Joan was chatting about whether or not she would prefer a girl or a boy.

"Do we have a choice?"

"How about twins?" she said giddily, not waiting for an answer. She suddenly stopped, motioning at the radio.

"Thought I heard the name Hunthausen."

By then the distant voice was drowned out in a field of static. Not until we emerged from the canyon did we hear the news. Because he was relatively unknown, and owing to the remoteness of his diocese, few observers expected the surprising announcement. The fifty-three-year-old Montana native would become the fifth archbishop in Seattle's history.

Speechless, I watched the color drain from Joan's face. She placed a hand on my knee, squeezing firmly.

Although there had always been the possibility Dutch would be moved, neither of us had taken it seriously. Not at all ambitious, he was considered too progressive for further advancement up the hier-archical ladder.

"Who makes these decisions?" she asked, her voice breaking.

"Sounds like the Holy Spirit had a hand in this one. At least for Seattle. Our loss. Their gain."

"Come on, hon. You know what I mean!"

"Jean Jadot. He's a Belgian archbishop. Paul the Sixth's delegate to the States. No doubt he read the report from the folks in Seattle profiling the type of man they wanted. He has to submit three names to the pope, but Paul relies heavily on Jadot's first choice."

"Some choice! It's awful," she said, looking out the window at the trees whipping by.

"Actually, it's an excellent appointment."

"How can you sit there so nonchalant?" she blurted. "You're so stoic about it."

I didn't understand my reaction either.

Joan asked when we would know about a new bishop, as if my answer made little difference.

"Six months. Maybe less."

Regardless, we both knew that whoever it might be, life would never be the same again.

At the core of my feelings was an all-pervasive emptiness, a sense of loss. For as long as I could remember, Hunthausen had always been there, the thread of his presence winding through all I was and ever sought to be.

"As an archbishop he won't have any authority over our diocese, but he can do more for the church as a whole," I said, trying to draw my emotions into focus.

"Well, I just don't want him to go. For your sake, most of all." She slung an arm around my shoulder. "This is the chance those who want to get a crack at you have been waiting for. With him gone, you could be left swaying in the wind."

She listened as I went over old territory. Most of the priests had supported Dutch's decision to permit us to remain. The people of the parish would stand by us.

Joan shook her head. "I'm sorry for reacting this way, but sometimes you only want to see saints out there. You're almost as blind to evil as Dutch. Well, maybe it's off center stage, in the wings, but it's there all right."

"See what's happened to you? If you hadn't met me, you wouldn't . . ."

"Wouldn't be so much in love! It's just that you trust the church more than I do." She paused. "You've got to call him."

"What?"

"Dutch. You need to see how he is."

"Yeah."

Alongside the road, row upon row of jack pines whisked by, their branches drooping mournfully with snow.

Two days later, I still hadn't called him, pretending that if I didn't the whole thing would turn out to be untrue. However, each time another story of the appointment was splashed across the state's papers, my heart skipped a beat.

When finally I did call, the archbishop-elect's voice carried an air of despondency. Since he had resisted initial proddings from the apostolic delegate, his appointment as spiritual leader of nearly a half-million Catholics came as a total surprise to him. At first, he felt like backing away, certain he wouldn't measure up to the task. Eventually, out of obedience to the pope's wishes, he consented.

"If God wants me to do this," he said, half-heartedly, "He'll have to make me big enough for the job."

"Maybe He'll change it to fit you instead."

Over the phone he took a deep breath, as though pondering whether to proceed.

"I nearly said no for two reasons. My mother is almost eighty and the idea of leaving her doesn't sit too well. Deep down, though, she wants me to go. The other, well, it isn't as easy. Quite honestly, this puts you and Joan in an awkward spot. I'm afraid there may be some among us who won't rest until this whole experiment is crushed."

"And us with it," I muttered.

"What?"

"Skip it."

"Anyway, the more I thought about it, the more convinced I

became that if what's happening there at Resurrection can't stand on its own merits, then maybe I shouldn't have permitted you to stay in the first place.''

I wanted to blurt out that he was missing the point. If merits alone were the deciding factor, the case for a married priesthood would win hands down. We'd be home free. Yet it all sounded so self-serving and foreign to the simple reliance Jesus called for.

Swallowing hard, I said nothing.

Hunthausen seemed worn. ''Whatever happens, you can be sure I'll talk to my successor about you. In the meantime, we'll just have to rely on God.''

The line went dead as a heavy curtain fell over one phase of our lives; neither of us was at all certain what lay ahead in the next act.

Were it not for the redwood sign jutting out from the close-spaced juniper and pine, a passing motorist might never know St. Thomas the Apostle Seminary was nestled back amid the lush vegetation bordering Lake Washington.

Since his installation in the Seattle Center, Dutch had abandoned the episcopal mansion for a small apartment behind the seminary. When he proposed that Joan and I spend the month of August with him, our response was immediate.

Not until the archbishop escorted us to our tiny rooms did we realize his residence was in fact a section of a former convent.

''These used to be cells for the nuns who did the guys' cooking and laundry,'' he explained.

I tossed Joan's suitcase onto the narrow cot in her room, where she stood with both hands on her hips.

''I knew you two were up to something. All along it's been nothing but a ploy to get me to enter the convent!''

Fussing about, Hunthausen helped her unpack. Crossing the hall to my own cell, I passed through a large common room, the floor strewn with mounds of mail and books. Except for an ancient Blaupunkt radio and a rocker I recognized from the days at Carroll, the room was bare.

Once we were settled in, the archbishop led us out a back door onto a walkway which circled behind a water tower to the edge of the lush foliage surrounding the seminary.

He took us down a worn trail into a rain forest; the vegetation was so dense we couldn't see the sky. Stepping over gnarled tree roots, we wound past patches of mushrooms, their snowy heads peeking above blankets of emerald moss. The trail fell downward until we reached the secluded lakeshore, where after skipping rocks across the waters, we climbed away from the lake. Along the way we passed a set of Stations of the Cross fixed atop sturdy posts. Each station, spaced about fifty feet from the other, depicted a scene from Christ's journey to Golgotha.

"I was a seminarian here," Dutch puffed. "It was during the war. I'd dreamed of being a navy pilot. Even learned to fly." He grinned, gently rubbing his thumb across a miniature foot of the Crucified. "But my confessor, Father Topel, thought God had other things in store. So there I was, loving it here but feeling guilty not being off with my friends. By the time I got out, the war was over."

We emerged from the forest onto a wide field, in the center of which sat a massive brick building, its five stories crowned by a pagodalike bell tower. The archbishop pointed up at the dozens of lifeless windows stretching along its walls like so many dominoes.

"My room was right up there. I used to sit by the window looking out over this field." He pointed to an overgrown stretch of rolling green. "It was especially beautiful just before dark. Right after the Angelus, the whole area was filled with seminarians strolling around, either praying the breviary or reciting the rosary."

I thought back to my own seminary days with a twinge of grief at their loss. I delighted in the quiet, contemplative atmosphere where, removed from the world, we had felt almost in another one. Where touching the divine somehow seemed far easier than before or since.

Picking up a few pieces of deteriorating tile which had slipped from the rooftop, Hunthausen explained that by the early sixties there had been so many students for the priesthood, the old building was converted into a high-school seminary. A new multimillion-dollar complex was then constructed across the hill where he now lived. Together, St. Edward's and St. Thomas's housed several hundred men and boys.

"The timing was poor. It was just before change started sweeping through the church. The days when parents thought having a son here was like a ticket straight to heaven for them." He stopped next to a bleached statue of the Virgin inscribed *Mater Cleri*. "No one saw what was coming. I remember looking out that window when the fog rolled in off the Sound, so thick you could barely see the black cassocks moving around. With the shortages today, it's like they all just walked into it and disappeared."

As we ambled across the field, heavy with the smell of lilacs, Joan asked him about the boarded windows of St. Edward's.

"It's closed. There are so few seminarians these days. In the next year or so we'll have to shut down the new one, too. Golly," he said, in a tone as close as he ever got to swearing, "the archdiocese is growing so fast we can't keep track of it. Yet the national vocations office tells us that whereas less than a decade ago we had over forty-five thousand people in our seminaries, now it's down to fifteen thousand and shrinking by the minute. With no priests coming down the line, coupled by the fact that over half of those ordained end up leaving . . . well, it doesn't take a genius to figure it out."

"At the university, kids turn on to the idea of doing something special with their lives. But a lifetime without intimacy isn't quite what they're looking for," I added.

Hunthausen stopped, throwing his hands up in frustration. "It's the same all over the world! Küng and the others warned us in the early days of the Council this was coming!"

Joan joined in, with the special way she had of entering the thoughts of another. "Meanwhile, the church keeps tossing out many of its finest. What's going on isn't right or fair. Too many people are paying for some ol' duffers' stubbornness! I'm sorry." She hastened on. "It's just that sometimes my frustration gets away from me. I know there are lots of reasons for the shortages, not all of them bad. Maybe someday it will even force the church to ordain women."

Dutch wrapped a beefy arm over her shoulder as we entered the driveway leading to St. Thomas's. "That's why what the two of you are going through is so important. We've just got to believe the Holy Spirit is pushing it along."

"He'd better be, or we're all in trouble," she replied airily.

For a moment Seattle's new archbishop looked terribly old.

Before long, we settled into a routine. Joan offered to lend a woman's touch to the archbishop's quarters, and in no time we were moving furniture, hanging pictures, painting walls. Each day when he returned from the city, we would either take a run through the woods or climb up on the seminary roof and together watch the sun sink into the Sound.

Whenever he could, Hunthausen broke free of the chancery office, and the three of us would venture out to explore the sprawling archdiocese. Whether in Port Angeles, Anacortes, Snoqualmie, or the metropolitan area itself, our lives bounced about in a jar full of joy.

On one such occasion, while taking a ferry to Bremerton, Dutch noticing a priest leaning against the railing, sauntered over to say hello. At first the rather stuffy fellow had no idea that the stocky figure in corduroys and sneakers, sporting a soiled fishing cap, was in fact his new archbishop. When he finally discovered who he was talking with, the priest gave Hunthausen a scolding look of disapproval matched only by a Marine Corps drill instructor sizing up a raw recruit. At once Joan started to giggle. The more she tried to smother her laughter, the worse it became until we were forced to excuse ourselves and go belowdecks, leaving neither of them with any idea what was tickling her so. It was during such times that the roar of the church cannons at home felt farther and farther away.

As the time approached to return to Montana, neither of us really wanted to leave. However, there was little choice but to let go of someone we had come not only to cherish but in a sense to cling to as well.

The morning we set out, it was still dark. Only when all but a few of the brightest stars clung to a milky sky, did we see the note folded under the wiper blade.

> Life's full of contradictions . . . try to rely on the Riddle
>   Maker—
> If you want to be rich, be poor.
> If you want to be full, be empty.
> If you want to be first, be last.
> If you want to live, die.
> If you want to find your life, you must first give it away.
>   Shalom,
>   Dutch

From the outset of our work together, Tim and I routinely set aside a day a month for reflection and prayer. Contemplatives traditionally refer to such pulling aside as "desert time." Not until our first such day since returning from Seattle did O'Mera mention the vicar-general.

"At first, I wasn't going to say anything," Tim said, closing his eyelids with a nervous flutter. "You know. More of the same ol' crap. But it's been eating away at me."

During our absence he and Gerald Himmler—the vicar-general of the diocese—had spent a few hours in the rectory at the table we now occupied. Himmler reminded me of a small gray owl with eyes far too large for his frail body. The task of administering the diocese pending selection of a new bishop had fallen upon the middle-aged priest.

"It was strange. He started off about your involvement in weddings and penance services. He kept prodding me for clues to what you were up to. Eventually accused you of having a well-planned, uncompromising game plan."

"Game plan? What's so suspect about falling in love?"

"Well, all I know is he made no bones about it. He's convinced you've had something up your sleeve ever since you executed your fateful decision."

"Fateful decision! For godsakes, Tim."

"Himmler's words."

"Meaning?"

For the first time Tim smiled. "Getting married. He thinks it's just the first step on your part to taking Rome on over celibacy. He said to remind you that playing the prophet is a dangerous game."

"Ah, you've got to be kidding. And I thought I was the only one who was getting paranoid." I managed a feeble laugh.

Tim went into the kitchen, rattling about in the cupboard. For a second I wondered about myself, questioning whether if in the struggle my motivation hadn't become muddled and ego wasn't taking over.

"Here." Tim handed me a porcelain cup of lukewarm coffee. "What bothered me the most was Himmler's bit about a letter some of the priests sent to the apostolic delegate. They complained about you still preaching, assisting with the sacraments. The whole ball of wax."

"They're still at it?" I thundered, slamming the cup down, startling both of us. "Who's they?"

"He wouldn't say. Just that there's a hard core who felt sold out and ignored by Hunthausen. They'd just as soon turn the clock back. According to our beloved vicar, they're the same ones who refer to him in four-letter terms. With all due respect, mind you!"

Tapping his spoon against the table, Tim told about reminding Himmler that the majority of priests supported Hunthausen's episcopacy, even agreeing with our own venture. The vicar had countered, suggesting that such support for us was calculated to place any future bishop who might wish to reverse things at Resurrection in a terrible position. Any such move on his part would encounter fierce resistance by the solid block of clerics we had steadfastly developed for our cause.

"I think he may have overestimated us! Besides, let's just hope it never comes to that," I said as rain began to sprinkle against the window. "Why do you suppose these guys wrote the delegate. What're they after?"

Tim coughed, tossing the spoon onto the table. "Your head for one thing. Himmler thinks they want to influence the selection of the next bishop. Someone who'll patch things up the way they ought to be."

"They're looking for a dragon slayer."

"At the very least, they're poisoning the well. What I can't figure out is how they account for Dutch's promotion if he was so awful."

I switched the subject back to the vicar, who sounded like a man caught in the middle.

"I'm not so sure he's in the middle," Tim said. "He's not in your corner, for sure; claims you manipulated Dutch into letting you stay. Played upon his goodness. Admits he counseled against it from the beginning."

"He has a right to that, I guess."

Looking uncomfortable, Tim sat back, folding his arms across his chest.

"As far as he's concerned, both of us live in a fantasy land. Says you've embarked on a 'perilous route.' He thinks there's nowhere but Resurrection where people would tolerate a married priest. Besides, in his mind, once you married you left the priesthood. His mental framework doesn't allow for anything else."

"Yeah, in his world everything I'm doing now is a violation."

"Oh hell, the whole thing is stupid," he said, pushing away from the table. Neither of us wanted to talk about it any longer, but I had a final question.

"Did you invite him to come to the parish some Sunday? See our side of things?"

He nodded. "Yup. But he's not about to."

"Then why'd he bother to look you up?"

"Usually he plays his cards close to the chest," he said emptily. "I think the real reason was to put himself on record as having slapped your wrists."

"Just in case . . ."

"Just in case he's being considered for the hierarchy. He talks as if he expects to get the nod . . . so he needs to cover his behind.''

I couldn't shake off a certain sadness, recalling a time with Himmler when we canoed over the polished glass surface of Seeley Lake. He spoke of a desire to leave church administration and start a house of prayer.

Outside, the rain was falling in sheets.

''Some desert,'' I said, not caring whether Tim heard me, wondering if God did.

Midway through the fall, we opened at last Resurrection's own center of worship, which when empty seemed full of the mountains rising just beyond its walls of glass, and when full felt empty of all else but those it housed.

Long before the smell of newness had left the building, the seats began to fill up half an hour in advance of Sunday masses with people anxious to secure a place. Normally by the time mass began, the center was jammed, the crowd quite often spilling out onto the sidewalks. If the center was already obsolete, the community itself exuded a power and vitality which was anything but. The confidence that reliance upon the rich heritage of Catholicism would indeed give the church a fresh face became contagious. Day by day, the community's response continually convinced me that the priesthood was where I truly belonged. Still, every time I preached or celebrated the liturgy, I wanted to pinch myself to make sure it was all really true.

If the exuberance of Resurrection constituted its nature, and the gospel its soul, an anonymous note placed on my desk hinted that our marriage had something to do with its heart.

> Knowing you are married has somehow made both of you priests more accessible. Seeing you are human, too, somehow makes the Christian life seem possible for me. Observing the love between you and Joan reminds me of the importance of those I love. I don't know what it all means yet, but one thing is for sure—your marriage has permitted many of us to relax a bit and makes this parish far warmer than I ever thought the church could be.

Whatever was happening, Resurrection was a happy community, all but oblivious to the persistent rumblings over its married priest, the epicenter of which remained unknown and distant from us all.

* * *

Paralleling our experience at Resurrection was a desire to discreetly share its valuable lessons to benefit the larger church. Not at all an easy task given the climate generated by Paul VI's admonition declaring the celibacy issue closed. Although the Vatican's doors were locked and windows boarded, certain factions within Catholicism were unwilling to let the question die. Such was the case with Jeffry Connley, my pseudonym for a priest and guiding force behind a major study on the American priesthood of the early 1970's.

The results of the intensive study commissioned by the nation's hierarchy turned out to be a source of embarrassment for many of them. Nevertheless, *The Catholic Priest in the United States*, with its focus on psychological profiles, found its way into nearly every rectory in the country, documenting among its findings that mandatory celibacy was a major obstacle to healthy personality development among large segments of the clergy. It really rattled the barricades.

Release of the report to the hierarchy's Committee on Priestly Life and Ministry coincided with the appointment of then Bishop Raymond Hunthausen to that same committee. Though Connley's work had a significant impact on Hunthausen, in the ensuing years the two men enjoyed little more than a passing acquaintance. Consequently, when Jeff, anxious to hear more about events at Resurrection, offered to meet with the archbishop and me, it was arranged at once. We met in the lounge of Chicago's O'Hare Airport while criss-crossing between independent engagements.

From the moment the gregarious Connley loosened his tie and settled his large frame next to Hunthausen, it was obvious that each viewed the other with sincere affection. Their backgrounds couldn't have been more varied, yet more the same. When Hunthausen was a boy stocking shelves in the family grocery, Connley was a toddler in knickers and cap. By the time Dutch emerged as an All-American quarterback, Connley was finishing up high school. Both men were characterized by those who were closest to them as bright and richly human. Growing up, neither had indicated more than a passing interest in the priesthood, yet by the mid-fifties, both were ordained, soon to be thrust into leadership roles which would follow them into the post-conciliar church.

A renowned professional, Connley glided into public consciousness on the tip of his prolific pen. At the center of those calling for renewal in Catholicism, he came to embody the combination of faith and vision which men like Hunthausen considered crucial if the church was to have an effect on a world catapulting toward the twenty-first century.

Now, outlining his findings on underdeveloped and developing priests, Connley's cherublike face reflected the range of human emotions. Whenever he laughed, which was often, I wanted to also. Whenever he frowned, I felt a scowl spread over my own face, too. Above all, he exuded a sense of wholeness and confident compassion that lay behind his milky-blue eyes.

At one point, just as a glistening 747 revved up its engines and was taxiing by the window, Connley said that as few as five or six strong bishops might unleash the spirit of the more than three hundred members of the American hierarchy.

The archbishop raised his voice over the jet blast. "Fifty or sixty?" When Connley held up five fingers, the startled look on Hunthausen's face brought a broad smile over his own.

"You're one of them," Connley quipped. "My friend Joe Bernadin's another. If only a few more would defend the need for the U.S. Church to step into the future without always looking over its shoulder toward Rome—well, just imagine!"

Noticing our reflections in the window, I felt out of their league and yet at home with these two men who had risen to prominence in spite of themselves. Preoccupied, I missed Connley's next question, assuming he had asked about the delay in naming a new bishop of Helena.

"We conducted a survey of the diocese and developed a profile of the kind we hope for. It was sent to Jadot over a year ago. Still nothing," I replied.

He leaned back in the chair, folding his hands atop his bowed head. "You go to the delegate for the type you want, now do you?" he teased with an exaggerated brogue. "And it's been over a year now, has it? Here, I've always supposed it took about nine months."

By the time we recovered from a chorus of laughter upon discovering he'd inquired about Joan's pregnancy, Connley was ready again for Hunthausen.

"The church gets hell-bent on preserving its institutional integrity. Meanwhile, the gospel's commitment to human growth gets sidetracked. We've got to avoid getting sucked into that quicksand."

He turned to me. "Take just one example. By insisting upon ordaining only males, and celibate ones at that, we end up settling for those who don't exhibit the grosser signs of unfitness. How did we ever get into this, where marriage is seen as a betrayal of priestly vocation?''

Noting Dutch wince, he spun around on the chair to face him.

''That's why I was delighted, Archbishop, when I heard about you permitting Mike to function so fully.'' He pointed out the window toward a whining jet. ''I bounce over the country in those critters. Everywhere people are saying the same thing. They are weary of loveless religion. At its core, so much of life's mystery is about the intimacy between men and women.''

Dutch removed his glasses, polishing them slowly on his sleeve. ''That's not surprising. If Jesus said anything, it's that the Spirit works through people in love.''

''It goes for priests, too, if they're to be developing people. Sure, they might end up married. Not necessarily, though. Many are likely to stay as they are and mature in their celibacy. Either way, the question's one of freedom. That's why what Mike and Joan are doing is probably bigger than any of us. It's . . . well . . . symbolic. Sort of a first beachhead on the shores of Mother Church,'' he said.

Coming from a man I had read and listened to since my first years in the seminary, this was flattering but didn't quite fit our situation.

''Maybe,'' I replied, feeling a bit self-conscious. ''But it's not like we rushed out there to hit the beach. It's just that being a priest is important to me like it is for you guys. Loving Joan is, too . . . so there really wasn't much choice.''

Connley seemed to be listening through his eyes, which held on to mine.

''Exactly! Your greatest asset is that you aren't pushing a cause. Just going about the task of ministry.''

We paused as a waitress set down three glasses of Chablis. Taking a quick sip, Connley picked up where he had left off, only more intensely.

''Still, the parish knows the risks and what your marriage stands for. A first's been set in place. That's what I meant by a beachhead.'' He shook his head, unable to conceal his frustration. ''Although I'm afraid there is no way the institution is about to come to terms with what's so right and creative.''

''Not if a few priests at home have anything to say about it,'' I added, going on to tell him of the correspondence addressed to Jadot and Rome.

Connley slammed his hand against the side of his chair with a loud smack. "By and large, priests are magnificent men. But with all respect, Archbishop, some are just mean old bastards! Of course they would have trouble with this. It upsets their applecart. The good fathers won't be looked upon in quite the same way if some are married. Or God forbid, women might get close to the inner workings of the church and take their rightful place! That's an iceberg lying just beneath the surface."

Hunthausen had been listening for some time. "Whatever the reasons, apparently some of the troops can only enjoy their choice of celibacy if others are made to suffer for disagreeing with it. I used to think the laity would have a problem with guys like Mike, but . . ."

"But we both know, Archbishop, the whole issue is of clerical origin and prolongation. Grab anyone off the street anywhere. They know the importance of marriage, family. All of which incidentally we've been saying's important for ages."

"The whole thing ticks me off sometimes. At least when I'm made to feel like the enemy," I said.

"Does that mean angry?" Connley asked.

"Yeah, I suppose. Like the other day when a young kid ran his sports car under a semi truck. There was barely enough time to give him absolution." Suddenly the memory of the boy's face bearing the blank stare of death jolted me. "When I got home, there was a letter from the chancery. They'd used a red marker to scratch out 'Reverend,' on the envelope. Then the vicar-general wanted to know why, since our congregation had doubled over the year, our collection hadn't. Yeah, I get angry."

"Sure it's petty," Hunthausen cut in, "but you can't let that kind of thing get to you or you'll end up being your own worst enemy, Mike."

Dutch cleared his throat, anxious to defend the clergy. "I don't know what the motives of some of the priests are, but they'll be okay with it eventually. It's just that so much is new to them."

"Agreed," Connley said. "Still, to some, anything new is intimidating. They come crawling out from under the rocks whenever they perceive a threat to the established order." He sat back, exhaled, then sipped his drink in silence before speaking again.

"In all honesty, I know of other priests—and you bishops surely do—who are not living the celibate life. At times the hierarchy just looks the other way. I'm not clear whether they agree in principle—

which is most unlikely—or are hindered by a drastic shortage of priests.''

He waved a beefy hand toward me.

''The whole point is that guys like him who are trying to be honest, and women like Joan, put their cards on the table and get nailed.''

''But the clergy have a hard time . . .'' Dutch interjected.

''Have a disease, you mean. We all do in a way and it can be terminal.''

''Disease?'' I asked, thinking aloud.

''Clericalism. Its roots run throughout the church.'' He looked at the archbishop somewhat sadly. ''I hate to say it, but right now we're losing the battle. Folly marches on. Still, there's hope, so long as there are parishes like Resurrection. You probably know better than I, that there are more and more of them.''

Without answering, Dutch reached into his jacket, checking his flight time. After walking him to the gate for Seattle, and saying good-bye, Connley put his arm around my shoulder along our way to the Northwest Airlines ramp.

''That guy is one of the most outstanding bishops in the American Church. Probably the best. Somehow he makes believing easier.''

We shook hands.

''That was pretty heady back there. Be careful in all of it, Mike, not to lose your sense of humor.''

He touched a nerve. In fact, I used to laugh more. Not only on the outside but deep within. Was I taking things too seriously? Developing a thin skin? Though he was forever on the firing line, the most appealing aspect of Hans Küng was his unbridled sense of humor. Testament enough of his reliance on a source of life beyond his own.

Though the Evangelists never say, Jesus must have doubled over with laughter, often. Surely there was a sense of mirth lying just beneath the surface of his days. How else did he ever get through them, putting up with the likes of people who condemned him for eating an ear of corn on the Sabbath? His critics might have appeared to him as so many crows, perched and aloof, cawing away over the cornfield. He must have laughed. Surely.

A harassed attendant called out my flight.

''By the way, what are you going to name the baby?'' Connley asked.

''If it's a boy, we've got it made.''

''And if not?''

''We'll name her Raymond anyway.''

*   *   *

"There! Feel? It's himself!" Joan cried, placing my hand beneath her stomach. "There he is again, the little rascal!"

A small ball rolled beneath the skin across her abdomen. Feeling a sudden kick, I remembered the sermon of the previous Sunday. There had been a message to deliver, but I couldn't come up with the right words. Drawing upon the example of Joan's pregnancy came spontaneously. Knowing looks from parents and grandparents told me they understood. God's actions are often visible only in their effects. Effects sometimes barely noticeable, other times hitting us with a swift kick.

By the final trimester, Joan began to call the baby "himself," following our visit with Grandma. Not one for silence in such matters, Annie McGuire said next to nothing about our expected child. Not until I asked her point-blank what was going on, did her eyes roll up, the cup of tea in her hand rattling.

"Well, it's just . . ." she stammered, looking down as if to read the leaves, a practice she firmly believed in. "Well, with himself on the way, now they'll all know. 'Tis all I'm thinking."

"Know what?"

As we were growing up, sexuality was something none of us talked about, especially Grandma, who told us only that we arrived in the world in strange places. My brother was discovered on a windowsill; I, in a cabbage patch.

Now her eyes were rolling, her brogue thicker than normal.

"They'll all know what you and this lady have been up to, Father, and . . ."

"Oh Gran," Joan cried out, throwing her arms about her with a fierce hug. "Well, some folks are just going to have to grow up now, aren't they? Whether they like it or not, 'himself' is on the way!"

From the moment we first heard a heartbeat, the quickening life within Joan was a source of joy, not only for us but for many in the parish as well. Preoccupied, we gave little more than passing attention to the triumphal installation of Elden Curtiss as the seventh Bishop of Western Montana. Scant notice, that is, until his blustery letter arrived.

As a first order of business, Curtiss intended to clarify my status within the church. To ensure that no one continued to view me as a married priest, it would be necessary to limit me to only those activities open to a layman. If a set of yet-to-be specified conditions were not acceptable, then my position at Resurrection would be forfeited at once. We would meet within the week to consider my decision.

The letter bore his episcopal coat of arms, a miter and pectoral cross, ringed by a Byzantine crown. Underneath, his chosen motto: "That They Might All Be One."

I arranged for an immediate meeting of the parish council. During our initial encounter in Oregon, Curtiss had indicated he would withhold judgment about our experiment at Resurrection, but he had apparently had second thoughts. His turnabout frustrated more than alarmed me. He was too new to the diocese actually to attempt something so reckless. Although sensing a potential crisis, no one on the council was willing to admit alarm either. There was, however, strong resentment over being issued an ultimatum calling for dialogue at what was unanimously considered the point of a gun—the first shot of which had already been fired across our bow. They were advised I would meet with the new bishop, but agreed that after coming so far, there could be no backing down.

The tires screeched against the hot pavement as Blake Robins negotiated a sharp curve running along the west shore of Flathead Lake. In the distance, a sole water-skier raised a glistening rooster tail from the waters stretching toward the gateway to Glacier National Park.

"I'd rather be out there than in here," Robins said, noting a temperature bordering on 100 degrees. As we approached the community of Kalispell, I checked my watch. The appointment with Bishop Curtiss was fifteen minutes away.

"What I can't figure out is why he wants to send a letter to the priests. It's not like you just got married, for cryin' out loud. It's been three years. Whatever you do, don't tell him about Hans Küng. He can't take him. Claims he's almost a Protestant," Robins said, reminding me of a recent note I'd had from Küng. In it, once again the theologian cautioned us to avoid any and all publicity, noting that even our parish bulletins were now being forwarded to archconservative groups in Europe.

We pulled up in front of the Outlaw Inn. Inside, several delegates to the annual conference of Diocesan Catholic Women milled about the lobby between sessions. Except for their lavender name tags, they might have passed for a group of tourists destined for the park nearby.

Blake pointed toward two newly ordained priests surrounded by a ring of delegates. "The ladies love baby priests. Can you imagine those characters wearing suits and collars in this heat! The conservative backlash is upon us. Pardon me while I avoid it,'' he said, stepping into a small gallery off the lobby as I took the stairway, smelling of ammonia, to the bishop's suite.

The door was ajar. I knocked and entered. Except for a pale gold lamp, the room was dark, the curtains drawn to avoid the heat. Curtiss was alone, leafing through a stack of papers. The last time I'd seen him—seated on a makeshift stage surrounded by thousands attending his installation—he also struck me as alone; terribly so. In a suitcase spread open across the bed, lay the same crimson skullcap, the *zucchetto*, he had received that evening.

No sooner had I sat down than Curtiss plunged abruptly into what he considered the alarming situation in Bozeman. Speaking over an air conditioner whining in the background, he advised me of a mandate given to him upon assuming the office of bishop. A directive to take care of the number one problem in his diocese, which the bishop of the neighboring diocese referred to as an outrageous scandal.

"You see, Mike," he said, leaning forward as if to pluck from the air the key to unlock an even greater chest of problems, "the heart of the matter is that there are those in Bozeman who see you as a married priest and we know it."

"Like I told you in Oregon, I resigned the celibate life, not the priesthood," I replied, trying to focus on his face partially obscured by the darkness.

His voice tightened. "Yeah, yeah. You know damn well what I mean. Talking with the delegate, I . . ."

"You brought this up with Jadot? Why, for heaven's sake?" I asked, the anger rushing to my temples.

His eyes flashed, blending in with the small aluminum spots on the wallpaper behind him. "Who said I did? At any rate, His Holiness is not about to accept a married clergy and therefore neither am I. Nope, it wouldn't be at all good for the church."

"Lots of others besides those at Resurrection would disagree."

"See. You . . . you . . . reformers . . . want to toss everything out. Celibacy is important."

"Sure, it can be, but so can . . ."

He waved me off. "The signs are there. As in the past, God will preserve things as is. It's too great a gift to forfeit because some priests can't control themselves."

"If it's such a gift, why does the church have to force it on us?"

"Listen, fella," he said, his voice laced with impatience. "No one forced this on you. But that's not even the point. It's not Paul the Sixth's will that priests be permitted to function after violating their vows."

"Pardon me, Elden, but that's so much crap."

His jaw tightened, a reminder of how much the use of his first name irritated him.

"What about the Holy Spirit's will?" I continued. "When Jesus was asked what was the most important commandment, he said 'love,' not 'celibacy.' The church has to face the issue!"

I regretted being drawn into this argument over celibacy, when he was actually asking me to give up the work of a priest.

"What's the problem? If I'm a dispensed priest with some restrictions—which I am. If the people of Resurrection see me as such—which they do. If the gospel is being preached and the Spirit seems to be coming alive—which it does. Isn't that what we're theoretically all about? Sure, they know I'm a priest. That's the whole point. My head didn't fall off when Joan and I got married!"

His jaw tightened. Fingering the pectoral cross around his neck, he glared at me. "There's still a problem."

"Obviously. But who has it? Not me. Not Tim, nor the parish."

We were getting nowhere. I stood up, taking a deep breath. For several moments the only sound was the high-pitched whir of the air conditioner. Finally Curtiss spoke.

"Look. Let's just back up here a moment. Trouble is," he said with a frosty smile, "you're a lot like me. We're both headstrong. Matter of fact, I have to admit that the work you are doing seems orthodox and effective. You come across as a real churchman, too, and that means a lot to me. What I can't figure out is how you let yourself get into an affair with a woman. You blew a real future. But that's water over the bridge. Cardinal Wright insists this breach is to be closed and my stipulations are a step in that direction."

A picture of the prefect of the Sacred Congregation of the Clergy, a noted reactionary to change, flashed in my mind. Rumor had it that Paul VI had promoted the nearly three-hundred-pound archbishop to the Curia to stave off a rising tide of criticism of him at home in Pittsburgh.

"Listen," Curtiss continued, more calmly, stressing that Hunthausen had made a serious blunder in permitting me to stay. "Unfortunately, there's no way we can rewrite that page."

"We?"

He ignored the question. "For now, we've simply got to clarify your role."

"Clarify?"

"Yes. Maybe Hunthausen saw you as a priest with a few limitations tacked on, but the fact is, when you married, you agreed to relinquish Sacred Orders for life."

"That's not true and you know it. How can you see . . . ?"

"The question is how Rome sees it. When you married, you left."

"Left what?" I asked as we circled one another verbally, looking for an opening. "I'm still at Resurrection. Still doing the same identical work. Who left?"

Slamming his fist down with a crack on the end table, the bishop said that Hunthausen violated the Roman rescript in keeping me on.

"He'd better not tangle with them!" he exploded, adding that if there was one thing the Vatican did not tolerate it was insubordination.

"Nor apparently courage. Concern for the needs of the people. Not even what's true!" I shouted back.

"God, you'd think you were on the side of the angels! Well, let me tell you something. The hierarchy is ice-cold to the notion of married priests. The fact is, either you agree to clarify this thing or you're finished!"

When I mentioned that our parish council was troubled with such threats, he assured me of his willingness to disband them altogether.

"If people don't like the church—it's teaching authority—then they should get the hell out!"

Speechless at witnessing a different side of Curtiss, I eased back down into the chair, the room suddenly much smaller. Still seething beneath the surface, he unfolded two sheets from the stack of papers he'd been thumbing through when I entered.

"Here. I want you to witness this."

I let the papers lie.

"Or?"

"Unless you sign, it's like I said. You're out."

My eyes swept the text staring back at me from the table.

"Looks to me like a toned-down repeat of the Vatican line. I can't agree to that."

"You and I will never agree," he said, matter-of-factly. "Anyway, it's confidential and will stay that way. I may need to assure Cardinal Wright of my position."

All at once it fell into place. His position. Not mine. His words.

Not mine. His stance would be on record as one I clearly understood. My signature would testify to that. But what of me?

"Honestly, Mike, I don't want to get rid of you. Besides, if I tried, all hell would probably break loose! I'm not about to walk into that buzz saw."

Curtiss sat back abruptly, and though strangely distant, listened, seeming to hear that any substantial modification of my role in the parish would be demoralizing to the community and telegraph the wrong signals about its new bishop. Even as I spoke it dawned on me that for him the issue was not what I did in the parish so much as how his stance was perceived by his superiors. A man of documents, he needed a piece of paper, a high wall protecting him from what he knew was the reality at Resurrection.

So while disagreeing, we agreed. A letter would go out to the priests indicating his position. In turn, I wouldn't encourage people to call me "Father." Nor would I wear a stole over my vestment during mass. Tim would continue to "preside" over the Eucharist. Whatever the verbiage, it was clear that precious little would have to change. With that, the threat of termination was withdrawn.

Curtiss stood, putting on the *zucchetto*, visibly relieved. "We can work well together down the line, but you've got to be careful. Even Broderick says things have gone too far too quickly. He thinks you're beyond the agreement with Hunthausen. You know what Himmler says?" he asked while we walked down the stairway leading to the buzzing lobby. "He thinks the archbishop lost more support over you than on any single issue."

"Bull. Dutch was the most popular bishop this diocese ever had. There was always that handful, though. Nothing he ever did was good enough for them."

As we entered the lobby, a woman waved, calling out to me, "Hi, Father."

Curtiss bristled, but let it pass when another stopped him, requesting a blessing for her religious medal. I took the opportunity to slip away.

"I don't get it." Blake Robins whistled as we settled into the car alongside the Outlaw's cowboy marquee. "Does our fearless leader have any idea just how far things have evolved at your place?"

"Beats me." I sighed, relieved the encounter was over. "We've invited him a couple of times to come down for a weekend, but he keeps putting it off."

"If he hasn't come by now, ten bucks he never will. He's going to keep his distance," Robins said, suddenly serious. "It sounds cynical, but if he's taking his marching orders from someone else, there's probably a trick or two up his sleeve. Why else demand that you sign his letter?"

"Document." I corrected him, half-heartedly.

"Sounds to me like he's trying to leave a paper trail to cover himself just in case."

Maybe he had a point. Still, Curtiss seemed more flamboyant than Machiavellian. Though he left me uneasy, there was something appealing about him. He came across as convinced of his position but paradoxically supportive of my remaining at Resurrection. What troubled me above all else about him sending another letter to the priests was Küng's warning that anything in print would end up in European hands.

Blake frowned.

"You know what kills me? You'd think some of the padres would be happy you stayed on. Instead, they're clucking like ol' hens. You're such a threat to them. They'd be strutting around flapping their wings if you left."

"Yeah, I suppose you're right."

Drumming his fingers on the dashboard, Robins paused before saying, "What's it take to penetrate the crust of these guys? Why do you put up with this crap anyway?"

"Death wish," I joked, but he wasn't smiling.

"No. Seriously. It's tough seeing you and Joan put through the wringer. You've already made your point. Sometimes I wonder why you don't just get out and get on with your lives."

The car was like an oven inside, calling to mind the Fat Lady sweltering on her porch swatting flies.

"Ever hear of the Fat Lady?"

"Run that by me again?"

I turned, squinting into the sun.

"We didn't get into this to make a point—though God knows one needs to be made. This probably sounds corny, but staying has become a question of conscience."

"Well said, Thomas More." He smiled, less intense. "Though it does sound corny."

"No. Really. Put yourself in my shoes. You go ahead and get married in spite of the fact that the church insists the people won't buy it. But, turns out they're dead wrong. By and large the folks out there in the pews not only accept it, what's more, they couldn't care less. Whether or not you are celibate is immaterial. All they want is for you to be a good priest.''

He nodded, about to say something.

"Hang on a second. Let me continue. To put frosting on the cake, you discover that the woman who took the plunge with you is helping you become a better person and a better priest.''

"Uh-huh. But alas, there's a fly in the ointment. When push comes to shove, the Curtisses of the world don't always care what the people think,'' he said.

"That's what is so damned frustrating about it all. The institution's always got to be right, even if it's wrong!''

Blake sat silently, a logging truck, then a Winnebago reflected in his sunglasses from the road behind me. He took a deep breath, exhaling thoughtfully.

"Don't get me wrong. I'm glad you're hanging in there. It's important. But you're standing on a slippery deck.''

"For sure. Though when both of us were ordained, we were asked to help renew the church. God knows I didn't dream that it might end up meaning . . .''

"Putting your ass on the line,'' he cut in, causing us both to chuckle and relax.

"All I know, Blake, is that in the end we all have to answer to God. I've just got to do what seems right even if the deck is slippery.''

He started the car, a familiar lightness returning to his voice.

"If I were in your shoes—and incidentally I'm glad I'm not—I'd hope to have the guts to do the same thing.''

"Well, the crisis is over,'' I said, looking at my watch.

"For now at least,'' he muttered, pulling out of the parking lot onto the highway.

The obstetrician glanced up at me from under his pale green cap and asked the question a second time.

"Father? What's her name?''

"Oh. Sorry. Michelle Raelene,'' I answered, still dazed.

"Raelene?''

"It means 'little Raymond'—after a friend of ours,'' Joan said, not looking at all like she'd just been through twelve hours of labor.

"Well, now you have two beautiful women in your life,'' the physician replied.

Indeed. Yet at times it all seemed so unreal. Even when Joan handed me our daughter, still covered with vernix, I wondered if someone would give me a pinch, and I would wake up to a priesthood that included neither of them.

Gently stroking the infant's head, I felt a pulse beat through the soft spot beneath her matted hair. For an instant, I wondered what kind of church she would grow up in. If there would be a place in it for her, as a woman and more so, as a priest's child. So far as Resurrection was concerned, the answer was clear. By the time we took Michelle home, we were flooded with booties, rattles, stuffed toys, and mounds of clothes. Everything came sharply into focus during her baptism.

Coincidentally, the last Sunday of October was also Halloween. It was three years to the day since we had waited for the call from Rome which never came; when any chance of stepping beyond impasse seemed lost. Now everything was possible.

We expected only a handful of friends to remain after mass for the baptism. However, by the time we put Michelle in fresh diapers, several hundred people were already crowding about the altar.

While Joan cradled our daughter, I dipped a thumb in the chrism, tracing the sign of the cross repeatedly over her.

"May your name be written forever in the book of life. May your ears be open to the Good News of salvation. Your eyes see what the prophets longed to see but did not. Your mouth full of the language of love. Your feet bearing the Good News of Christ Jesus. Your precious heart alive in the freedom promised to those called to be the sons and daughters of God."

Enveloped in the sweet smell of the chrism, Joan placed a hand atop Michelle's head, the ancient symbol of calling down the Spirit. Altar candles flickering in her eyes, she invited those closest to us to do the same. First Tim, then a river of hands. Tender hands which had sewn not only the vestment around my shoulders, and Joan's wedding dress, but the tiny baptismal gown as well.

Michelle's dark eyes floated toward mine, then closed as beads of water danced across her forehead.

"I baptise you, our daughter, in the name of the Father—and of the Son—and of the Holy Spirit."

So close I could feel the warmth of her breath, Joan whispered, "Amen."

Moments later a shriveled woman in her nineties hobbled over to

say she had waited all her life to witness such an event. Waited for
the church to permit its priests to have families, thereby affirming that
marriage was not a lesser state after all. Joan set Michelle in the
woman's arms and taking her cane, asked her to bless our first-born.

Nursing Michelle by the bay window of the living room, Joan
watched a persistent grosbeak tugging at the few remaining apples
clinging to our flowering crab. Since giving birth, her complexion had
taken on a pronounced luster. Always beautiful, she struck me at that
moment as doubly so. After a few minutes, she tiptoed over to the
bassinet and tucked her slumbering bundle beneath a fuzzy pink blanket
before returning next to me on the sofa. Our relationship with Bishop
Curtiss apparently on an even keel, we were going ahead with plans
to depart after Thanksgiving for a mini-sabbatical to Holland. While
Joan had arranged to observe the counseling centers of two universities,
I intended to complete a manuscript on contemporary liturgy. Curtiss
promptly agreed to assign a priest to assist Tim on weekends during
my absence.

"It bothers me that Elden is so anxious to see us go. Especially
when he confesses qualms about the Catholics in Holland in the first
place," Joan said, voicing a recurrent concern.

"Come on now . . ." I replied, half-listening.

"Maybe I'm starting to get cynical. It's just that so much of
what I once bought as substance in the church has turned out to be
nothing but shadows. Sorry, but I don't trust the boys at the top like
I used to."

I repeated an earlier conviction that Curtiss would be okay. After
all, the letter he finally wrote to the priests was essentially supportive.
It helped keep the wolves at bay.

"Perhaps," she said with a touch of foreboding.

Michelle stirred, and I went over to wind up the mobile above her
crib. Leaving her mesmerized by twirling elephants and bouncing
clowns, I settled next to Joan.

"Maybe this thing is getting to you more than you think. We've
got to keep our own eyes on the clowns, too—you know, a sense of
humor. Otherwise this tug of war with the church begins to color
everything we see and do."

"No more than it does now," she answered as one who had given
it all more than enough thought.

I massaged the furrow spreading across her forehead. "Lady? You
are loved. Believe me."

Joan reached over, stroking my cheek. "Father Miles. You know what first drew me to you? Your gentleness. The way you treated people. You made me feel so special."

"And?"

Her eyes clouded over.

"Sometimes I don't feel that way anymore. It's like we've become second to the stupid little wars with the church. We even take them to bed with us. Shoot, we don't even laugh as much as we used to."

Unprepared for the intensity of her emotion, I leaned over and kissed her on the ear, whispering, "You've just got a fit of postpartum blues. Say we don't laugh as much? Try this!"

As I tickled her in the ribs, she began to giggle, then flipped me to the floor, where we wrestled until exhausted by the effort.

"Now that we've made up for the laughs," I puffed, "let's not worry about Elden. He doesn't need those wars any more than we do. Besides, he's covered with his document. We'll be just fine."

Even while saying it, I was sure she didn't believe it, nor in a sense did I. Not really.

We said our good-byes to the parish. Within forty-eight hours, Huub and Tine would pick us up at Schiphol. Scurrying about in a last-minute frenzy, I had forgot that the Senate of Priests was holding its monthly meeting in the parish center. Passing by their conference table, I was nearly as surprised to see the bishop as he was to see me.

Curtiss leaned over, whispering something to Tim, who then got up from the table with a message that the bishop wanted to talk with me immediately.

"He thought you were already gone. Beats me what's on his mind. He's been owly all morning."

I went into my office, switched on the lamp, and waited. We hadn't seen one another since Kalispell. No sooner had Curtiss stepped into the room than his pursed lips telegraphed something serious. Pacing back and forth, his movements abrupt and tight, he launched into a summary of a recent conversation in Washington with the apostolic delegate. After reviewing Curtiss's report on my status, Jadot had suggested the Vatican was already conducting an investigation of the case.

"Investigation?" I stammered.

"Close the door and for godsakes, keep it down," the bishop shouted, the muscles rippling along his jaw.

I pushed it shut.

"This is for your ears and Tim's. No one else. It's absolutely confidential. In fact, I shouldn't even be telling you. I was furious. What right do they have coming into a diocese without telling the local ordinary?"

"What's going on?" I stammered, still confused. "We've been married three years."

"You tell me. I'm not sure whether it's Jadot's idea or coming from higher up."

"He's pretty damn high. How much higher can it go?"

He waved me off. "All I know is there's an investigation."

"Because of the clergy. Right?"

"Partially," he replied, citing what he considered a scheme among certain priests in the diocese to get rid of me, a plan launched well before he became bishop.

"The delegate keeps getting complaints from some of them. No doubt so does the Holy See. I've told you before, what sends shock waves is the suggestion that you're functioning as a married priest."

There was something in his tone which I'd heard before. Heard time and again in the seminary, where secrecy and mistrust prevailed between the administration and students. After all, Curtiss had entered the seminary while still a teenager. I wondered if he had ever trusted anyone, ever felt trusted himself. Questioned whether now in fact he distrusted the very system which received his unequivocal allegiance.

The bishop sat down, running his fingers along my desk. Concerned about publicity, the delegate had assured him the ongoing investigation would be absolutely secret. To avoid detection, the chief investigator had either been disguised or come from within Bozeman itself. He wouldn't say which, though unusual circumstances normally called for an outside cleric to melt into a community disguised as an ordinary layman.

"The investigator? Has he been here yet?" I asked, still stunned at the revelation.

"No way of knowing."

"Lord help us! I thought this kind of thing ended with the Middle Ages. This thing smells—it has no place in the church of Jesus Christ!" The force of my anger took both of us back.

"You underestimate Holy Church. She's been around a long time. Besides, institutions have a right to defend themselves. Over the years I've been an investigator on two separate cases myself."

"It's so sick."

"Things like this go on every day in the government, Mike. There's the FBI, CIA, and . . ."

"We're talking about the church, for crying out loud!"

"Don't lecture me," he replied with a stiletto glare, thrusting his glasses up over the bridge of his nose. "We have to respect authority. It's a question of loyalty. Something your swelled ego has a hard time with."

"What about conscience? The gospel?"

"Don't be so damned pious. You're not the only one who pays attention to the gospel. Face reality. The fact is, the investigation is going on. You're being watched. You're just lucky I even bothered to tip you off."

I didn't respond, instead wondered why he was telling me at all. Was he dealing straight or from the bottom of the deck? Perhaps he was using the pressure of possible recrimination to eat away bit by bit at the reality of married priesthood in Resurrection. Was he concealing the whole story, or was I the victim of my own suspicion? Was Curtiss the point man for others above him, or had he simply wandered across a minefield not of his own making and was now warning me away from its path?

"When's the damn thing end?" I asked harshly.

"The investigation? Who knows. Of course there's always the chance they could order your dismissal."

"And?"

Adjusting a purple cuff link, he held his sleeve up against the light, and sighed. "Well, with my oath of obedience, I'd have to carry it out."

I suggested there was another way. We could get Hunthausen involved. Perhaps he, Curtiss, and a few other bishops in the Northwest could tell the delegate to let well enough alone. He was unconvinced, insisting again that no one, including Seattle's archbishop, should be advised of the matter.

"Well, if it ever came to them ordering my dismissal, you can be sure Resurrection wouldn't take it lying down," I suggested wearily.

Curtiss sat bolt upright in his chair and riveted his eyes on mine.

"Make no mistake about it. If I have to close this place and start from scratch, I will! They aren't running the show here, I am!"

The thunder in his voice must have startled him, for he pulled up short. When I suggested delaying the trip to Holland, he eased off. We should go. Things were not about to come to a head. Not yet, at least.

The bishop stood, flashing a quick smile. "Meanwhile, you have my word, nothing will happen while you're away. But you've got to start cooperating a little. I've bent over backwards to help you. It's a two-way street. You've got to help me a bit, too."

He hesitated at the door. "Incidentally, that reference in your parish bulletin about the sabbatical helping you grow in the priesthood? Within a day of its printing, copies were on my desk with a note signed by nine of our senior clergy protesting this business of Resurrection viewing you as a priest."

"Who would bother? It's so bloody petty!"

"Men who know the law and love their Catholic church."

He closed the door, unaware that in mentioning the bulletins he supplied a missing link. Each week our bulletins were printed at Holy Rosary Parish. Courtesy of Father Paul Metzner.

Despite the Vatican investigation, we went ahead with our plans and departed for the Netherlands. Though apprehensive, we remained confident that Curtiss would keep his word.

We took a small flat overlooking Alphen aan den Rijn, a small community between Leiden and Utrecht. Each morning over espresso, we would peer out our third-floor window into the misty Dutch dawn as bicycles zigzagged through skiffs of snow, leaving traces like so many threads across white lace.

Whenever we could, we strolled through nearby parks and along canals, where children skated on ice seemingly as thin as onion skin. Whether wheeling Michelle through outdoor markets draped in Christmas lights, or munching hot cashews on streetcorners, we thrived on this opportunity to focus on one another.

On Sundays we boarded a sleek yellow express train for the thirty-minute journey to Leiden, there, in the half-light of a medieval cathedral, to worship with the university parish—the Ekklesia. Although the community was still vibrant, there was a gray edge to the otherwise colorful atmosphere I remembered from three years earlier. Before long, we discovered that the Dutch Church, once heralded as pregnant with potential, had seen its dramatic attempt to renew Catholicism aborted. Each step along the road of change matched tit for tat by a fearful and cautious Curia. The result was further polarization between

Rome and what was once heralded as the Cinderella church of the Western world.

If there was a warning contained in the winter mood which hung over Dutch Catholicism, it was overshadowed by the joy of living outside the pressure-cooker atmosphere Joan and I left behind in the States. Christmas proved to be an exception.

From the moment we had arrived in Holland, Joan and Tine developed an immediate rapport, an élan born from a world of shared experience. So, following a foggy morning spent traipsing along the seashore of Katwijk aan Zee, we joined the van Doorns for a holiday dinner.

By the time we finished the meal of roast duck, steamed apples, and miniature potatoes, Michelle was fast asleep, clinging to a fluffy red blanket presented with great pride by Erna and Frans, the van Doorn children.

Throughout the evening, an aging Reformed minister entertained us with stories ranging from Christmas in old Holland to his imprisonment for speaking out against the Nazis during the Occupation. It was in prison that Walter Huisman became convinced of the need for Protestants and Catholics to join together in the bonds of their common faith amid a world increasingly impatient with their historical differences. Committed to the unity of Christians, the short, balding native of Utrecht now served as chairman of the Dutch Council of Churches.

Once Huisman discovered that unlike the Ekklesia, Resurrection Parish was directly under the auspices of the Catholic hierarchy, he was delighted to hear that I remained its pastor.

"Marvelous. Truly marvelous news!" he said with a disarming gentleness. "I know of nothing like it anywhere. Not even here in Holland."

The spark in his eyes faded a bit when Huub advised him of the ambivalent posturing of Bishop Curtiss and the ongoing investigation, which we felt free to discuss outside the country.

He tapped a finger against a gold foretooth, something he did whenever struggling to express himself in English.

"Investigation! Surely you make an exaggeration. These are not the days of the Inquisition."

When first informed, Huub's reaction had been identical, until he recalled similar situations. He reminded his visitor of the probes of Hans Küng and Huisman's close friend Edward Schillebeeckx.

Rubbing a hand through his silver-streaked hair, Huisman smiled in my direction. "Well, then you're in good company! They are among your Roman Church's finest theologians. But you are just . . . ah, how do you say . . . ?"

"A pastoral worker," Huub interjected from the far side of the table.

"Yes, and yet they examine even you? Poor Rome, she is so nervous." Smiling once again, Huisman placed two lumps of sugar in his tea. "We need to sweeten her up. There are well-meaning people in power now who can only imagine the road to heaven if it is lined with the bleached skulls of suspected heretics."

Staring into the tea, as if searching for a leaf to explain the past, he recalled attending the Vatican Council as an official observer. Whenever he spoke of his friend John XXIII, his eyes lit up. Since the portly Angelo Roncalli, unlike other popes, did not have a lengthy curial background, he had seemed more willing than those working under him to let go of the temptation to control and dictate events.

"I'm afraid the need to rely upon themselves and not trust the Holy Spirit is almost instinctive with those in high office. Especially the closer they get to the throne of Peter. They tend to forget the story Pope John told on himself. Whenever he went to bed burdened with worry, he'd say: 'Relax, Angelo. It's not you who run the church but the Holy Ghost!' "

A distant look crossed his face. For a moment, he appeared lost in the memory of a tender era.

"How we loved him! Just when many of us were wondering if the Roman Church misplaced its heart, along came John. He knew that even Catholics were losing confidence in the prevailing system. Meanwhile, the cardinals thought they'd elected a caretaker pontiff."

"Well, he surprised them, to put it mildly," I interjected.

"At the same time," Huisman said, wagging a slender finger in my direction, "we can't forget that he was quite a traditionalist. More than many would like to think. Although he knew that the history of the church is a history of *veränderung*—how do you say—change? He also understood that his flock didn't want to renounce their traditional belief."

"Nor do we now," I replied. "If by that we mean the essentials of our faith. In that sense, parishes like Resurrection can be considered quite orthodox. The trick is not to mistake relatively recent trappings for genuine tradition."

Huisman was enjoying himself. Much as a teacher prodding a student, he asked for an example or two.

I pointed to the ornate clock suspended on the wall just behind Huub.

"Tine tells us that's from the days of Napoleon. Just about the same time the French introduced confessional boxes. Yet we sometimes cling to the box as if Jesus dragged one around with him throughout Galilee!"

"Ah, so you are for getting rid of confession. We reformers were right all along!" he said, winking.

"No, of course not. It's just that we tend to think of so many things as essential when in fact they are of relatively recent vintage."

"For example?"

"Well, the confessional box, or Roman collar, or fish on Friday, or Lord knows how many other things."

Still in a jesting mood, Huisman pointed his spoon in Joan's direction. "I mentioned to your husband earlier that if I were pope, I'd give the church fifty years of freedom, carte-blanche. Just to make up for the nearly four hundred years of Counter-Reformation restraint!"

"Maybe Tine or I will work our way up to pope," she said, enjoying the fantasy. "Then we could change a few rules here and there!"

As quickly as the smile crossed his face, it disappeared. "Ah, but they are deathly afraid of women. Still, I remain optimistic, for in Catholicism rests the hope of all churches. In time, we'll see the triumph of John's council . . . in time."

Illuminated in the candelabra, a sudden frown spread across Huub's face. He wasn't quite so optimistic. "When our bishops here in Holland suggested the option of married priests, the cardinal in charge of the Curia's office of the clergy . . . ah, he is . . . ?"

"Wright. Used to be in Pittsburgh," I replied.

Huub told of the cardinal cautioning a newly appointed bishop in Rotterdam to keep his finger in the Dutch dike to prevent the renewal movement from washing away ecclesiastical authority.

"He was one of two conservative bishops handpicked for the task by Rome. It hit us hard since we only have seven to begin with."

Noting the surprised look on Joan's face, Huub threw up his hands with a broad smile. "Yes. That's all we have in all of Holland. Compared to so many in America. They aren't as busy here anymore, of course. They used to ordain up to three hundred boys a year. This year there will be a handful, if that.''

Huisman added that the situation in France was equally as bad, with only one priest for every dozen or so parishes.

My mind went back to the conversation with Connley and Hunthausen, and Jeff's forecast of the demise of the clerical priesthood. Joan nudged her elbow against mine. Huisman was referring once again to the investigation.

"In the future, lives like yours could be commonplace, although today you must stand alone. Even if they threaten to cast you out as a heretic. It must be *peinlich*—I mean to say, ah, painful for you. Especially when it comes from the same church which you love.''

Our silence was answer enough. He glanced around the table as the clock chimed the hour.

"The American monk Thomas Merton? You're fond of him?''

"Yes. Very much so,'' I answered.

"Well, it was Merton who said, 'Many have gone away injured from the house of God.' He was correct. Even so, what you do is important. Parishes like the Ekklesia, and the one you have, are bridges from the old to the new.''

"But all Rome knows how to say is no! Always no!'' Tine said, startling us, then burying her face in her hands. "I'm sorry, but the big church doesn't care at all about the kind of persons we are here or that Jesus Christ is important to us, too. I'm so tired of it at times. How do you Americans say it? Water, water . . .''

". . . everywhere, but not a drop to drink,'' Joan replied, casting a sympathetic glance toward Tine, who was already standing to pick up the dishes.

Huub pushed back from the table to help. "Sometimes it makes us to feel that the big church wants only that we are docile. To have the instinct of sheep.'' He went over to pull a blanket across Michelle, sleeping soundly beneath the ornate tree. "Such instincts are lacking even in little children.''

He followed Tine around the corner into the kitchen as Huisman reached into his jacket, then lit a small cigar, releasing a musty aroma which hovered over us on a thin sheet of smoke. Leaning across the table, he touched Joan's hand.

"It is important to all of us that what is happening in your lives survive. We must pray that your current bishop will listen to his flock. Tell me, how did he rise so quickly toward the top?''

"He isn't rising, he's swimming," Joan said, half-heartedly.

All along she had contended that Curtiss was protective of his career, aspiring to even higher office. I wasn't sure.

Over running water, Huub shouted from the kitchen, "Walter thinks we have stumbled rather badly here in Holland, and that it is now up to you Americans to lead the way."

Saddled with such hope, neither Joan nor I felt so confident, and left that evening of Michelle's first Christmas, thankful that the test of our own promise waited some six thousand miles away.

For the first time since my brutal attempt to break off our relationship seasons earlier, Joan unpacked her brushes and started painting again. At daybreak she would perch on a stool next to an easel, and there, with the light spilling across her face and down her shoulders, attempt to capture its earliest rays. In those quiet moments where daydreams intrude, I would drift back and picture her before time and stress had robbed her of youthful velvet, and before crow's feet etched their way beneath her eyes.

Whenever research drew Joan away to the university, I found myself involved with yet another woman. At first, the prospect of being alone with an infant was nearly as unsettling as not being with her at all. Gradually, in the interchange of diapers, baths, and warm bottles, I found not only time to discover more about who our daughter was, but through her to chance upon undiscovered parts of myself as well.

One such evening, as Michelle slept quietly next to a ticking clock, I lit a candle and sat next to the window watching for the six o'clock train. My writing was going well. It was the New Year. We were happier than at any other time in our lives.

As evening began to fall, I could see Joan trekking across the soccer field separating our flat from the terminal. In her arms was a bundle, no doubt filled with dark breads, cheese, and fruits from the market in Leiden.

We met at the top of the stairs. I took the bags as Joan looked in on Michelle, then returned to warm herself next to the fire, her hair smelling damp from the drizzle. Though her cheeks were cold, her lips were warm.

"Oh, I almost forgot," she whispered, backing away from our embrace and reaching into her jacket. "This was downstairs in the box."

Not until I tore at the envelope marked *Staatsbedrifj Der Pitt*, did I realize it contained a telegram. Scanning it quickly, I began crumpling it into a ball, then gave it to Joan. She held it next to the candlelight, reading aloud.

"Bad news. Bishop's made his move. Call at once! Tim."

She looked up, the rosy color draining from her face. It was as though an uninvited guest, leering off behind the curtains, had stepped center stage, reciting dated lines. I wanted to hold her but felt immobile.

"So much for Elden Curtiss and his word," Joan said bitterly, placing the telegram over the candle flame, where it shrank into flakes of ash.

I went into the bedroom and placed a call to the States.

His voice heavy with sleep, Tim admitted a sense of betrayal. "Curtiss is demanding that I get up in front of the parish and tell them you can no longer exercise the role of a priest here and . . . get this . . . that you took it upon yourself to ignore the law of the church. He doesn't dare say anything publicly about Hunthausen. Then he plans to publish a list of new restrictions on you in the diocesan paper."

"And if we don't go along?"

"You're canned. Since he doesn't want to get saddled with it, he wants me to act as his official representative and fire you."

" 'And they shall divide brother against brother . . .' "

"What's that, Mike? Couldn't catch it."

"Nothing," I said, struggling to pull my feelings together. "What happens if you refuse to give me the boot?"

Over the miles I could see his face leaden with tension. See him take a breath and swallow hard. "He says he'll suspend me. At the very least, he'd transfer me out of here."

"Dammit, always the threats! Always the blade hanging over us!"

He explained that Curtiss apologized for acting in my absence, insisting he was obeying directives from an undisclosed source, that he had little choice.

"Like Pilate. He wants to wash his hands of any and all blame!" I said with mounting rage. "Whose directives?"

"The bishop mentioned Rome, but nothing about Jadot," Tim, said, shouting through the crackling wires. "I'm not sure if the delegate is calling the shots or the Curia, or just who."

Again, the question of the chicken or the egg. Was Rome using Curtiss or vice versa? If he was only a cover, then why not identify the source and have it done with? In any event, someone, somewhere, was determined to force us to retrace our steps at Resurrection.

Tim's voice was fading. "Something smells about this. There are some missing pieces which just don't come together. What drives me up a tree is the unilateral way His Grace has of doing things. No consultation with anyone, and precious little concern for you or the people here. Then to try and pull this off while you're conveniently out of the country! He told me that if you don't go along, it might be better for you to just stay in Holland. The whole damn thing's sick!"

We both agreed there was little choice but for us to return at once. By the time I rang off and returned to the living room, Joan had already started packing.

Two days later, sandwiched in the van Doorns's Volkswagen, we bumped along the narrow streets of Leiden and out into the countryside. En route to Schiphol we whisked in silence past hedgerows and windmills dusted with snow. Once in the terminal, Huub wrapped an arm about my shoulder, gently pulling Joan close with the other.

"Remember, in your hearts you always have one another. Then whoever is after you will not have power over you." He kissed Joan and held Michelle up for a final squeeze. Along the way to the KLM checkpoint, Tine stopped at a flower booth before rushing over with a bouquet.

She started to say something and realizing she couldn't, thrust the flowers at us, turning away. Moving through security and down the gangway to the glistening KLM DC-10, we looked back to wave, but they were gone.

We flew from a misty Dutch evening into the half-light over the ocean, toward a Chicago afternoon. A stewardess stopped by to place a blue blanket over Michelle and Joan, asleep next to me. For a moment in the amber glow of the overhead lights, they both looked terribly fragile, like pieces of fine-spun crystal that even the slightest lurch of the plane would shatter into tiny fragments.

Why indeed, I wondered, were we abandoning the tranquillity of the Netherlands for the bull's-eye back home? Then again, it wasn't fair to leave Tim and the parish alone with our battle. I began to resent my insistence on remaining a priest. Quite possibly what some saw as devotion to the ministry was simply compulsive behavior, downright bullheadedness. What right did I have to drag a wife and child into the spider's web of conflict which my effort to hang on seemed to spin? What started out as a naïve dream of fusing two loves was disintegrating into an endless hassle. Maybe it was time to quit being an albatross around everyone's neck, cut the cord with the church and be done with it!

I rose, maneuvering through the narrow aisle to the washroom. The tingle of water against my face brought to mind another day, nearly buried by subsequent events. The day of the eagle and the frigid waters of the Gallatin River when I had been convinced of a baptismal experience. Through bloodshot eyes, I stared into the mirror, seeing anything but baptism staring back.

When I returned, the aroma of baked ham floated through the near-empty cabin. The attendants were starting to serve dinner. Just before waking Joan, I wondered if she felt special any longer. I wanted to hold her close and seek forgiveness.

She woke, stretching lazily.

"Someone's been loving at a distance. I could feel you," she said, setting Michelle on an adjacent seat. "Don't you think God loves that way—distant? Watching?"

"I guess so."

She sat up.

"Just before falling asleep, I thought of that black swan. Remember?"

I did. It was a chilly evening when we crossed the bridge in the *avifana*, a waterfowl sanctuary outside Alphen. If not for the feeble thrashing we might not have seen her, out there, beyond our grasp. The swan had broken through the ice covering the canal, trapping her wings beneath its surface. Exhausted from the struggle for freedom, she looked up at us only once before laying her long neck back onto the ice hardening about her. By the time we located park attendants, it was nearly dark. We never did find out whether they had saved her or not.

"Anyway," Joan said, laying her head against me, "when I fell asleep I had a dream. Probably shouldn't be telling you, but need to. The plane got into trouble. We started to fall toward the water. Thinking of you and Michelle, I wanted to live more than ever. We grabbed for you, but you weren't there."

She took my hand just as the stewardess slid the steaming trays in front of us. We waited until the big-boned Dutchwoman passed down the aisle.

A quizzical look spread across Joan's face. "What would happen if Michelle and I died? You know, an accident or something?"

"Good God, honey!"

"No. No. Just tell me. If we were gone, could you get back in the good graces of . . . what's Tine call it? The big church? Would they leave you alone then?"

Her eyes were steady, unwilling to let go of the question.

"You mean if this piece of tin fell into the drink and went down to the bottom of the sea with both of you in it and I survived? Which I wouldn't want to do, by the way!"

"But if . . ." she pushed.

"Well then, yes. If you were dead, the church would probably welcome me back into the club."

"That's what I thought," she replied, her voice hollow but firm.

Savoring the fragrance of Tine's bouquet, she picked it up, quietly stroking the petals. "That's why you've got to hold on, hon. Stick in there and fight something as twisted as that every inch of the way."

Braced for confrontation, we returned to Bozeman, suggesting nothing more to the parish than we had come home earlier than anticipated. To limit the concern, we again chose to inform only the parish council of the intimidation emanating from the bishop's office.

The immediate reaction of Kirby Walsh surprised us more than any other. For the first time, he suggested that the ongoing struggle was possibly counterproductive.

"You've got your own lives to lead. This schizophrenic thing with the church will wear you down. Besides, there's Michelle to think of. Maybe you ought to say the hell with them and get out."

I wanted to tell him that since opting for love, and even more so since our marriage, all the signs pointed toward going on with our journey. Wanted to say, too, what it meant to be given strength and pulled by something deep within me, which I prayed was God's own Spirit. Then again, we all understood that Walsh wasn't throwing in the towel, just that his personal concern for our family's well-being transcended any desire to have us remain in the parish.

He wasn't alone. A pained expression spread across Kevin Doherty's face. I had seen it hanging over him only once before, when a virus attacked his infant son without warning. By the time I arrived at the hospital, the boy was in the throes of a fever and having violent convulsions. Prognosis? Guarded at best.

For two days, Joan and I took turns watching at the bedside of what seemed like a fragile doll stitched together with tubes and needles. Kevin and his equally distraught wife were always composed. Yet in such moments, I sensed a part of their awful fear. Felt it as my own whenever I touched the burning body with the sign of the cross. What if, I wondered, the child lying there, so vulnerable, were mine? Flesh of my flesh? Bone of my bone? I identified with the anguish the Dohertys were going through, more than I might have without a child of our own. They seemed to know. The trauma passed and their son recovered, leaving a lasting bond between us.

Kevin's pained expression at the news of what now drew us home from the Netherlands spoke mutely that the bond had not weakened.

Gay Pomeroy wasn't so quiet. Always up front with her feelings, the fiery wife of the physician who had delivered Michelle summed up the parish council's sentiments.

"What I don't get is why Rome—Curtiss or whoever out there— is supposed to be upset. If they'd put half the effort they're expending on Mike and Joan into working to make the church come alive, well . . . just imagine! God, you'd think we were the enemy! All that's happened is two people fell for each other. Correct me if I'm wrong, but isn't loving what Jesus was all about?"

But Pomeroy, who had become Joan's closest friend, wasn't about to let me off quite so easily.

"I shouldn't say this, Father, but . . ."

"No. Come on, go ahead," I said, unsure of what was coming next from the olive-skinned Italian.

Taking a drag off her cigarette, she exhaled thoughtfully.

"Okay. Here goes. You're not exactly a Caspar Milquetoast. You can be pretty aggressive. I don't know if anyone else feels this way, but even before you went to Europe the strain was beginning to show on you. I guess what I'm trying to say is that you have to be careful that your own frustration doesn't get in the way of loving, either, even those you disagree with."

Though gently put, she was right on target. I thought of Christ telling the story of the man who, purged of a troublesome spirit, failed to fill up the ensuing void with goodness. As a consequence, he was overtaken by seven other spirits far more evil than the first.

Not only would I have to work at casting out a vindictive spirit occasioned by the mounting frustration of our circumstances, but even more, fill up the ensuing void with compassion and patience. After all, the parish had a right to expect far more from me. As with any priest, they hoped for someone who had something special. Someone who radiated just a bit of the joy which came from feeling the presence of the same One who had knocked the Apostle Paul from his high horse outside Damascus.

Walsh asked if despite the harassment we could stick it out. There could only be one response. We would stay with it, if they would. To a person, the council was instantly supportive.

So we agreed. Tim would not get up before the community of Resurrection and say what Curtiss demanded. Together we would stand fast in the face of still another threat of dismissal. In no way could the parish be party to what we all considered was a direct assault on its deepest values.

Still, we would try, despite our own convictions, to listen to the other side and be flexible. Knowing that while we had to struggle for what we believed, how we did so would determine the kind of Christians we were and would become.

Together we waited with swelling apprehension for the feared confrontation. Days later, hearing of our abrupt return from the Netherlands, Curtiss called.

His voice was brittle.

"I've decided to write an article for my regular column. There's pressure on me to do so."

"The cardinal again?"

He ignored the question.

"Why won't you say from where?"

"The article will be about you, but not . . . it'll be about men who have left the ministry to get married."

The bishop sounded rushed, preoccupied. "It won't be in the secular press, just my own newspaper."

I waited for more, prepared for his previous insistence that Tim criticize our four-year experience from the pulpit and read a statement to the parish severely limiting my role. Waited for him to inquire about my decision whether or not to go along. Waited for the battle the council dreaded, yet expected. Instead, Curtiss never mentioned the issue, acting as if his action, which had drawn us home from Europe had never happened. In all, it was quite anticlimactic, leaving me at once relieved and emotionally limp.

A few weeks later the bishop's article appeared in the local Catholic newspaper under his regular column entitled "From My Perspective." It contained his by now familiar position.

Priests who had married were unfaithful to their vows; unable to live in the total dedication the church required. Such men, though still priests, could not function as such, nor could they be leaders of congregations. However, they could share in the ordinary activities of a layman. Such was the case at Resurrection.

While the column referred only obliquely to us and even then did not speak of the facts of our circumstances, it might have been much worse. Broderick advised me to ignore it, indicating that Curtiss's primary intent was to protect his career. If things were to blow up, he would be on record as siding with Rome all along.

Broderick laughed, but there was no joy in it. "He also wants to put as much distance between himself and you as possible."

So the crisis fizzled, leaving intact my role and work in Resurrection.

Still, the gnawing questions persisted. If Curtiss had all the pressure he claimed to have to act decisively against a married priest, how could he not only let the pressure go, but help camouflage it as well? Was the pressure really on him, or was he in fact its source? Above all, what happened to the much-trumpeted investigation?

While the immediate crisis faded, in its wake came the silence of a cold war. I was dropped from the invitation list to all official gatherings of the clergy. Communication with the chancery dried up. There was even a subtle shift in attitude among some priests who once praised the step into married priesthood. It was Tim who first spotted the shift and who offered the most plausible explanation.

"It was easier for guys to hang in there when Dutch was bishop," he said. "Now Curtiss is their bread and butter. He pays the salaries; makes the assignments. For some at least, not to side with him is to go against their own best interests."

He was right. It was a tough bind, even for the most resolute.

Throughout the ensuing months, both Joan and I felt stronger and happier. Within Resurrection, the fact of our marriage was so commonplace it occasioned only passing attention. As such, the reality of just how far we had ventured out upon Catholicism's limb was obscured by the flurry of activity surrounding a large parish. While the icy silence from Bishop Curtiss was eerie, at times we managed to convince ourselves that the cold war meant no war at all.

As Resurrection grew, so did the demands on my time. Though time with the family shrank in terms of quantity, its quality increased. Somehow we managed to find a delicate balance which kept work and life in harmony. Watching Michelle learn to crawl, take an initial step, or struggle with a first word, I couldn't help but wonder how long it would have taken for my own ministry to shrivel up without the well-spring provided by her and, of course, her mother. Each day we prayed simply to be left alone, but when the silence from the church was finally broken, we were for the most part unprepared.

"Bishop Curtiss has agreed to let Pat Langley stay" were the first words out of Tim when he returned from a brief stop at the chancery office in Helena. "He's going to announce it to all the priests next week at the annual assembly. I don't get it."

"That makes two of us," I stammered, my mind racing back to an earlier time.

Throughout our seminary years and after ordination, the lanky, athletic Langley had remained one of my closest friends. Within days of his assignment to assist Blake Robins, Pat confessed to having fallen in love months earlier and wanting now to pursue the same path we'd taken in Bozeman. After all, a precedent had already been set in our case. Christ the King was a progressive parish; Robins favored optional celibacy. Pat intended first to seek a dispensation; only upon its reception would he then seek to stay on. If denied, he would leave the priesthood.

Lying just behind his sapphire blue eyes, I had seen a sense of defeat, a sadness we both shared. Although we both had considerable reservations about the prospects for his success, we rarely discussed them. After all, the odds stacked against him were staggering. Profoundly troubled by the presence of one married priest in the diocese, there was precious little chance the bishop would permit yet another. Though not expecting him to get to first base, I outlined for Langley every step Joan and I had taken along the way.

"It just doesn't fit," I repeated to Tim. "If Elden's getting all the so-called heat because of us, why would he just double his troubles?"

In my last conversation with Langley just weeks before, he hadn't said anything. If he had received the dispensation and talked with Curtiss, why hadn't he told me? What should have come as good news filled me instead with unease, a feeling that only deepened the following day when the bishop called asking to see me during the annual assembly in Missoula.

Curtiss appeared haggard as we exited through a side door of St. Francis Xavier's onto the sidewalk. It had been months since we last talked.

"Over a hundred priests in there, all trying to get at the same coffeepot," he said, swinging alongside me. "I want to get back as soon as the break is over, but wanted to talk with you about Langley. As well wired as this diocese is, you've probably heard?"

I had.

"At first, I suspected he was up to the same funny business that character next door tried a couple of years back. Remember?"

I remembered allright. Over the course of his hospital rounds, Burt Kramer—a popular figure in the neighboring diocese—fell in love with a woman who had been partially paralyzed in an accident. Citing the example of our situation in Bozeman, his community pleaded with the aging bishop, indicating their desire to retain him as a married priest. They considered their approach an utterly practical one: That a family man be allowed to serve the family of God. Their petition was rejected on the spot, and Kramer joined the rising statistics of departures.

Curtiss was still talking.

"He did a lot of damage, letting the whole business out to the press and all! Whatever made him think he could stay? Well, Pat's different. He's not trying to hitch onto your bandwagon. He knows it's not going anywhere. I've talked with him several times. We've even prayed together over it. As you might imagine, at first I was adamant against it all." He winced. "God knows there's enough fallout from your situation! He checked with the clergy here in town and they're willing to go along. They want him preaching, too. OK. Besides, that's no surprise. Most of them joined in on your deal and would probably still throw a fit if anything happened to you."

Frowning, he stopped and thrust a finger at my chest.

"But you should know for your own good that the support you once had is shrinking mighty fast. People realize you are way outside the limits and that I'm being pushed to get rid of you."

Then switching back to Langley, he acknowledged our friendship. "So you'll be happy to know that since he's willing to support me, I've agreed to reciprocate."

I froze in my tracks.

"Support you?"

"Well, you know. Meet me halfway." He started across the street on a green light. I pulled at his arm, feeling it tighten.

"He's not so damn stubborn as you are, Mike. He knows how important it is that the people understand once he's married he simply

can't go on willy-nilly functioning as a priest, with total disregard for
the universal church.''

The muscles rippled against the bishop's jawline while he explained
the next step. He would compose an announcement to be read in Christ
the King and all parishes in the city underlining that Langley—having
decided to abandon the priesthood—would be employed as a counselor
and music director.

"Music director? You've got to be kidding!"

"He's lucky to stay there at all. We'll have his position clearly
defined and explained from the start. He'll toe the mark so there's no
scandal.''

I was confused. If the bishop was under fire from Rome, his priests,
or whoever, then everything he was saying still made little sense.

We circled through a park, turning back toward the brownstone
walls of St. Xavier's, with Curtiss still talking.

"I know you two are good friends. That's why it's imperative you
agree to the same terms he has, or else.''

"Or else what?" I asked with a sense of déjà vu.

"Or else I may be forced to reconsider my decision about letting
him stay. Simple as that.''

The prospect of a friend being turned away at the last moment
because of what might be interpreted as my own intransigence was
unsettling. Then again, there could be no further compromise without
wiping away what had been achieved, and in effect saying that the
past years at Resurrection had been a mistake.

He opened the door and we moved quickly down the hallway into
the school gym, where the priests were already seated for the bishop's
annual summary of diocesan finances.

"What if I can't go along?" I asked tersely, knowing at once that
I could not.

He stopped, motioning toward the clergy.

"Even the flaming liberals out there won't be able to accuse me
of not being receptive to you, once they hear I'm keeping Langley.
They'll finally see that you're the troublemaker.''

Curtiss stepped up toward the podium, then leaned over next to
my ear.

"Looks like the question's changed. It isn't whether Pat will be
able to stay, but whether or not you will. Agree to my terms or else.
The choice is yours.''

Turning away, he left me feeling more confused than ever.

*   *   *

Later that same afternoon, I spotted Langley in the gym winding
his way through the throng of clergy. As he passed beneath a basketball
hoop, I thought back to our days together in college when he had
captured the attention of sports writers as the finest forward to play
for the Fighting Saints in a decade. Once during the Frontier Conference finals, I was seated behind the backboard when he took the free-
throw line in the final seconds of a decisive game. There was melancholy in his eyes that didn't change even when the ball split the net
and the gymnasium exploded with cries of victory. As he approached
now, I saw the melancholy in him still, but this time with an edge of
sadness.

He was more guarded than defensive, discounting at once the
suggestion that we might be used as opposing pieces on the bishop's
chessboard.

"Hey, lookit. Everyone knows our situations are different. Even
Curtiss can't pretend apples are oranges and get away with it," he
said, utterly sincere.

I needed to tell him of the Vatican investigation, but could not.
Besides, he was so obviously relieved at being able to stay in Christ
the King, it seemed unfair to cause any rain to fall on his parade.
Rather than say anything more and risk venting my anger boiling just
beneath the surface, I decided to wait and talk with Blake Robins.

"Don't get me wrong, Blake," I said later that evening, slipping
off my shoes and sitting cross-legged on the couch. "God knows,
ninety-eight percent of the bishops in this country would've tossed him
out at the first suggestion he intended to marry. But it just doesn't
fit."

Not looking up, Robins worked away at his fingernails. "You've
gotta keep in mind that Pat's case isn't the same as yours."

"Tell me about it. Music director for godsakes!" I could still see
the sadness in Langley's eyes. Wished I had said as much to him.

"He didn't have a choice. He would have stayed as a janitor to
get a foot in the door. He . . ."

Impatient, I cut him off.

"That's just it. He's ordained to be a priest, not a janitor! Where's
his passion? By saying yes to a hollow shell, he's not opening a door
but slamming one shut, and not just on himself. Curtiss knows I can't
agree to the same conditions and . . ."

"Come on! Give the guy a chance. He just wants to stay on!"
Blake said angrily.

"At any price? He's a pawn! Listen, if he wants to get into this arena he has responsibilities, too. Pat has to look at the big picture and how it forces us at Resurrection into a corner."

Robins got up, tossing down the nailclipper and pouring us a glass of wine.

"Geez, you make him sound like he's sold you out for thirty pieces of silver. Come on. Pat intends to gradually work his way back into as much of the action as possible. He's a damn good priest."

"The best," I said wearily. "Still, Curtiss isn't letting this happen out of the kindness of his heart. You know what he told me today?"

Listening patiently, Robins shook his head.

"What's gotten into you? All of a sudden blowing his threats out of proportion. He's been making them since day one. Things will be okay."

Maybe he was right, I thought. Perhaps I was clouding things after all.

"Whatever happened to the Christian life?" I muttered as he switched on the television, and we spent the rest of the evening watching the Orioles whip the Yankees.

Pat married in mid-October. The ceremony was preceded by the promised stipulations to the parish from Bishop Curtiss. For the wedding the groom wore a leisure suit. The bride seemed content.

That same night I had a dream. Although the robed figures gathering around the high altar knew I was already ordained, Elden Curtiss, questioning the sacrament's validity, insisted upon a second ordination. Suffocated with the prospect, I managed to stall until the ancient ritual began without me. As the ceremony continued, I edged forward, drawn by a desire to be accepted again, then froze. A headless figure was reading in a booming monotone from the Gospel of Matthew. ". . . 'In those days brother will betray brother.' " I couldn't breathe. Unable to take another step, I felt Pat edge me aside to kneel before the bishop's outstretched hands.

Once Paul Metzner moved on to a new assignment, the city's two parishes hosted their first joint social. We were well into an evening featuring everything from barbershop quartets to children's theater when someone mentioned that the new priest from Rosary had arrived.

An amiable hulk of a man, George Barnes wandered easily into the festive crowd, leaving his companion silhouetted in the doorway. Through the shadows I saw the glitter of a pectoral cross. Though

Elden Curtiss had been in Montana for over two years, when Tim interrupted the music to announce his presence, it was the first time most everyone there had seen their bishop.

Cordial but reserved, Curtiss moved to a far corner of the room while chatting with Tim. After managing to get away, O'Mera pulled me aside.

"He was passing through town and Barnes persuaded him to stop. He won't stay long. Just wants to look the place over. He's really antsy, but it's a chance for us to break the ice."

Perhaps because we were on the familiar ground of Resurrection, I felt at ease going over to introduce Joan to the bishop. In my mind I had rehearsed the event countless times. Though Curtiss never once mentioned her name, I wondered now whether sparks would fly or things would go smoothly. Though stiff and a bit forced, they smiled at one another, as if through an invisible glass shield, before drifting along the safe highway of small talk. The exchange was uneventful until Michelle reached out from her mother's arms, grabbing hold of the cross strung across the bishop's vest. Abruptly he pulled away, and seconds later when she reached out again, he stepped back, removing the glittering symbol of office. At first, Joan thought he was going to let Michelle touch the cross, but when he coolly slipped it into his pocket, she excused herself, leaving the two of us. No sooner were they gone than Forrest Ullman and his wife stopped by to say hello. When they left, Curtiss shouted over the background din into my ear.

"I can't tolerate this. Everyone who comes up to me talks as if you're still a priest. It's what I dreaded all along. You were warned . . ."

At that instant it struck me just how separate our two worlds truly were, and how much I had underestimated the breach. The distance between his cathedral and Resurrection Parish was immense. It wasn't so much a matter of which of us was right or wrong, rather that our experience of the church was a vastly different one.

A family came over to introduce themselves. I waited while one of them knelt to kiss his ring, then I thanked the bishop for coming and rejoined the party.

Later, Joan confessed that Curtiss was much as she expected but for his eyes, which reflected an indefinable fear, with hardly enough warmth to melt the ice between us.

Like a row of dominoes, all hopes of reducing tension continued to topple, one by one. One event was to prove decisive.

* * *

When she started showing up at the Saturday afternoon mass, I noticed her at once. Slender and tall, in her late forties, and carrying herself with confident grace, Maureen was the kind of woman who caused eyeballs to click. Somewhat shyly, she referred to herself as a "migrant" from Rosary Parish. It wasn't long thereafter that her husband and five children joined in the migration.

That was months before she started to look so thin and haggard. At first, I thought she was dieting. Not until she didn't show up at the parish for a few weeks on end, did it dawn on me something might be wrong. It fell to her teenage daughter, a girl of budding beauty herself, to inform me tearfully of the biopsy. The news was not good; like a prairie fire, her mother's cancer was running rampant.

From then on, each Wednesday afternoon immediately after a series of premarriage instructions, I visited Maureen. The contrast could not have been sharper. Going from back-to-back sessions with couples in the dawn of love—where conversations typically centered upon ways of resolving the anxiety caused by the church's birth control ban, or the dilemmas incumbent upon mixed-religion marriages—to her bed of pain, was always a jolt.

One such afternoon, the room redolent of the disease, she acknowledged her cancer was terminal.

"At least I'll die here at home," she said, propping herself up against the brass headboard of the bed.

Although her savage struggle was reducing her to bones, hearing her verbalize what we both knew was coming stopped me cold. I sat next to her, atop the heavy quilt which she found necessary even though October was unseasonably warm.

"It's going to be fast. I've got the hundred-yard-dash type," she quipped, pointing at a picture of her daughter sandwiched between the mirror and frame of an aging dresser. "I used to be in sports . . . Nancy's the runner in the family now. That was taken two years ago. They grow like weeds, don't they, Father?" Biting at her lower lip, she fell into silence.

"Hey. You okay?"

"It's nothing. Just thinking that I'll never see her grow up. The boys are going to be all right. It's her . . . she needs her mom, and . . . well, you've got a daughter . . . you can understand." The tears welled up into her eyes, but when she saw the same was happening to me, Maureen wiped them away, shifting moods.

"I'm embarrassed with that dresser, Father. Just look at the dust!"

"You ought to see mine. Besides, I didn't notice. Who are the rest of them?" I asked, referring to a series of snapshots ringing the beveled mirror.

"Garland and me." She smiled, pointing to a faded black-and-white photo. "He'd just come back from the service."

The lean, wavy-haired G.I. looking back at us bore little resemblance to her now balding, paunchy husband.

"Except for your glasses, you haven't changed all that much," I said, inching closer to the picture.

"Then you haven't looked too closely in the past months, have you, Father? I've only dropped about forty pounds. My legs are swollen and my hair's falling out."

I flushed but needn't have.

"Only teasing," she said. "Besides, whatever that forty pounds was, it wasn't me. Whenever I look in the mirror these days—which isn't often, mind you—it's scary, but then I know very well that behind the sunken cheeks and yellow skin, I'm still inside there, the same me. That's the part that will live on when it's over. Right?"

I nodded, just as she winced with familiar pain.

"Hurtin' much?"

"Lately it's not so bad. Only when I get the hiccups. Never had them before the mastectomy, but, boy, have they made up for lost time! Speaking of time, Father, I don't have much more of it, so we'd better chat."

That afternoon we finally talked about death, in particular, her own. No longer was it something far off, only a threatened possibility. Except for an occasional attempt at words of comfort, I sat back and listened. Once again her concern was for the children, for Garland, how they would react and go on. As the peculiar orange tint of twilight spread across the room, I searched inside my jacket for the small pyx containing the Eucharist, just as she brought up the matter of her own funeral.

"I'll always remember a sermon you gave a year or so ago. The one on Lazarus. Somehow I never thought of Jesus weeping over the loss of a friend like that. I tended to think of him as always under control. You know, he's God and not a bit like us." Weary, she started to cough but insisted on going on. "Anyway, Jesus rising from the dead has been part of the faith for me ever since I can remember. But Lazarus? Him coming back to life? Well, that really hit me . . ."

"Yeah, I know what you mean. The heart of the church's faith is that like Lazarus you, too, will be drawn right through death into life."

Taking her hand, turning the pale gold wedding band hanging loosely on her finger, I added, "I know it's easy for me to say, sitting here healthy and all, but I honestly believe that the same Jesus who drew Lazarus from the tomb will do the same for you."

Weakly, she squeezed my hand, her grasp at once warm yet clammy. "I want you to preach at the funeral. Please use that gospel story when you do."

I agreed, fearful she was becoming overtired. "Ready for the Lord?"

Nodding, she closed her eyes, waiting to receive communion. Unfastening the clasp from the tiny gold-plated pyx, I started to remove the eucharistic wafer inside when Maureen abruptly clasped a hand over her mouth, turned away from me into the pillow. Within seconds, her frail body was heaving, wracked by a slow, persistent cough. Not until I noticed the crimson spots on the pillowcase did I realize she was coughing up blood. Eventually she managed to lean up on an elbow and motion toward the bathroom where I found a damp washcloth. I began to sponge the blood away from her mouth. The siege finally over, she flopped back against the bed, exhausted.

Placing a cool cloth against her forehead, I felt utterly helpless. Despite her pain, Maureen recognized my own.

"Are you okay?" I stammered.

"I'm fine, but you look a little scared, Father," she said weakly.

"Aren't you?"

"Not really. We're all dying. Some just a bit sooner than others."

When she smiled through the dried blood caked on her lips, I smiled back, laughing nervously. "Guess you're right."

"It's nothing to laugh about, though," she said gently.

Embarrassed by my difficulty in coping with her loss, I looked away.

She tugged at my sleeve. "No, no. I didn't mean it that way. It's just . . . well, it's kind of hard to die when I'm the one who's doing it. It's something you think about but in the end have to do all alone."

"Someday I'll have to do it, too," I said, moved by her conviction. "The Lord went through it alone, too, but in that somehow took upon himself our own death . . ."

Her gray eyes suddenly intense, she asked me to hand her an ornately framed, enlarged photograph from the far wall. The picture was of a fawn, peering innocently through a camouflage of high autumn grass.

"My son took this a few years back. It's my favorite. Probably because of the autumn colors . . . the old grass. Dying grass . . . but such a beautiful surrounding for new life." Her eyes glistened as she added, "I want the funeral to be about life, not death."

"For sure."

After assuring her it would be, and praying with her, I got up to leave.

"Promise me about the funeral. Upbeat, life over death."

"Of course . . . promise," I stammered, choking back my emotions while leaning over to give her a slight kiss on the cheek.

"Good-bye, Father Mike, see you soon," she said wheezily.

Pausing at the doorway to admit a nurse, I turned back to Maureen. She was already asleep, clasping the picture against her chest.

The next time I saw her was two days later. Summoned by her physician in the midst of evening rounds at a local rest home, I broke away immediately. The look on Garland's face when I arrived at the family home told me it was all over. Silently, we entered Maureen's bedroom, where she lay perfectly still, the quilt pulled up beneath her jaw, slack in the peculiar relaxation of death. She had gone into a coma; the end had come quickly. Just before sunset she had slipped toward God and was gone.

We talked, sought to exchange words of comfort. Knelt to pray. Only when I reached the car, just about to drive away, did her daughter remember. Rushing up, her eyes bloodshot, she clutched something against herself.

"Mom insisted you have this . . . we'll get it copied. Here. Please . . . she said you'd understand."

Trembling, I turned over the frame, revealing the photo of the fawn staring wide-eyed through the grass.

Tim and I prepared to celebrate the funeral mass, one reflecting Maureen's lifelong devotion to the church and her conviction that even in death there was life.

When I finally noticed the two priests in the congregation, I was too caught up in the events to pay much attention. Not until we were closing the grave did I see them once again, off in the distance among the spruce trees.

"May perpetual light shine upon her. May you, Maureen—who loved and trusted in the church of your faith—may your soul and all the souls of the faithful departed, through the mercy of God, rest in peace. Amen.''

Detaching the cross from the glistening casket, I handed it to Garland and the children. By the time I looked toward the trees again, the two figures were gone.

No sooner had I returned to the parish to enter her name under the column inscribed *"Mortis Domini"* than the phone rang.

"This is the bishop!"

His voice was shrill.

"Yes?"

"What the hell do you think you're doing? That funeral! There was no distinction between you and any other priest. Once again you've gone too far, fella.''

For a second I didn't know what funeral he was talking about. It couldn't be Maureen's. The grave was still warm. Then I remembered the two priests. I gripped the phone as he started in again.

"Your role in that funeral was absolutely scandalous!''

"Look, Bishop," I stammered. "This morning's service was no different than any I've done since way back when Dutch was still here.''

"One mistake doesn't justify another.''

"I only did what Maureen asked of me. She was dying. We were close and . . .''

"I don't care what she wanted. She's dead!'' he shouted.

"Maybe you ought to ask her children instead of your spies how they felt about the funeral. What about talking to her husband?''

"I resent you calling them spies. They're just doing their duty. As for her husband . . . if he can't live with the rules . . . then he can just . . . just . . .''

He hesitated, then slammed down the receiver, leaving me stunned and shaken.

Five minutes later Curtiss's secretary called asking both Tim and me to schedule a meeting in the chancery.

It was a damp Wednesday morning when Tim and I drove toward Helena, where we expected Curtiss would demand I make a decision to state publicly the errors of my ways and agree to abide by further restrictions.

Throughout the two-hour journey we discussed that decision. Although I might submit to such minutiae as standing farther away from the altar, or not wearing a stole, when it came to substantive demands, there could be little compromise. There was no way I could accept token involvement in the mass and other sacraments. To do so would divorce me from intimate contact with the people of Resurrection during peak moments of their lives. To do so would not only place a significant burden on Tim, but also make a mockery of the past and place in jeopardy all we had come to believe in. Least of all would I sanction public statements repudiating Hunthausen's alleged errors. At the same time, we were confident there might be a slight thawing of the cold war, expecting that the pattern with Curtiss would most likely be the same. He would become volatile, characteristically acting out his feelings. In the end, though agreeing to disagree, we would then go on as before, each of us hoping that someday the other would grow weary of it all and give up.

Joan did not share our optimism. Just before Tim and I left for the encounter with Curtiss, she was in an unusually pensive mood.

"Just meeting the man—there was something about him," she said, struggling to wrap words about her instincts. "It was in his eyes. More than fear. Almost panic."

She asked me to be careful.

"Of what?"

"Of his fear."

The bishop's secretary, a young bespectacled priest, nervously ushered us into the episcopal office, announcing that His Excellency was on his way from his private chapel. Tim observed that the floors in the chancery were always cold as we settled into soft burgundy chairs separated by a table supporting a bust of Pius XII. Seconds later Curtiss entered, ordering the secretary to hold all calls while we waited for someone else. Tim and I exchanged glances—wondering for whom?

The bishop, obviously distracted, was brusque, his speech brittle. When Gerald Himmler entered, he appeared at once relieved.

"I've invited the vicar-general to sit in," Curtiss announced.

Withdrawing a tablet and pen from his briefcase, Himmler noticed my quizzical expression.

"His Excellency wants a witness to the proceedings."

"Witness? For what?" I asked, hearing the sudden tension in my voice.

"For the record," Himmler replied.

"Aren't we just talking over your conditions?"

No one answered.

Tim looked over at me, his fingers drumming on the arm of the chair. Clearly the bishop and his vicar knew something we did not. Remembering Joan's counsel to be careful, I took a deep breath and waited, but couldn't help jumping a bit when Curtiss sprang from his chair and began pacing about the room.

"Let me begin with the *status questiones*," he said, as if reciting from a script already written. "Ever since coming to the diocese, I've tried to work out a suitable arrangement for your ministry." He stopped at my chair and then twirled away. "I took all the documents to Washington with me last week and talked with the Holy Father's delegate."

"The delegate!" I stammered. "You're going to end up forcing him to act!"

"He was just speechless when I told him about that funeral, among other things!"

"Why'd you go to him?"

Silence.

The remainder of the monologue covered the same ground we had been over for two years. The words snapped from his lips. I had failed to make proper distinctions between lay ministry and priestly ministry. I was a source of confusion and irritation to priests within and members of the hierarchy outside the diocese.

Curtiss stopped, placing a hand atop the bust of Pius XII, staring down at me with steely resolve.

"So, what I'm about to say has the full support of His Eminence, the apostolic delegate." He cleared his throat and paused, the only sound Himmler's pen racing to keep up.

"Mike, you've made many contributions to the life of the church. I've honestly tried to cooperate with you so those contributions might continue, but . . ."

His tone sounded like that of someone reading an obituary. My muscles began to tighten. Across from me, Tim's brow was deeply furrowed.

"So, there's no choice but for me, as spiritual leader of western Montana, to declare that your ministry at Resurrection and in this diocese is officially terminated."

Terminated? Initially I thought it might be just another threat. A pregnant silence suggested otherwise. He repeated the word which this time crashed into my brain like a cannon shot. *Terminated*—the cantor's first note from the dirge had at long last been intoned.

The bishop sat down next to Himmler, who looked away from me. Only the unconscious drumming of Tim's fingers against the chair interrupted the stillness.

A familiar melancholy rippled through me. A sadness not only for myself but for all of us. Maybe the matter was beyond the bishop's control, had been all along. Like it or not, the chain of decision was now linked directly to Jean Jadot, the pope's personal representative.

Shaking my head, I managed to whisper a reply, "Deep inside I'm a priest. From the beginning all I've wanted to be is who I am . . . and try to serve the church."

"What was that?" Curtiss asked tersely.

For a split second, I saw the fear in his eyes Joan warned me of.

"Ah, nothing. What I can't understand is that what we have at Resurrection has been going on successfully for nearly five years. If you—the church—whoever the 'they' you always talk of—wanted to get us, why wait so long?"

Perhaps reading defeat in my washed-out tone, the tension strung in tiny knots about Curtiss's face began to unwind.

"Mike, don't take this personally."

"Oh no? It's me who's being set adrift," I said, still trying to recover.

He motioned to Himmler to keep on taking notes; then, his finger cutting through the air to underline a point, he turned back to me.

"Even if I hadn't opposed this from the outset—which the record will show I did—we still would've come to this. Hunthausen made a serious mistake in permitting you to marry and stay. Common sense would have indicated . . ."

"Common sense!" I cut in. "Love and the gospel aren't common sense?"

Curtiss folded his arms about the pectoral cross strung across his chest.

"We've been over this a thousand times, and . . ."

"At least that." My voice was trembling. "Dutch saw our case as an opportunity for the church to quit tossing its priests into the trashcan. But you? Oh no! With you, it's been a mistake. How did you put it when we first met? 'The major problem of your episcopate.' "

"This damn thing is bigger than either one of us. We're talking about the Roman Catholic Church, not just your corner of the world! Besides, I have to listen to my priests. They've been terribly upset."

"I've yet to talk with one priest who is the least bit bothered by Mike and Joan." For a moment, I had forgotten Tim was in the room. His voice startled us all.

"You don't talk to the same priests as I do, Father! There are plenty who still feel *aut casteat, aut peceat,*" Curtiss snapped.

At the words "let him be chaste or let him burn," a strawberry spot the size of a half-dollar formed over the furrow on Tim's forehead as he struggled to contain his fury.

"God, but I'm sick of hearing of these disgruntled priests, all wrapped up in something which doesn't concern most sane human beings. It's like a broken record! In Bozeman, his marriage is simply a nonissue."

"That's not true!" Curtiss's voice was high-pitched as he leaned forward within a few inches of Tim. "There are lay people who are troubled. Maybe not among that Resurrection bunch, though there's bound to be some, but . . ."

"But where?" Tim asked.

"Elsewhere."

"One or two cries of discontent and you make a federal case of it and run off to the delegate. My God, no wonder you've got pressure on you!"

"Listen, Father," the bishop shot back. "This guy is a sign of contradiction to our people, a scandal!"

"So was Jesus," Tim replied, surprising me with an unusual tenacity.

Curtiss turned to the vicar, who until then had appeared reluctant to enter into the fracas.

"His Excellency means that Mike confuses the people. They can't see him living one moment like an ordinary layman, the next, sharing in the priestly state."

"State!" I blurted, unable to contain myself. "So help me, Gerry, you sound like a seminary textbook! People know me as a person. As an honest-to-goodness human being. So what if they see me wheeling a grocery cart or carrying Michelle around, then see me at the altar on Sunday? God forbid that folks will get the idea priests are just like them! Then 'Father' won't be able to stay perched on his pedestal."

The vicar started writing again, choosing not to get any closer to the heat of the conflict than he had to. Behind him, the pendulum of a gold-leaf clock swung back and forth along with our moods. Already an hour had passed.

The bishop proceeded to review our history together, insisting that he had little recourse given my attack on priestly celibacy. At no point did he broach the subject of the further restrictions he had once demanded. What we originally presumed to be the point of our gathering was now moot.

I stood, hoping to ease the tension snapping at my nerves.

"What's most troubling is seeing all of us at Resurrection treated like lepers." I sighed, looking out the window over the chancery lawn. "We're not the enemy. If there is one, it's out there . . . somewhere. We're supposed to be a part of the same faith."

Curtiss leaned over to push a white button beside his desk. Nearly before it stopped buzzing, the secretary appeared, only to depart, return with a stack of papers, and depart again. The bishop tossed the papers onto the table where our coffee had long since grown cold.

"These are the documents of your case. From day one you've missed the point. It's not a question of right and wrong. Of enemies or friends, but of obedience to me and the Holy Father. Either you are or you aren't."

I ignored the papers. "What of faith? It isn't right when we're forced to choose between belief and our own church. Everything we believe forces us to disobey . . ."

"See! He admits flounting authority," Curtiss blurted, motioning triumphantly to the vicar. "We are to obey the church. Absolutely."

"Obedience to Christ first."

"They're one and the same!"

"Not always!"

Again the bishop looked to his vicar, shaking his head incredulously, before turning back to me. "Why can't you see the issue is authority?"

"It's more than that. It's also whether we're meeting the needs of the people and . . ."

Impatient, Curtiss interjected, "Tim's told me how effective you are as a minister. And the parish"—he paused, measuring his words—"well, why not say it? Resurrection is probably now where the rest of the church will end up someday. But"—he slapped a clenched fist into his palm—"it's not where Roman Catholicism is today and therefore you have to go. Period."

O'Mera muttered something.

Curtiss spun, facing him. "What did you say?"

"I said, what you want to do is destroy the village to save it. Mike has to go. The people of Resurrection are to be shattered. We will have one less priest and all in the name of celibacy! When will it all stop?'' he sputtered.

"Listen, Father O'Mera. I've about had enough of you! Believe me, I won't forget this!''

Shaken, Tim took a gulp of his cold coffee as I wedged in between them.

"You said the issue was authority. All along I thought the church was about the gospel, whether or not we live it.''

"Oh, cut out the holier-than-thou nonsense!'' the bishop blurted, his cheeks flushed.

The scratching from the vicar's pen ceased. Seeking to change the subject, he asked why we hadn't prepared the people of Resurrection to accept the restrictions Rome placed on dispensed priests. I replied that while we discussed them, we didn't accept them from the outset. To do so would have meant my surrendering the priesthood. Besides, compared with the everyday concerns and needs of the parish, the Vatican's posture was largely irrelevant. Satisfied, Himmler picked up the pen and began writing once again. His manner irritated me.

"Doesn't anyone care what the people think? There are a couple thousand of them in Resurrection, yet no one asks them what they want. Neither of you people have really been in the place. How can you sit there and make judgments?''

"We know damn well what they think,'' Curtiss flared. "Trouble is, you won't cooperate in getting the errors out of their thick skulls, and so here we are!''

"You mean about my not being a priest after marriage?''

"Of course.''

"We've been over it *ad nauseam*! No matter what you want them to think, they know the truth.''

"Truth? Who's to say what's true?''

There was little use and we knew it. The termination was irreversible. If I cooperated and said nothing to Resurrection, it would not become effective until the new clergy appointments in June.

It was Tim who mentioned that if the parish got wind of the news, there would surely be resistance.

Curtiss's response was steady. Subdued.

"Let me assure you, Father, that Holy Mother Church is prepared to take any and all measures to erase this scandal.''

"Would you mind translating that?'' Tim asked with an air of sarcasm which infuriated the bishop.

"Certainly. For starters, we'll get you out of there. But that's only the beginning. I'm prepared to see the entire parish dismantled from the ground up. We'll start over completely from scratch before we accept this affront to holy celibacy."

The blood drained from Tim's face.

I took a deep breath.

"You're willing to rape the whole parish over this?"

He didn't answer.

"Elden . . . what are you afraid of?"

"Not of you, buster! If you so much as lift one finger to fight this—if you cause any trouble at all . . . Well, let me lay the cards on the table . . ."

He then pledged to personally prevent me from exercising even the most token ministry. Anywhere in the United States. Ever again.

"Do I make myself clear?"

"What you're saying is, you'll blackball me," I replied, taken back by his certitude. "No matter where my family goes, you'll be on us. Yeah, I know what you're saying."

His eyes were riveted on mine, and for the first time I knew what Joan meant about the danger of fear teetering on panic.

Hours later, drained from a morning I could reveal to no one but Joan, I arrived home. Michelle was in the kitchen standing tiptoe on a stool, about to help her mother stuff a turkey for roasting the next day. Hearing the news, Joan fought back tears. Slowly wrapping the turkey, she placed it in the freezer, knowing it would be impossible to enter into the spirit of Thanksgiving. For the sake of the parish, we agreed to remain silent about the termination, concealing our remorse as we once did our love.

PART IV

But hush, for I have lost the theme,
Its joy or night seem but a dream; . . .

—W. B. YEATS, *A Man and the Echo*

It was one of those passing remarks which tend to get lost in the heat of emotion. In the days following the meeting with Curtiss, there was little else I could think of. He had been standing in the chancery door speaking to Tim on his way out. "I guess both Mike and I always knew it would come to this."

Quite possibly he knew all along, but what had blind-sided me? Certainly, I knew from the outset the Catholic Church would resist a married priest entering its sanctuaries. Had Joan and I permitted romance to shield us from harsher realities? Were we simply naïve in not expecting failure?

Of course, we knew we were taking a major risk. The early months of our marriage were like walking a tightrope. If the institutional church had severed the wire then, it might not have come as such a shock. However, after surviving five years, we did not expect a purge. If there had been one serious mistake, it was in assuming that despite Elden Curtiss, our status was a *fait accompli*. While the hierarchy might not sanction our precedent, we simply didn't believe that they would toss it away either. Besides, even the most resolute authorities would think twice before risking the repercussions of attacking such a firmly rooted situation in a community like Resurrection.

We had been wrong all along. While there were always threats, the actual termination notice took the wind out of me. Again, the question why? Had the parish's acceptance of us clouded our perception of the larger church and of just how intimidating our breach of an eight-hundred-year-old tradition truly was? Had that very acceptance blanketed us in a comfortable illusion, destined to turn into our shroud? More painful yet, could a major fault line be traced directly to me? Had I in fact pushed Curtiss too far with my unwillingness to compromise any further? Had my own pride rather than the step beyond celibacy now put our dream on the line? Yet, there seemed little choice. Since coming to the diocese, the new bishop had pecked away at my ministry as if by design. First at the outer edges; then, more recently, boring into its very soul. Despite the limitations of my own perception, there was no shaking the feeling that Curtiss knew from the day we met that Joan and I would have to go. Yet who had made that decision? Would he own up to it? Was it, rather, the apostolic delegate? Or did the road lead to Rome? To the Curia? Perhaps even to the pope himself?

Such questions hounded me throughout the days, followed me into restless nights.

Tim, too, was showing the strain, admitting that the bishop's naked threat to remove him from the parish was a jolt.

"I guess I could've handled that one," he mused with a trace of anxiety in his voice, "but what if he carried through with the other? For me to be suspended from the priesthood would kill my mother."

"He wouldn't dare. You have more friends among the clergy than he'll ever have. The lid would blow off the diocese," I replied, noticing his nails were torn down to the quick.

"No. I think he's fanatic enough to try anything if pushed. Then that business about completely dismantling our parish. There's no way he could do it, unless he was saying what I think he was?"

"Excommunicating the opposition? Yeah. It'd be a last resort but that's what he's getting at. He threw that little gem at me once before."

The Adam's apple along Tim's throat moved as he swallowed, then swallowed again. "He pushes my buttons with that stuff and knows it. I'd feel guilty the rest of my life if it happened."

"It won't."

"Don't be too sure. The hierarchy have all the horses. All the power in the crunch."

The now familiar knot in my stomach tightened.

"They remind me of parents who know they are losing their grip on the world around them, so they take their frustrations out on the only ones they still have control of—their own flesh and blood."

"That's what I'm afraid of," Tim said. Reminding me that Curtiss was a loose cannon. That zealots usually were.

* * *

Although Joan and I knew it could be our final Christmas at Resurrection, we were swept up by the sheer energy of the season. Each Sunday as we lit still another Advent candle, we put aside any thought of the shadow lurking behind our Bethlehem star. What that same star had come to mean was captured on Christmas Eve in a picture that said what words could not.

Every seat in the parish center was taken, the walls lined with those who somehow managed to squeeze in. Yet there wasn't so much as a sound as the two women moved through the translucence of a single blue light, completing their dance celebrating the Nativity gospel. I stepped forward to speak of fresh hope passed down through the eons of time to our own moment of Bethlehem.

Suddenly Michelle, her mother momentarily distracted, toddled up the aisle, shouting, "Daddy! Daddy!" Before I could react, she crossed in front of the altar and stood tugging at my chasuble. There was little I could do but pick up our two-year-old, who then rested her head against me throughout the remainder of the homily. No one seemed to share in my embarrassment. It wasn't until the Creed that Joan was able to work her way through the congregation and retrieve Michelle. Only later did we realize that for us, at least, that unexpected event and the community's reaction captured the promise of Christmas.

It was nearly midnight by the time we finished decorating the tree. Tiny wooden shoes from the Netherlands. A fragile glass star given to Michelle on her first Christmas. A porcelain seagull passed down through my family.

"Remember the Cliffs of Moher? Those two gulls? They kept rising on the wind in front of us like dancers," Joan said, stringing the porcelain piece over a branch of spruce. "They were so free. So utterly free."

The sweet smell of pine enveloped us, the tree lights glistening in her eyes.

Joan pulled a blanket over our daughter, curled at the bottom of the tree.

"Time's slipping away. We have to talk about it, you know."

"It?" I asked, knowing full well what she meant.

"What you're going to do?"

"You mean about Curtiss? I can't believe the guy!" I blurted, then caught myself. "Oh, what the hell, it's not just him. He's there because the institution wants him there. If you don't mouth the party line, no one seems to listen, much less care.''

Pondering where to hang a tiny angel, Joan's voice was flat. ''I'm starting to really hate it, you know. It's awful to say, but just seeing what it does to people.''

Immediately, I wanted to rush in, at once denying her feelings while protecting the church.

''Come on now. You've always loved her. There's a difference between what a few clerics at the top of the pyramid say and the church.''

She waved off my protest.

''You didn't answer the question. What are you going to do?''

I thought back to the meeting at the chancery. Recalled the look on Tim's face when the bishop threatened to shut the parish down.

''They've got leverage on us. The bit about getting rid of Tim and all. Maybe we've given it our best shot.''

''If you're thinking about quitting, remember, that means leaving the priesthood. They're one and the same,'' she said, still in a monotone.

She touched a raw nerve. Despite the fact that we were married and had a family, I had never been asked to leave the priesthood like thousands of others throughout the world. Now I was about to be forced out, a reality I didn't want to face.

Joan scooted across the floor to sit next to me.

''It seems so long ago when we first talked about it. If you are ever out it will tear you apart. I'm afraid of that and fearful you'd end up resenting me.'' She glanced at Michelle. ''And her, too.''

I ran a finger down across her forehead, tapping her on the tip of the nose.

''Know what? I love you, lady.''

''Yes. I know that.''

''Do you? Honestly, if we could turn the clock back, I'd do it all over again at the drop of a hat; if you'd have me. If they push us out, we'll have one another and that's worth more than all their pious titles, crosiers, and miters combined.''

''They know what you cherish,'' she stammered. ''That's why the threat to ban you from any kind of participation in the church if you offer even the slightest shred of resistance. Oh yes, they know what you care about all right.''

''At least part of it.''

Joan stretched out her legs, resting her head against me.

"Then again, maybe they know more than part of it," I said. "When ol' Elden said he'd see to it that you, Michelle, all of us would be blackballed in Catholicism, he was going for broke."

"Could he do it?"

"He might try, but I doubt if he'd pull it off. People are too good."

"Well, if they get you, I won't have any part of their holy church again!"

"I couldn't live with a price that high," I whispered.

"You're always trying to protect me, Father," she half-teased. Then she raised an issue which had been troubling her all along.

Since first advising us of the termination, Curtiss had insisted upon confidentiality. A request neither Tim nor I questioned at the time, and one which Joan now challenged.

"It's a way to neutralize you. If no one in the parish knows what's going on, then there's no resistance."

She was right. Priests were taught to keep things close, especially in the inviolate domain of confession. Of such confidentiality there could be no question. However, we were also accustomed to keeping any number of church issues in-house; that is, among the clergy. If a bishop requested silence from a priest, silence was expected. Yet in our case, such secrecy could only disarm us, prevent resolution of the issue on any terms but those given by authority. On the other hand, there were valid reasons for keeping the parish in the dark. All along, we had hoped to avoid unnecessary worry. Furthermore, if we were to let the cat out of the bag, a spotlight might be turned on us that could further upset the hierarchy and hasten the termination. Still, with the wheels already in motion, what choice did we have but to bring it all into the light of day?

"What did you say?"

"Just mumbling a line from Maureen's funeral."

"Please. Can I hear?"

"No one lives for himself. No one dies for himself. We live and die together in the Lord," I replied, glancing at the porcelain gulls spinning slowly amid the soft glow of tree lights.

"Mean what I think it does?"

"Well, all along we've been preaching that the people, not just those at the top, are the church. That's basic Roman Catholic dogma! The nameless ones . . . you know, those who put the checks in the collection plate every week—they're the church. In Resurrection they went out on a limb with us in the first place. So now they have a right to know what's going on!''

She nodded in agreement. They had to know. So, too, should Archbishop Hunthausen. Besides, neither Tim nor I had actually agreed to Curtiss's insistence on secrecy.

"Michael. You still haven't answered my question. What do you want to do?''

I reached down alongside us and touched Michelle's cheek, feeling the breath of sleep against my hand.

"What kind of church is she going to inherit? One where as a woman she's a second-class citizen? Worse yet, one which views the love between her mother and father as a scandal to the faithful?''

Michelle stirred, drawing her favorite teddy bear in close.

"If we didn't believe that the Holy Spirit was somehow involved in our finding one another and in the miracle of my being able to stay, then neither of us would have plunged into this mess in the first place. Maybe we are caught up in something far bigger than we realize. Whatever, I just have to believe the Spirit is still in it.''

"Then you want to stand up against them getting rid of you?'' Joan asked tenderly, running her hand across my own.

"There's no choice. Being faithful to the church doesn't mean lying down and playing dead. Besides, there's you, hon, and there's no way in hell that I can sit back and watch those turkeys attack you, too!''

"Why are they so afraid of love?''

"Full of questions tonight, aren't you? Maybe we should have heeded Joseph's example—bundled up Michelle and high-tailed it for Egypt long ago.''

Joan leaned forward, brushing her lips against mine, whispering, "By the way. Merry Christmas.''

Archbishop Hunthausen did not appear concerned in the least about potential repercussions for himself in lieu of my pending dismissal. While he hurt for us, he was not so surprised.

"Maybe Elden was right all along. That we should have seen this coming,'' he said when my call caught him at Sea-Tac International. He flared up only once, and it was at Curtiss's suggestion that the apostolic delegate was exerting pressure from behind the scene to remove me.

"That's not the way Jadot operates. Of course, I know this is a little different, still it doesn't sound like him. He's usually right up front. Nope. He's a better man than that."

In the next breath, Hunthausen confirmed what I had long suspected. Since his style as well as his perception of the church was far different from that of many colleagues, he never mentioned our case to the delegate. As one who instinctively looked to the grass roots for his directives and not always the institutional church, the archbishop assumed that if Jadot had trouble with the events at Resurrection, he would hear about it soon enough. In his decision not to seek agreement before endorsing my request to marry and remain, Hunthausen had avoided putting the delegate on the spot.

"So it's possible Jadot never knew what was happening at Resurrection until long after the fact. Maybe not until after you were appointed to Seattle?"

"Sure. Though that's hard to imagine. You know, it's an unfortunate time for this whole thing to come to a head. The pope is quite ill and the Curia is supposedly in charge. For some of them, the only winds blowing come from the right."

In the background I heard the final call for his flight. Just before breaking away, he advised me to inform the parish of our plight. "The problem is that as soon as you do so, you bring the thing out of the closet and lay it in the media's lap."

"You mean, married priesthood?"

"Well, that doesn't concern me so much as what it does to your family. It just exposes you to the kind of publicity we've tried all along to avoid. You jump right from the frying pan into the fire. Still, I don't see how you have any choice. When you do tell Resurrection, though, do so without any suggestion of confrontation. Leave how they react up to them, and the Holy Spirit." He paused, then went on hurriedly, his voice starting to crack. "Tell Joan I love her and give Michelle a kiss."

I was about to tell him of the threats against us and the parish, but he had already hung up.

Time was running out. Despite the decision to inform the parish, I continually put off doing so in the vain hope that Bishop Curtiss would call to say the whole episode was a mistake.

The first weekend in March dawned against a slate-gray sky, as a chinook wind reduced the snowpack to murky streams running down the streets. Prior to the first mass, I remained within the office putting the final touches on the sermon. Outside, Tim's occasional laughter rose above the buzz of the congregation. He was much too loud, a tip-off that inside he was full of butterflies.

As Michelle toyed with the tassels of my cincture, Joan and I went over the talk one final time. I would focus on the gospel of the day —Matthew's account of the temptation in the wilderness. Only toward the end of the homily would I bring up the termination, keeping in mind Hunthausen's admonition to lay out the facts without setting a tone of confrontation.

I slipped on the violet chasuble.

"Here, give Daddy a kiss," Joan said as Michelle wrinkled her nose and pecked me on the cheek.

It was time. Opening the door to join the congregation, I was immediately relieved. No longer would we keep the door closed on our constant struggle with church officials.

Midway through the mass, the lector handed me the heavily bound copy of the Scriptures before sitting down next to her husband. They smiled. I tried to.

Glancing out over the crowd, I spotted a young divorcée with her son. The same woman who only recently had managed to let go of her guilt and sense of rejection enough to start receiving the sacraments again. In the row behind her, a graduate student, about to complete his preparation for an Easter Eve reception into the church. I feared what they both might think of that same church now.

Seated alongside a far wall was a Protestant minister who along with his family worshiped with us frequently. I recalled the Swedish-style stroganoff they had prepared to celebrate our wedding. As dinner guests of the local Lutheran, Presbyterian, Episcopalian, and Methodist clergy, we shared a common feeling of jubilation. I shuddered to imagine how the same group would receive our present news.

"The Book of Ecclesiastes tells us there is a time. There is a season for every purpose under the heavens." My voice felt strong, controlled.

"A time to be born. A time to die. A time for loving and for hating. For war and peace. For keeping silent and for speaking out. Today is a day for speaking out, for this is the Gospel of the Lord."

As I elevated the Scriptures while the community stood for the proclamation of the Word, my eyes fell first on Kirby Walsh, then toward the back of the room on Terry Doherty. Even though the parish council knew of the bishop's frustration with my role, they believed the issue had blown over.

Maybe it was the stark weather, but when everyone was seated, the room was swallowed up in an unusual stillness, punctuated only by Tim's nervous cough behind me.

Matthew's gospel spoke of the time in the desert when a young Jesus encountered the Tempter wearing the face of a friend. Initially Satan offered bread—the comfort and security of a worry-free life stretching into old age—if only Jesus would be content to stay in his proper place, and give up the dream. Unable to shake him, the Tempter then raised the ante and lifted him to the parapet of the temple, there to be enticed with the promise of power, the glistening gemstone in the crown of success. Again he refused. The face of friendship dissolved into one of raging cynicism as the Lord of Flies held out the trump card. He would go to the core of the young man's soul and reveal a glimpse into a perilous future. Therein to taunt him with the folly of relying on the promises of what might turn out to be a powerless God.

"In the desert, Jesus realized that the ultimate tragedy for him, as for any of us, is not so much to do the bad as to fail to reach for that which we know to be good. Turning away from the face of temptation, he entered the synagogue and there, before the elders, reached for the ancient and living Word which from then on would chart the course of his future."

Outside, a persistent sun broke through a bank of clouds, its misty light streaming through the windows. The shift of mood took me from an uneasy calm to the edge of anxiety. I disregarded the remainder of the homily—explaining that what was to follow was not at all easy to say, that in seeking a way through the days before us, we, too, would have to reach for our deepest values. From then on, the words jumped out ahead of, and almost in spite of me.

"Nearly a decade ago, I came here with a deep love of the priesthood. Also the conviction that the risk of intimacy which the gospel calls us to is worth all it takes. Still, I was unprepared for the gift of love shared freely with me by a remarkable woman. At times it appeared as though there was no way to resolve the dilemma of living out these two loves in a church which forbids their union. No way until . . . you."

A lump swelled in my throat; for the first time my voice started to tremble.

"Quite honestly, loving her has brought me closer to you. I'm a happier priest, that's for sure."

I glanced at my watch, then waded into the murky waters of the termination. Though we had not sought attention, certain sectors of the hierarchy had been focusing on Resurrection for some time. Since the arrival of Elden Curtiss, the pressure had been unrelenting.

"The bishop has a great deal of difficulty with us. Though we couldn't tell you, that's why he canceled the confirmation here last spring."

I paused, feeling my own breath pushing against the center of my chest.

"It's not that the bishop has the black hat and we the white. We can't judge him. It's more that the glasses he wears give him a picture of a church in which structure and established order are priorities."

While explaining the law of celibacy and the questions raised by Curtiss, a wall of resistance rose within me the closer I came to broaching the subject of the termination.

"At any rate . . . ah . . . the bishop's decided to bring my ministry here to an end a few weeks from now. It's not a transfer to another parish. There won't be another one. As far as he's concerned, this is the end of the line."

A few quizzical looks darted through the room. Momentarily I wondered if they had already guessed. Within an instant, several audible gasps and wide-eyed expressions left little doubt that the congregation was taken by complete surprise. Their faces were much like those of a family informed of a sudden accident.

"How does it make me feel? Angry, but not bitter. Not yet at least," I said, attempting a smile which wouldn't come. "Maybe it's because I've seen so much of the mind-set lying behind this action. A mentality embedded at the core of the institutional church. No, I'm more sad than bitter. Sad for a church which is so afraid of love, and treats its own like this!"

From the back, Joan shook her head, backing me off from a rush to lash out. Above all else, the parish had to be given the leisure to react on its own, as free as possible from the momentum of my own feelings. Nevertheless, they had to know the truth as we saw it.

"This exile, or termination as they call it, involves not only me. Not only Joan and our two-year-old daughter . . . but Tim, and all of you . . . None of us asked to be in this spot, but here we are. In choosing how we react it seems to me we can do no less than Jesus did in that desert . . . try to see what it is the Holy Spirit calls us to do."

At last the veil was lifted. For the first time it struck me that quite possibly we stood at a juncture in the history of the American Church which might not come again for years, if ever. Though the future was uncertain, it promised to plunge us into the very heart of what Catholicism was all about.

Relieved to be finished, I turned back to the altar, glancing up at the Lenten message etched in black letters against the stark white of the wall.

"Remember man that thou art dust and unto dust thou shalt return."

Individually and collectively, the reaction among the parishioners of Resurrection was the same. Dazed, all but speechless, no one seemed to know initially just how to react to the unexpected revelation. However, a common denominator of painful outrage bound the community together. For the time being at least, they appeared willing to rely upon the parish council for a sense of direction.

Within twenty-four hours of the Sunday announcement, the council came together. Their mood was calm, more somber than volatile. For the better part of an evening we seesawed back and forth exploring options to the bishop's mandate, ranging from acquiescence to outright defiance.

Forever philosophical, Drake Shepler fell back on his conviction that Curtiss couldn't be serious about moving against us. Beneath the rhetoric, his voice was hollow, as if the reality of the termination threatened to rob his soul of a tender picture of the church implanted at baptism.

"Before we get too upset, let's be honest. We knew all along there was a chance something like this could happen. It's just not as bad as it sounds. Maybe we ought to give the bishop the benefit of the doubt."

Everyone at the table waited, hoping that Shepler had stumbled upon something we had overlooked. He twisted a curl in his beard.

"Don't get me wrong, but we've got to try and see this from the bishop's perspective. There's a chance he's caught in the middle. For him, Mike is in violation of the law, pure and simple."

"I don't follow your point," Kirby Walsh said impatiently. "Obviously if we paid attention to the Roman rescript as Curtiss wants, Mike and Joan would've been gone a long time ago. Saint Peter had a wife and kids. Hell, he couldn't even pass muster today!"

Walsh's slender wife, who always reminded me of a china doll, reached over, touching his arm. He backed off.

Across the room, Kevin Doherty cut in, his dark eyes flashing.

Hidden behind his sharp, youthful features was a hint of the genes of his ancestors, those who had survived the potato famine in Ireland and fought the British in the back streets of the north.

"What did we hear Sunday? We have to ask ourselves 'what is the gospel thing to do?' That's the same question which helped us leap over hurdles before this one. Don't kid yourselves, Elden Curtiss doesn't give a damn whether Mike's ministry is effective . . . whether we have more students coming to mass now than universities much larger than ours . . . whether or not people are returning to the church in droves. Oh no! Celibacy is more important than all of that. This . . . this . . . man is not really a bishop if he thumbs his nose at the gospel! So, what should we do? For me, the answer is clear. We've got to say no to them," he said, slamming a fist down on the table.

Kevin was not alone. Yet, whenever others echoed his stance, Tim and I exchanged glances, silently questioning our decision not to mention the repercussions threatened by Curtiss at the first sign of resistance.

Throughout the discussion, Esther Gilmore maintained an uncharacteristic silence, appearing increasingly troubled as the evening wore on. Once troubled by most any change in the church, she was finally convinced that Eucharist in the hand, nuns without religious garb or even a married priesthood would not undermine the substance of her faith. The stocky mother of three, known for her easy compassion, eventually emerged as a popular figure in Resurrection. It was Joan who finally prompted her to speak up.

"I just don't know," Esther said, looking around for Tim, a close friend since their days growing up together in Butte. "Maybe it's the way I was brought up, but the bishop's word was always law. You know, he's a successor of the apostles, and . . ."

"Most of whom were married, incidentally," Kevin interjected.

Esther agreed, massaging her hands spent caring for others in a lifetime of nursing.

"I love Mike and Joanie, and would do anything to keep them. But if it comes to out-and-out disobedience of my bishop, well, we were always taught that's a mortal sin, and I just can't go that far."

A couple of the others appeared to nod their heads in agreement.

"Well, it hasn't come to that," Kirby Walsh said impatiently. "Though if the response so far from the parish is any indication, it may. I don't know about the rest of you, but what began as a trickle of resentment on Sunday is beginning to turn into an absolute torrent within this parish. They aren't going to sit by and let it happen, nor am I if we can help it!''

He turned toward Tim.

''Frankly, it makes little sense for us to talk about what we're going to do without knowing where you are.''

''I wish it was anywhere but here,'' Tim chuckled, his smile fading as quickly as it appeared. ''The reaction you're talking about is there, no question about it. At first, the people were hurt, now they're plain angry. Trouble is, that's kind of scary.''

''Scary?''

''Well, you know. Elden is so unpredictable.''

''Well,'' Walsh said, forgetting that Tim had not answered his question, ''we have to wait and see how His Excellency reacts to our knowing about his secret fiat. Then we've got to make it obvious to him that we intend to keep our priest *and* his family. That much we agree on, right?''

When everyone agreed, Walsh spoke to Joan, seated next to him. ''Down the line, you and Mike have to tell us how far we can go to keep you. You're the ones with your feet being held to the fire. You should have some say as to whether or not you're willing to risk getting burned even more.''

I thought of Hans Küng saying the future belonged to those willing to act decisively. But whatever we decided to do could have repercussions on others. We needed time, but there wasn't much left.

With that, the meeting wound to a close, the only decisions procedural ones. The council agreed to coordinate Resurrection's response and to suggest that those in the parish who desired to do so could write the bishop expressing their opinion of the events. Meanwhile, the council members would return home while we all thought about what to do next.

Early next morning, a reporter from the state's largest newspaper called, interrupting my attempt to help Michelle through her French toast. He had talked with Elden Curtiss and several parishioners. There would be a story. Tightening up inside at the prospect of publicity, I repeated a few statements from the Sunday homily and excused myself.

Moments later, the phone rang again. Caston Broderick was abrupt.

''Elden is furious over the *Gazette* getting hold of this. He's also livid with you for telling the parish.''

''What'd he expect me to do, disappear in June without a word?

Besides, I tried last week to let him know, but he didn't return the calls."

"Well, all I know is he'll come unstrung even more if there's publicity. He wants this baby handled out of the public eye."

Caston then took it upon himself to urge me to take up the question of my termination with the Senate of Priests.

A day or two later, I heard the *Gazette* slap against the storm door. Through the pane, its bold headline leaped out from the front page.

BOZEMAN MARRIED PRIEST MAY BE ON WAY OUT

The article reported the issue of marriage and celibacy in the priesthood was so sensitive that the pope had halted all discussion of it. I was quoted as saying the bishop and indeed all of us were caught in the tensions of a changing church . . . We were at a crossroads of what had been and what might yet be coming. Consequently, we all felt the pain. The rest was fair enough, reporting Resurrection to be perplexed and altogether stunned by the bishop's action.

"Hold on. That looks like an out- and-out distortion," Joan said, reading over my shoulder. She pointed to a quotation from the bishop that in scanning the article I had overlooked.

Bishop Elden Curtiss said in a telephone interview that . . . since Miles is a dispensed priest, he is hired directly by the church council and is virtually immune to his orders. "He is quite free to be active," Bishop Curtiss said. "But I haven't any direct responsibility over him."

"It looks like he's fudging a bit," I said, utterly confused.

"But I don't understand."

"Neither do I, unless it's his way of keeping the press away."

"But he doesn't seem to be telling the truth. Michael, he's not. Since we were tots we were taught to look up to them. At my confirmation, when the bishop came down the aisle, one of the kids thought he was God—really! Now it all seems so far away."

Unable to look into her dry-eyed stare, I held her close, momentarily eased by the warmth beneath the cotton of her robe. The *Gazette* article slipped to the floor between us and with it the last vestiges of her childhood.

When the invitation came, it couldn't have been more timely. While passing through Bozeman, Archbishop Hunthausen called. We arranged to spend the day skiing.

We made a full-bore assault on the hill. It wasn't until late afternoon, when we slumped exhausted next to the fireplace of the Bridger Bowl Chalet, that there was time to talk. We were on our second glass of beer when Hunthausen asked if there wasn't a way to compromise even more with Curtiss.

I bristled.

"The middle ground has shifted so often that it's not there anymore. Elden's starting point is that we were outside church law from the beginning. As far as he's concerned, we're lepers."

"You're in good company then," he chuckled, trying to lighten things up. "Christ embraced the lepers. Anyway—he admits you're doing good work."

"That's not the question, though, is it? Broderick says Curtiss is frightened the whole episode has already jeopardized his career. He's got to get rid of me. Just sweep it under the rug."

The archbishop repeated his question about finding a way out of the dilemma.

"There isn't one. In his last letter to the priests, he even admits that he's been talking with Rome all along. The two of us have been at it for so long, neither trusts the other. Besides, I'm not so sure I would ever want to work with him again, even if it were possible."

Hunthausen rubbed a hand back and forth over his windburned forehead.

"What do you want to do?"

It felt good to smile.

"If wishes were horses . . . Go off to a monastery for a few months. We need to step out of this, get some distance. Pray over it. But it's impossible."

"Realistically, then."

"Maybe we should slip away quietly. If the church gets me, at least Resurrection will survive."

"That's not what you want to do, though?"

"No. What I really want to do is fight him every inch of the way!" I muttered, staring into the fire. "To just accept it is to let evil triumph. And that's what it is . . . evil."

I loosened my neckerchief as the festering emotion oozed out of me in a clot of words. Finally I pulled back.

"Trouble is, an out-and-out confrontation would put the whole parish at risk."

Dutch reached for a fistful of pretzels, emphasizing that above all else the survival of Resurrection was paramount.

"I don't want you catching any flak, either," I added.

He shrugged it off. "Nonsense. Don't let that enter into it in the least. Unfortunately, I don't have any jurisdiction in this diocese any longer, or we'd try at least to turn things around. So it's up to you to do what you want to. Trouble is, I'm not sure you have a handle on just what that is."

"Some of it depends on what the people of Resurrection want. If only the powers that be would listen to them," I said, for a moment forgetting that the archbishop was one of those very powers. "Sometimes I wonder what's the sense of going on. I'm so tired of it. The whole system is sick! It'll become the grave of God if it keeps up!"

A few students at an adjacent table glanced in our direction. As I lowered my voice, they turned away, their hands once again carving out memories of deep powder.

Hunthausen unbuckled his ski boots. Settled in.

"Don't forget what your friend Hans Küng says . . . *simul justus et peccator.*"

"Yeah. The church, at once holy and sinful. You'd think the holy would win out once in a while! But the institution doesn't care what I think, or what the people want. Oh no. None of that matters but their almighty celibacy. Their eleventh commandment, which they carted off the mountain behind Moses. Heavier than the stone it was carved into. No matter. Küng was right on that one, too. The law is immoral!"

"You know as well as I do, as Roman Catholics we need to have law," he said, slightly irritated.

"That's not what I'm talking about. It's when the law denies freedom and human dignity."

"I just can't agree with you, Mike. Celibacy makes many of us more free, and it's a sign of hope to the world."

"Okay, granted. But you're talking about real celibacy, freely chosen. I'm talking about something else. Most of it's reluctant and in lots of cases no more than comfortable bachelorhood."

Hunthausen kneaded his brow, the way he often did when wrestling with whether or not to say something. He let out a long sigh and remained silent.

Outside, a purple hue reflected off the icicles encircling the chalet, matching my mood. A Sno-Cat, its lights bobbing along like yo-yos, passed beneath vacant ski chairs.

"Sometimes I feel at the heart of the institutional church there's nothing but ice," I said regretfully, but unable to soften my feelings.

"Why even stay with it? We say lofty things but when push comes to shove, the bottom line is preservation of the system."

Hunthausen studied me, a shadow of sadness just behind his gaze. For an instant, I wondered whether I had failed him, disappointed the confidence he had placed in me all along.

"Mike, I think you are distorting things a bit, but it's naturally hard for you to be objective."

"Well, why do you stay?" I asked, reaching for the pitcher and pouring a final glass.

His voice was clear. Not at all defensive.

"You mean in the church? For me, it's home. Yours, too. That isn't to say I don't understand when some opt out, but a fire was ignited at the Second Vatican Council and . . ."

"*Aggiornamento*? That's one fire with less heat than that creek out there," I said, knifing through his sentence.

Troubled at my outburst of frustration, he straightened up in the chair, moving closer to the fire.

"The church has her seasons. We're in winter right now."

"Winter kills. Think of all the priests out there who've been clobbered merely because there's a woman in their lives. Look at what Curtiss will do to an entire parish. It's not just him. Paul Metzner is still at it. Broderick tells me there's a bunch of them that can barely conceal their glee with my getting the boot. And Joan—talk about scandal! The hypocrisy of the church has stripped away her innocence!"

"Careful. You're sounding less and less like yourself and more like someone on a crusade."

While suggesting my sentiments were understandable, the archbishop maintained they were too harsh.

"Don't forget that beneath that snow out there, the flowers of spring are already starting to grow. Whatever you do, Mike, leave room for others—that includes Elden—to change."

I had said enough, and in the morning would probably regret it. Still, I wondered if this time winter hadn't lasted too long.

When I told Tim about the importance Hunthausen gave to involving not only the parish but also the priests in our efforts to reverse Curtiss's decree, he agreed at once. Even more than the archbishop, he remained convinced that without their backing, we would fail. Yet we were faced with the fact that several former supporters had reversed themselves 360 degrees with the advent of the episcopacy of Elden Curtiss. This, combined with what appeared to be a lack of concern for our plight among the majority of the clergy, left us skeptical about marshaling much assistance. We were pleasantly surprised. As the days wore on, first a handful among them and then more began laying their opposition at the chancery doorstep. Gradually the wheels creaked into motion in an effort to bring our case before the Senate of Priests.

If support was slow to mobilize among the clergy, just the opposite was true within Resurrection. By the time the parish council convened to settle on a way to approach the crisis, an avalanche of individual letters questioning his decision had already reached the desk of Bishop Curtiss.

"I can remember, growing up—to question church authority was a capital sin," Drake Shepler said, leafing through a stack of carbon-copied letters sent to the council. "These people have to feel mighty strongly about this even to write a bishop—much less say what they do. Just listen to this."

Like a monk chanting a contemporary litany, he went through a psalter of words, characterizing the mood of the mail.

"Hurt . . . troubled . . . disgusted . . . shock . . . pain . . . anxiety . . . sorrow . . . pity . . . tragedy . . . loss . . . damage . . . horrid . . . error . . . injustice . . . shock . . . shame . . . ! That's the one that really gets to me," he added. "Shame."

Next to him, Yvonne Shepler dabbed her eyes, then straightened up, taking the stack from her husband.

"There are other feelings in here, too. Like reconsider . . . reverse . . . Listen," she said, turning toward Joan, "also, gentle woman, inspirational, mother, friend."

Around the table, others related the personal stories of housewives, students, and friends who continued to protest what was generally acknowledged as a bombshell.

Tie loosened, sleeves rolled up, Shepler looked like he had been through the wringer and then some. He managed to toss a smile at Tim.

"No denying it. People here see you two as a team. We all do. No one is about to stand by and see it destroyed. Just look through those letters. Even the bishop can't ignore this kind of outcry. He's bitten off more than he can chew."

Jane Harlow cut in, her voice changing octaves as it did whenever she felt intensely about something—which was often.

"Sometimes I regret getting elected to this group. Our phone's been ringing off the wall. Folks just don't understand what all the big fuss is about. They agree that having a married priest is valuable; then again, no one knocks celibacy. It's just not that important to them one way or another."

Just across the table from her, Tim piped in, pretending to be wounded by the strawberry blonde's candor.

"Here I am, celibate for twenty years, and it's not that important one way or the other she says!"

Everyone lightened up for an instant, happy for the chance to do so.

"Well, if it will make you feel better, Tim," Yvonne said, shuffling through the stack of letters, "there are a few in here who admit to being mighty shocked when they found out one of the priests was married. In fact, one lady said she was in the parish a year before she even knew it. She was in line behind Joan for communion. You must have been seven or eight months pregnant, Joan, because she mentioned it. Anyway, when she heard Mike say, 'Honey—the Body of Christ,' she started asking around. It was a jolt. By that time she was so taken with the place that she sat down and asked herself what difference did it make and decided none."

"That's supposed to make me feel better?" Tim winced, a broad grin spreading across his face.

This time the room exploded with laughter, with the exception of Kirby Walsh. Preoccupied, he leaned forward, elbows on the table.

"All kidding aside, we're talking about the bottom line here. Celibacy is not the issue and Curtiss has to realize that. It's more a question of whether or not the men at the top will listen to us or anyone for that matter. What the church needs today is a massive act of faith— not in its structures, but in its own people."

After the topic had been batted back and forth repeatedly, Kevin Doherty brought up the question raised a week earlier.

"Okay. No one disagrees that we want to keep Mike and Joan with us, but . . ." He turned to me, unfolding his hands much as a priest about to pray. "What do you want to do?"

Throughout the week we had been over it again and again. In a sense, it would be easier if we bowed out quietly. Besides, we knew resistance might well produce fallout that would affect the entire community, troubling families which already had enough concerns; drawing taut the frail thread between belief and unbelief. Just how far we could permit Resurrection to move down the uncertain road of confrontation weighed heavily on us. Then again, neither of us relished the prospect of admitting that—faced with the iron glove of ecclesiastical power—in the eleventh hour we had backed away from our deepest convictions.

Joan nudged me beneath the table. They were waiting for an answer.

"What do we want? To be left alone by all of them. To be free to minister, supported instead of feared by the bishop and clergy. Not viewed as so much straw to be thrown into the fire," I said.

Barely audible, Joan started to respond. The room grew still.

"Curtiss, and whoever else is so upset with us, can't be allowed to succeed in this. If they do, it's like raising a victory flag over the chancery proclaiming that Archbishop Hunthausen and all of us were wrong and that those at the top of the clerical heap—who always have to be right—are right once again!"

Her voice trembling, she asked me to continue.

"I guess you get the point. None of us wants an explosion, but deep in the marrow of my bones I really feel called to be a priest. Nowhere in talking with you or in the most personal times of prayer, have I had any inkling that it's God's will for me to get out."

"So what are you saying?" Kevin prodded.

"That religion is more than crossing *t*'s and dotting *i*'s."

"And?"

"That rather than kick the dust off our sandals and move on, we want to stay and face them head on, not just for us, but for you and for the sake of the faith our kids will inherit. Only, though, if you want us to."

Kevin let out a low whistle. "Whew. Need you ask? Believe me, we want you."

"Amen," Jane Harlow added.

Around the table the sentiment was unanimous.

Before adjourning, someone suggested that Bishop Curtiss might indeed be subject to pressures none of us were fully sensitive to. Therefore, it was imperative to request an immediate meeting with him, with the hope of opening lines of communication to seek a way around the crisis.

John Barry agreed to draft the invitation. As an established and sought-after attorney, Barry being legal counsel to the diocese, would be guaranteed an open ear in Helena. The invitation would outline the council's major reasons for objecting to the termination, while remaining sensitive to the awkward position my ministry imposed upon the bishop.

A direction had been established.

Once alone in the center, Joan and I glanced through a stack of letters Yvonne had set out for us. One of them, written in pencil with several erasures, covered an entire page.

> Dear Bishop:
>
> We are only kids from the parish. Five of us have received our first communion from Father Mike. The sixth was baptised by him. We are good friends of his and Joan's, too. He has a tiny girl, Michelle, that he wants to raise Catholic. We really like them. They are very nice persons.
>
> We thought you would like to know that everybody comes to hear Father Mike talk. He is a good priest and without him our church would be lost.

The unevenly scrawled note was signed by six children, not yet in their teens.

Eyes moist, Joan pointed at the bottom of the page.

> P.S. Please listen to us. Please answer us.

The only answer from the bishop's house was no answer at all. The flood of letters, now joined by those of former parishioners scattered throughout the country, was greeted with nothing but silence.

Although the issue continued to plague the parish, preparations for Easter Week blunted the questions still hounding me. All but one would be pushed aside. If the Holy Spirit was involved with Resurrection and if the precedent we created was ultimately for the good of the church, then why were we in constant conflict with that same church? Was it possible that the Holy Spirit was not with us at all? In fact, was trying to tell us so? Then again, a mustard seed must have been planted because something vibrant and good was growing. Then there were Joan and Michelle. Whenever I looked at them, there was no way to say what we had done was all wrong. While there might be many roads to the one God, I knew of none without love. How then explain the abrasive tension with the institutional church? An unexpected note hinted in part at the answer.

The card was from my cousin, a Franciscan priest who ever since our ordination together had been laboring among the Papago tribes in Arizona. His brief message seared me to the core.

> Sorry about the hassle up there. It's called "breaking the bread."
> A tough but necessary part of the process of being consumed, and that's what priesthood is about anyway. *So don't start feeling sorry for yourself.* You're only getting what we asked for back there ten years ago when Hunthausen laid his hands upon us.

He was right, yet I wished he was wrong and prayed that ours would not be the path of the gospel's burnt men. One that would wind directly into the mouth of consuming fire.

Toward the end of Lent, Bishop Curtiss still had not responded to any of the hundreds of letters reportedly piled upon his desk, among them, that of Forrest Ullman.

Forrest made a point of coming to the center one afternoon for what I guessed was an effort to show me his composition.

> Most Reverend Bishop:
> It is regrettable that such a letter as this must be written and incidentally it is the first one of this nature I have ever had to write during my nearly eighty years as a member of the Catholic Faith.
>
> I was born and reared in the Gallatin Valley and attended Mass here as a child. I have learned more about Jesus and the Bible in the 4 or 5 years I have attended Resurrection Parish than in all the years before.
>
> I now know that God loves me, instead of waiting for me to commit a mortal sin to cast me in an ever-burning hell. My life has been changed after years of fear. Now I am not afraid.
>
> The men who are responsible for this wonderful parish are Father Mike and Father Tim. To terminate Father Mike's ser-

vices under the conditions you have spelled would be a grave mistake and surely a disaster for all of us here.

I thanked him, still not sure why he had come. Forrest seemed as shaky as his script. He revealed that, impatient with the lack of response, he had called the chancery office. He was informed that Curtiss was out and would not return the call; that the issue was to be handled by the proper authorities and not the laity.

His voice cracked as he took the letter back into his gnarled hands.

"I attended mass even before any Catholic steeple was in this valley. All my kids went to parochial schools. We've always tried to give money and time . . . then to be told to mind my place!"

Embarrassed for his sake, I implied it was probably all an unfortunate mistake; most likely he had got a crotchety secretary. He would have none of my excuses. Shorter than me, Forrest reached up and put an arm around my shoulder. There was no avoiding his eyes, but then there was no need to. They were twinkling.

"Know what, Father? I'm not afraid anymore. When do we picket the chancery? I'll lead the charge!"

Without another word, he turned, hobbling away on his cane.

Although letters from the community continued to go unheeded, one did receive a response. When John Barry called asking to see Tim and me, we both knew that whatever the reply was, it was not good.

Normally leprechaun-like, with a hint of glee about to break out, Barry was somber when he slumped into the booth at the Bacchus Pub. In his letter to Bishop Curtiss—written on behalf of the parish council—he had suggested that, in light of the community's anxiety over the termination, the bishop agree to celebrate Sunday mass with the parish and then meet with the council afterward.

John spun a damp mug around, leaving a mosaic of rings across the table.

"Chrissake . . . ah, excuse me . . . but geez, it was all fairly simple. Something must have really set His Excellency off. All I can think of is I mentioned that as a lawyer it looked like due process was not being observed in Mike's case and we wanted to talk with him about it. Anyway, I got a call today from someone up there telling me a letter was on its way from the chancery. I'm fired as the attorney for the diocese. No reason given, just boom, like that!" He slapped his hand down with a loud crack and then started to grin. "No doubt about it, the guy plays for keeps. Wonder if he bothered to check before canning me to notice that all these years I've been doing their legal work free of charge!''

As always, Holy Week molded the community together in an attempt to find fresh ways to express its drama. One proclaiming victory over defeat. Hope over despair. Life over death. The Good News.

Whether it was weaving splashy banners, baking bread for Holy Thursday, or putting the finishing touches on a contemporary film-and-sound Passion meditation, everyone wanted to be involved and to forget.

From the moment groups of self-conscious and giggling children began distributing palms to the rising crescendo of ''Hosanna,'' until three dancers converged to light the paschal candle on Easter morning, the week came together with a power that each year surprised me. Invited to write and lecture nationally on Resurrection's liturgy, I had yet to find a way to put the joyous experience into words. This time the joy would be short-lived.

While all signs pointed to it, it was not until the bishop broke his silence with a letter scratched out on Easter eve that we knew for sure that the clash we had hoped to avoid was imminent. There was little question that the hundreds of appeals he received from the people themselves had had little impact.

Once again, Curtiss pledged to remove Tim and see to it that my future in Catholicism would be thwarted if we failed to cooperate. Such cooperation on my part included a new twist. Not only would I be removed from the parish, but I was also to state publicly that we had circumvented the law.

Curtiss concluded—

''If I must stand alone on this issue, which I am prepared to do, then the results will be devastating to everyone involved. I am prepared at this time to revamp the entire structure at Resurrection and start over if it is necessary.''

An unsettling shadow passed over Tim's face.

''Well, at least he's accepted the invite to meet with the council.''

''We've got to tell them the stakes as soon as possible,'' I said, trying to keep the lid on my despondency.

Although the council knew of my desire to resist, Tim and I both realized little choice remained but to tell them what sanctions might be leveled if we carried out our resolve.

We again convened the parish representatives. While Tim read aloud the bishop's letter, the faces around the table remained expressionless. Kevin Doherty asked if Curtiss was suggesting he would excommunicate people. Reluctantly Tim and I nodded, knowing full well that everyone in the room had been raised in fear of this, the church's most extreme sanction. Looking around, I was surprised to see just how far Catholicism had come. Even though they'd just heard a bishop of their church clearly suggest the ultimate weapon, their faces reflected concern but little fear. The penalties reminiscent of a church from a different age failed to have their expected impact on one still struggling to be born.

Jane Harlow tossed a pencil against the table, her dark eyes flashing.

"While we're celebrating Holy Week that guy's up in Helena cranking out a love letter! God, I just can't believe this!"

Others began to echo similar sentiments, but Jane wasn't finished.

"He wants Mike to make a public apology and then he's still going to toss him out. Then if we speak up, he'll go after us. We're supposed to sit there pretending wrong is right, then cuddle up like chickens under his wing! What's it coming to when the church is so desperate that it has to start throwing out entire parishes! Well, he won't be able to do it. What's he going to do, take away the building? Fine. Let him. He can't take away God or rip us away from one another."

Such sentiments became a chorus, giving vent to suppressed feelings of disbelief and anger. Not until Drake Shepler pointed out that in agreeing to meet with the council the bishop had left an opening for resolution, did the mood shift. By the conclusion of the hastily arranged session, everyone seemed determined to meet with Elden Curtiss promptly and to do so in an atmosphere of cordiality. In the meantime, I agreed to visit with him alone. The reasons were compelling. By assuring him that the parish leadership wanted to work things out and avoid a deepening crisis, it might diffuse some tension before his journey to Resurrection.

Once the room was empty, Tim asked me to remain behind. Clearly something was still eating at him.

He struck a match and lit one of his rare cigarettes, sitting back with his feet propped up on the table.

"I think it was a good idea that neither you nor Joan said much tonight. What amazed me was none of them even suggested that you should fold up your tents and step aside. No one crumbled!"

"Yeah, but Esther and one or two others looked pretty uptight,"

I said, leaning back on the hind legs of the chair, wondering what he was getting at.

Before long, Tim was chatting about his widowed mother, her life wrapped around devotion to the church. Both of us knew how important it was for Irish mothers to have a priest in the family. Tim was Eileen O'Mera's pride and joy.

"Needless to say, she's having a helluva time with this thing. She can't understand it at all. For Mom, any bishop is the next thing to God. She'd come unglued if she got wind that I might be suspended."

I wanted to say that, if anything, Eileen O'Mera was a survivor, but remained silent.

Tim drew on his cigarette, as if trying to swallow what was inside him.

"It's not so much her as the parish. Shit. How can I say this? We've been friends for twenty years, but . . . well, you know."

I shook my head. "I'm not sure I do."

"It wouldn't bother me that much if Elden tried to suspend me," he continued gravely. "I'm more worried about the parish. We're talking about a couple of thousand people. It could be worse than we think. Can you imagine one of the university kids going home on vacation and saying, 'Guess what I did last week, folks? Got myself excommunicated!' "

The way it came out started the two of us laughing, but not for long.

"Come on, Tim. Curtiss is bluffing. That's one threat even he couldn't get away with. It's what I was trying to hint at tonight."

His lips tightened.

"I wish you were right. Honestly, I believe he's reckless enough to try it if we dig our heels in. God almighty, we just can't stand by and let that happen. If it ever came to that . . ." He paused.

"That's where you draw the line?"

"Yeah. At that point, we'd have to split company. I wouldn't be able to support you that far," he said, exhaling and grinding the cigarette against the side of an ashtray.

Tim filled in the blanks. Even though the parish was united, if it came down to outright defiance of the bishop's orders, the threads of unity might come unraveled.

We both agreed such a scenario could happen. What was essentially a conflict with authority might easily divide the community within itself. Neither of us wanted to see it go to such lengths. Still, something was askew. I decided to stop tiptoeing around and follow a hunch.

"What will split the parish is if we are divided on whether or not to take a stand. Somehow I feel all of this has more to do with you than just concern for your mother . . . or Resurrection."

He sat back, crossed his legs.

"What do you mean?"

"I'm not sure. Just that you're talking about backing off pretty early in the game."

Tim's head bobbed up and down in agreement, as if he had suddenly stumbled on something in front of him all along.

"Maybe. You know I like to play things safe. Cover all the bases. I guess when it comes down to it, it's a personal thing with me. I might argue with Elden and try to change his mind, but there's a point where I can't just say no to my own bishop," he said carefully.

Closing in on the heart of things, neither of us wanted to bruise the other in the process.

"I'm not sure what you're saying," I said.

He cleared his throat, eyelids fluttering.

"Perhaps it's a cop-out, but saying no would go against my conscience. In a sense it would separate me from the church to defy my own bishop."

"No doubt Curtiss is counting on that with both of us," I said, struggling against an impulse to argue it all out. After all, why were our integrity and faith being called into question for standing up against what we perceived as a serious injustice and a departure from basic values? Did obedience mean carrying out the dictates of authority even if it also meant trampling on the faith and convictions of an entire parish?

It wasn't the time to argue. Only one more question remained.

"What if the parish decides to say no to Elden?"

"They'd have to do it without me." He chuckled half-heartedly. "You know something? We're in different circumstances. Tonight you can leave here and go home to Joan. All I've got is the ministry. When I die, there won't be a Michelle to weep over my grave—I hope you understand."

It had been an intense half-hour. Although Tim had drawn his line, we both prayed the time would never come where we would be forced to stand on opposite sides of it.

Seated in the waiting room adjacent to the episcopal office, I felt torn. On the one hand, there was an undeniable friction between the bishop and me, as natural as that of flint against stone. Then again, I felt a begrudging affinity for him, spawned by his dogged determination and flamboyance. One thing was for certain, I thought, as his door swung open, Elden Curtiss might be many things but he was never dull.

His greeting was brusque and cool. We sat, but not before he pointed out a mound of manila folders on his desk.

"Letters from Bozeman! Thank God they at least sent them to me and not the press. That's about the only good thing about them. If we needed any proof that that bunch of yours is confused, we have it now. Nearly every letter refers to you as a priest. How many times have I said they see you in priestly ministry? Well, now I have the documentation to prove it."

"Oh, for crying out loud!" I said, not concealing my frustration. "Do we have to go through this again? You're missing the forest for the trees. They're just trying to tell you how they feel, and . . ."

He cut in.

"The whole foolish letter thing is probably orchestrated by you anyway. Then you want me to trust you. Why should I, with all this going on?"

Before I could protest, he was already turning another page in his agenda. Moving brittlely to the desk, he returned with a stack of mail, tossing it on the floor in front of me.

"Your fans. Take a look. They're all the same. My God, it sounds like you have a cult going on down there. Did you ever teach them that the Lord does the work and gets the credit, not us? That he works through us; that any one priest can replace another? These letters go on and on about you and Tim as if they can't live without you! It's ridiculous."

Again I started to say something, but like a Roman candle the bishop continued to explode. Rather than erupt with him, I surrendered to a certain sadness for the man across from me; a pity based on my conviction that both of us were victims of our times and circumstances.

"You know what you've been pushing in that parish, mister? It's not the Church of Rome, but a cult of personality! Ninety-five percent of that crew would follow you and O'Mera even if you set up for Holy Mass out in a field somewhere."

He sat down, struggling to control his anger.

"I may have to purge them yet."

Over the next several minutes he covered everything from my alleged anti-Roman reputation to permitting those who had been divorced and remarried to receive the Eucharist. Again he sprang from his chair and retrieved a few news clippings from his desk.

"And look at these! Saying how you celebrated this wedding, or that funeral. People are upset!"

"People?"

"Not just priests," he shouted, flipping the articles onto a coffee table. "Although you should know, most of them feel you're a man who doesn't keep his word."

"I'm not tracking you."

"The agreements about presiding."

"Tim was at those weddings, too!" I replied, more frustrated than angry.

"Big deal, if you still do most of the ceremony!"

Curtiss rose, pushing back against the chair, his knuckles white.

"We've been over this before. It can't go on. People all over the diocese still see you as a priest."

"I am."

"You know what I mean. If there are distinctions, no one seems to notice or care. You've made it into a farce."

"Well, what the hell is it if it isn't just that?"

Neither of us looked away from each other as for an instant the comedy of our mutual fate seemed to show its face.

I seized the opportunity to tell him that in his accepting the invitation to meet with the parish council, the road to reconciliation was now open.

At the suggestion, his clenched fists relaxed. The white tips of his knuckles dissolved. Where seconds before we were spinning down into the same old vortex, the bishop reversed himself. Sitting down with a slight smile, he pushed at the letters strewn on the floor with the toe of his shoe.

"I tend to get carried away, but these things just show they don't understand the Church of Rome."

Whether he was expecting me to announce that the parish was about to bolt into schism, fighting to the last man, woman and child, or simply that his momentum was spent, he seemed enormously relieved. The mood in the room shifted dramatically, revealing another side of the man but one no less complex. Suddenly he was no longer a representative of the official church speaking to a defrocked priest, rather—if not quite as one man to another—certainly as cleric to cleric.

"We're dealing with the laity's ignorance of such matters. Their shallowness if you will. They have to understand I'm trapped. I can't act unilaterally on the celibacy requirement, even if I wanted to,'' Curtiss said, unfolding his arms, revealing dark spots of perspiration.

"That requirement's immoral. Whether you agree or not, we've found a way around it and can't simply stand by now and watch it die."

Sensing he would listen, one by one I touched upon the stones that constituted the wall between us, beginning with the Second Vatican Council, which repeatedly admonished those in power to hear to the voice of its people. A Council that envisioned priests immersed in the life and conditions of this world. Not strangers, but servants willing to take on the tasks of Catholicism's renewal; tasks whose importance would be proportionate to their difficulty. A Council prepared to blow layers of dust away from the gospel, unleashing its power once again.

Curtiss listened intently, appearing to step out of his episcopal role. The more personal I became, the more often he nodded his head. He seemed to appreciate what it meant to feel called to the life of the priest, called at times in spite of oneself. Of being seized by something or someone far bigger than either of us.

Yet if there was a common ground, it started to shift beneath us.

"You know, Mike, all of this aside, it really is a shame you got married. We could've used someone like you for bigger things in the church."

"Run that by me again."

"Well, maybe I shouldn't ask this. But . . ." He paused momentarily then leaned forward intently. "Tell me. While you were trying to decide whether or not to marry, did you ever consider that someday you might have become a bishop?"

"If you mean did I go into this with my eyes open? Yeah. Sure."

He sat back, folding his arms behind his head.

In the long silence which followed, he stared flatly at the ceiling overhead. While touched by his attempt to share something personal, I was at once put off. Eventually he seemed to notice, continuing with a conciliatory tone.

"In a way, it's not fair that both of us should be taking the flak on this, when the archbishop . . ."

The fragile balance holding our conversation together wobbled at the mention of Hunthausen.

"If it's necessary for me to say he was wrong—publicly—I'll do it. You know, they're keeping an eye on him . . ."

When I asked who "they" were, his hand shot out as if to swat down the question like a fly in the air. He thought for a moment before responding that the apostolic delegate was "watching Hunthausen like a hawk" to see that he remained in line.

"Dutch takes the gospel seriously," I said nervously. "If those above him can't deal with that, there's something wrong with them, not him."

"If the Vatican had known he permitted you to stay, he would never have made archbishop. That's a fact," Curtiss added quietly, almost secretly.

"But he'll go to heaven, that's for sure."

Curtiss blinked, flashing a porcelain grin.

"God, but you're an idealist! Sure. In the long run, I suppose. But that's not the point."

As always, he was faithful to his background and training. So too, I thought, were we all.

Just then his secretary buzzed. An appointment was waiting. Placing a hand on my shoulder, Curtiss escorted me to the door.

"At least you can appreciate my position. When it comes to church law, there's no choice. Can you imagine what would happen if we didn't carry through on you? I'd be in hot water! Look at Broderick. He's done himself real harm by being part of this."

The muscles along my back tightened at the prospect of the chancellor's career going down the drain along with us.

"Anyway," the bishop continued in a singsong tone, "after you are out of that parish, we'll all be better off. Take a year or two out, then maybe we can find something for you to do. It would be a shame to lose you altogether."

It was confusing. Either he had mistaken my suggestion at reconciliation for acquiescence, or he was pushing his same decision but more gently.

I turned around, seeing the stack of parish letters scattered on the floor.

"Just so we understand one another. The feelings in those are genuine. The council is willing to talk about the termination. No one is accepting it."

His only response was a trace of tension spreading across his face, with a glint of the now familiar fear. Once again I wondered if by leading the Trojan horse of institutional conformity into the diocese, he underestimated the Curia inside it, which now threatened him as well as the rest of us.

* * *

Leery of any publicity, the parish council agreed to Bishop Curtiss's request for a closed meeting. Arriving alone, he took a seat on the edge of the circle. Throughout the introductions, he seemed distracted, staring into the main arena of the center, where a large banner, proclaiming "He Is Risen, Allelujah," bore the face of Christ.

Anxious to begin, Curtiss distributed individual packets containing "documents" pertaining to the case. Although my last impression of him had been of a man relieved at the prospect of communication rather than confrontation, there was little evidence of this as he launched into what amounted to a blistering lecture to the council.

As one accustomed to control, the bishop made it clear from the outset that the termination was irreversible. The normal Vatican rescript refusing priestly ministry to a man contracting marriage had been ignored. It was necessary to respond to the "technical" scandal existing in the parish and erase the confusion.

Surprised by the barrage but mustering a diplomatic air, Drake Shepler finally interjected.

"Frankly, Your Excellency, you're making it sound like a dead issue. We thought you came to talk this through, to see if we could work it all out. We represent over two thousand people in this community who disagree with the firing of Mike. You have hundreds of letters, and . . ."

"Letters of defiance!" Curtiss stammered, unable to relax.

His jaw tight, an equally determined Drake Shepler insisted that as a Catholic parish Resurrection had a right to be heard. In return, the bishop fired still another salvo.

"Please quit referring to it as your parish! It is first and foremost mine. That's basic ecclesiology. Besides, you can't call yourselves Catholic unless you are in union with my will. To be in disharmony with me is to be fractured from the church herself."

Convinced that Curtiss needed to clear all personal agenda from his docket, Shepler backed off. No one said a word until the bishop wound down. At that point, Bill Leason gathered together the threads of the council's own agenda.

Peering over his glasses, the young, normally laid-back professor of business sought to dispel a few assumptions.

"If there is any confusion—as you put it—about Mike's role here, it's coming from outside the parish, not within. We know he's a priest, for Pete's sake."

"There it is again!" Curtiss said, slapping his hands together. "How many times do I have to tell you. The scandal here is that you still want him as a priest."

Leason feigned a smile.

"The only scandal is the way the church keeps hounding him."

Beneath the surface, Curtiss seethed. Trapped by his own frustration, Leason appeared not to notice. Shepler did.

"Bishop, we know how difficult it must be for you to just walk in here alone. You're to be complimented. Some of us thought you might come with a small army," he said, managing a grin.

A pencil-thin smile etched across Curtiss's face. "Well, to be honest, it did feel like walking into the lion's den."

All at once both he and the rest of us felt more at ease. Shepler continued.

"If we're really going to lay the cards out on the table, we'll admit there are some in the parish a bit perplexed with Mike's situation. I'm talking about newcomers who are here for quite a while before they find out one of the priests is married. That could be where some of the confusion you refer to is coming from."

For the first time, several others in the circle chimed in, saying more or less the same thing. While newcomers in the parish had to deal with an unprecedented situation, once it was explained to them, there was rarely, if ever, a negative response.

Never one to hold back, Jane Harlow added a footnote.

"Matter of fact, Bishop, most of them say it's high time the church got off its duff!"

The room rippled with nervous laughter.

"No, seriously," she continued, waving for silence, "that's what I hear over and over. It's what my husband says—even Mom, and, believe me, she's not a flaming liberal. She thinks we still should be eating fish on Fridays! But as for Father Mike getting married . . . she's all for it . . . thinks the church is long overdue."

When the bishop disagreed, repeating that because of marriage I could no longer be a priest, the conversation turned full circle and became polarized.

Stephanie Moss, a brunette dietitian and mother of two, could no longer restrain herself. Educated since childhood by nuns, raised in a family which found its center in the faith, her voice now cracked with emotion in an outburst as true to her convictions as it was a surprise.

"I've been a member of this parish from day one. We're not dummies and we aren't going to live a lie, either! Mike's a priest and always will be, no matter what you would like us to believe. I'm tired of the clergy always saying the people are the church, but when it comes down to the nitty-gritty, acting like they own it and the rest of us are just hangers-on!"

Taken back, the bishop glared across the circle at her. She didn't flinch. Nor did any of the women around her. In my mind, I could hear a chorus of female voices echoing from the letters of protest strewn across the chancery floor. Women who, like Stephanie, were proof that the hierarchy was losing its grip. Losing its control over the lives of Catholic women everywhere, suddenly with minds of their own. Now I knew, in part at least, the origin of the familiar shadow of fear which passed over Curtiss's eyes.

In an attempt to smooth things over, Gay Pomeroy took a deep drag from her cigarette, then broke the icy silence.

"Maybe part of the confusion, Your Excellency, lies within the church's teaching. I remember the *Baltimore Catechism* being drilled into me. How did it go? 'Once a priest, always a priest'?"

Curtiss sat up in the chair; his words were measured.

"That's true. Once a man has received the sacrament of Holy Orders, he is a priest forever. Mother Church has always taught that."

Slowly grinding her cigarette out in an ashtray, Pomeroy asked, "How then can your law change that which Catholic doctrine says is unchangeable?"

Curtiss shook his head in disagreement. "In the first place, it's not my law. Rome reserves the option wherein a man can be disposed of his office, deprived of the clerical habit, and permanently reduced to the lay state."

"If I can put that in plain English, it sounds like an invention of law to fit the institution's needs."

"We have to be able to get rid of those who are unfit," he countered.

"You can't imagine the good Mike's doing. How's he unfit?"

"Need we ask?" Moss cut in.

Losing patience, Curtiss pointed in her direction. "If he marries, he forfeits his right to engage in priestly ministry, period!"

Not about to let the opportunity to jump into it again slip by, Moss fought back, her voice shrill but stronger.

"That's not what the church has always taught, though. Even in the Eastern rite, priests are still allowed to marry. If we look at the gospels, they . . .''

"We're talking about the law of the church, young lady. The one you claim to be part of!''

She persisted, pointing at Joan who until that moment had gone unacknowledged by the bishop.

"That same law would even keep Peter, the first pope, out! You're saying Mike can't be a priest because of her. Just because she happens to be a woman. Well, you don't have any idea how much that woman has given to us over the years, or how much we care for them. We've all grown because of their love. Now you come in here and want us to lie down while you tear out their hearts and ours!''

Expecting us to intervene, the bishop looked first to Tim, then to me. Neither of us said anything, having agreed from the evening's outset to stay out of the discussion. If there was a point where the meeting might have come apart, it was just then. However, for some reason no one could later account for, Curtiss checked himself, leaned back, and almost physically removed himself from the mounting tension.

"You misunderstand. I've acknowledged all along that Mike is an excellent minister. So, too, is Father O'Mera. But in the minds of Roman Catholics, a priest is special. He's a sacred person, and being married doesn't . . .''

"Doesn't make him so sacred anymore,'' Moss interjected, wiping away beads of perspiration from her forehead.

Sounding more like a teacher than someone in a heated argument, he continued as though he hadn't heard her.

"Being married makes him, well, the same as everyone else. Don't get me wrong. He's still a priest, but we're talking here about image. About what Catholics have come to expect. Besides, the Holy Father is terribly worried about efforts to desacralize the priesthood. There is a sacredness there. It must be preserved if we are to remain faithful to Christ and his church. That's why celibacy is vital. It points to a sacredness.''

The bishop held up both hands to ward off a chorus of objection. Tim got up and opened a window, sending a cool breeze through the stuffy room.

"I've always thought what made a person a good priest was being a leader. You know, in things of the Spirit,'' Kevin Doherty stammered, searching for words. "I don't know as much about theology as you do, but it seems to me sacredness isn't so important as finding someone who can work with people, preach so we can apply it to our lives, and is a believer in the best sense. If that's what a priest is, then Mike darn well is one!''

His face utterly expressionless, but shaking his head in what appeared at times to be agreement, Curtiss declined to respond.

Terry Doherty looked up from the afghan she had been knitting for as long as any of us could remember. The wholesomely beautiful competitive runner and full-time housewife now took up where her husband left off.

"We know Mike touches us where it matters—in the heart. Yet people like you tell us to ignore all of that and go along with getting rid of him because of Joan and their baby girl. It's so darn stupid it makes me want to scream,'' she protested, waving her needles in the air as if to carve out each word.

Like a mentor admonishing an erring student, Curtiss strained to keep his patience.

"Tradition tells us that the call to ordination is a call to celibacy. There's not one without the other. Rome believes this. We bishops do; therefore, the church does, and you must.''

"Even at the expense of the Eucharist?'' she asked airily.

"I'm not following you.''

"There's already a shortage of priests. Back home they just closed two parishes. No priest, no mass. I was raised to think the Eucharist was more important than celibacy, but I guess I was wrong.''

Frustrated but again catching himself, the bishop explained that it was impossible for Roman Catholics to conceive of priests as married, since their experience failed to include such a precedent.

"Exactly,'' Bill Leason exploded. "That's the point. How can there be a precedent if no one is permitted to have one? What we have here is that very breakthrough. Someone who's given new meaning to the term 'Father.' Don't toss it away!''

Someone else mentioned similar situations, such as communion distributed in the hand and general absolution of sins, without individual confession, in which precedents were first established and only later sanctioned by church law.

Curtiss acknowledged the dilemma. "It's painful for all of us, but if we want to belong to Mother Church, then we have to pay a price.''

The room spilled over with reactions, each in his or her own way objecting to a price which seemed too high.

When it was over, the bishop shrugged.

"There are pressures you have to understand. Believe me, it hurts me as much as you to see Mike have to go."

Grasping what struck him as an opening, Kirby Walsh sought to lower a drawbridge over the moat separating Elden Curtiss from the council.

"Then maybe we don't have to keep throwing away the gifts of men who fall in love. There's not a major corporation in the world that would keep tossing out people with years of training and experience. They'd go bankrupt! But the Vatican does it every day! Well, we can't let it happen here. We want to work with you and find a way to turn this dreadful situation around."

Curtiss hesitated, just long enough for Drake Shepler to add, "Besides, if we don't find a way, the image of Catholic authority will be severely tarnished. You have a chance to emerge as a true leader in this parish and, who knows, maybe the entire American Church."

So it went for the next few moments until the bishop agreed to accept suggestions from the council for a way to salvage the situation. Upon reviewing their proposals, he would meet again in thirty days. With that, he abruptly gathered his stack of documents and excused himself. Without batting an eye, Elden Curtiss had seemingly taken a first step over the moat.

After the center emptied out, I remained behind with Tim to digest the evening. Although the strong support of the parish had apparently persuaded Curtiss to question his course, we both felt that without significant backing from the leadership among the clergy, any attempt to salvage the situation was destined to fail. The Senate of Priests' discussion of our case was now only days away. We agreed; the result of that encounter was crucial.

By the time I arrived home it was after midnight. Still preoccupied, I flicked on a light only to stumble over Michelle's shoes lined up toe-to-toe on the stairway. Weary, I sat down next to them, toying with the frayed laces. In the stillness which comes only from a house asleep, each scuffed shoe began to tell me something. A full day had passed without my seeing our daughter. Even during those days in which I did, she was all but lost in my focus on our latest struggle with the church. I tried to picture her, only to find the tiny face eluding me.

Upstairs, I placed the shoes next to Michelle's crib, waiting in the darkness until the shadows dissolved from her fine, shoulder-length hair. I brushed it away from her face, feeling the privileged softness of a child's skin and promised never to forget her again.

Crawling beneath the comforter, I pressed against Joan, felt her breath, which seemed as one with Michelle's a room away. Wanting to tell her I was sorry, I sought out her lips through the inky blackness. Kissing them lightly, I sensed there how much we had aged.

As a member of the Senate of Priests, Tim traveled up through the Swan Valley along the rim of the Bob Marshall Wilderness and into Kalispell. When he phoned us to report on the proceedings, he seemed markedly relieved. Serving as a barometer for clergy throughout the diocese, the Senate reported widespread anxiety over the termination. Conjecture as to its wisdom further aggravated an ongoing morale problem and was creating conflicts between friends. Some felt the situation was out of hand, ecclesiastical law, in their view, having been seriously breached. Others insisted that the whole affair raised questions so fundamental to the central mission of Catholicism that the termination could be viewed as nothing less than a tragic mistake.

Tim shouted through the receiver as he always did when talking long distance, "Talk about opening a can of worms! No one questioned the value of your work, though most admitted they didn't know what, de facto, you really do. Some of the most supportive have been in our parish and that really helped, though what they reported seeing raised a few eyebrows here."

The senators debated for an entire afternoon, during which the bishop complained again of pressure from the apostolic delegate and hinted at still more from the Vatican.

Tim continued. "Half the troops think he's bullshitting about all the outside pressure and just doing what he intended to do all along. They see Resurrection as symbolic of the post-Vatican Two era and therefore what happens to all of us as crucial. The big hassle was whether or not you have been faithful to the original setup with Dutch. I assured them you had, but things aren't static. It's evolved. That's the rub with the older crew. In their minds the spirit behind the agreement was too loose. They know you're as much a priest as any of them, but resent the hell out of you working as one."

Still, the major consensus of the Senate appeared to be that the course of events leading to my dismissal ought to be reversed. They adjourned on a unanimous vote, requesting me to appear before them to express a side of the issue they had not heard. Bishop Curtiss agreed, but only after repeating for the record that he would not be pushed or manipulated on a matter which had as much to do with the universal church as with the diocese of Helena.

"Elden said he, not the Senate, would make the decision whether you sink or swim. Needless to say, His Grace was not at all pleased. A guy with his background gets pretty uneasy unless the priests are lined up behind him. He knows the ducks aren't necessarily all in a row. Frankly, I think the old boy's backing down," Tim said, his voice heavy with relief.

"Sounds like it," I answered exuberantly. The bishop had to know that dissatisfaction with his manner and rhetoric was no longer confined to scattered sectors but was spreading. Even religious women were beginning to complain about a clamp-down. The last thing he needed was to get himself boxed into a corner and into a tangle with the Senate. He was beaten.

I wanted to run home and tell Joan it was worth it. Tell her that either it all made sense or it didn't, and that, yes, God was listening and did care. Assure her that there were others out there who would not sit idly by watching our downhill slide. We were going to make it. Not in spite of the church, but because of it!

Drawing a red circle around the fifteenth of May—the Senate's next session—I knelt in front of the altar for a quick prayer of thanks before heading home.

Spring arrived late to the Gallatin Valley, ushering in a spirit of guarded optimism. Things were looking up; there was an undeniable momentum toward reversing the termination. Advised that negotiations with the bishop were under way, the mood within Resurrection inched upward. The council's white papers were nearing completion. Elden Curtiss was in Chicago for the National Bishops Conference. Rome was light years away.

As the pressure eased, we simultaneously began to rediscover ourselves as a family. A new world opened for Michelle, which she attempted to call by name. Whether expressing delight in a nest of robin chicks, or the tickle of grass beneath her feet, each early word tumbling from her lips drew from us an easy joy that was once as dormant as the tulips which now poked their heads through the earth like so many bouquets of lollipops. The cloud obscuring the sunshine in our own lives was slipping away. Saturday, the second week of May, began on just such a note.

Reaching through a shaft of sunlight, Michelle cradled a small glass of juice carefully. Just as the doorbell rang, it slipped from her grasp, spilling across the lunch table. Tim was on the front porch, white as a sheet. Recognizing something amiss, Joan invited him in and folded the French doors to the living room, leaving us alone. He stood with his back to me, thumping a fist quietly against the wall.

"Shit. Oh, dammit to hell!"

"Tim?"

"Dammit anyway!"

"Curtiss?"

"He called me a few minutes ago. He wanted to make sure I got his letter first," he said, staring blankly out the window.

"And . . . ? Come on, what in hell are you talking about?"

He turned, square-jawed and tight, flipping me an envelope bearing the familiar coat of arms.

"You better read it first. The bastards brought out the big guns."

Addressed to Tim and the council, the first line told the story.

The following directives regarding the ministry of Michael Miles have been received from the Roman Congregations for the Doctrine of the Faith and for the Clergy.

I looked away. Through the doors, the sunlight now settling across Joan's hair recalled another day atop the Cliffs of Moher. Cradling Michelle on her lap, Joan tickled her nose, then squeezed her close. How could I tell them? Explain that if not for them, the Vatican would never have heard of Bozeman, would not be so relentless in the chase.

Numbly I read on through the Curia's edicts, given under the seal of Paul VI, Bishop of Rome.

. . . he may not remain in active ministry at Resurrection Parish.

. . . may not exercise a ministerial role reserved for those in Sacred Orders.

. . . may not preach the homily or administer the sacraments.

. . . directed to see that all violations of these directives be eliminated immediately.

. . . consequently . . . Terminate immediately.

The words rolled in front of me, as across an undulating sea.

Rome had come in on the side of Elden Curtiss. In one way it was no surprise. We had survived longer than any of us might have expected. Then again, the intervention caught me emotionally unprepared. Unable to look up, I fought back the tears.

"Whew, they play for keeps, don't they?" I sputtered.

Still white, Tim punched me gently on e shoulder.

"We'll talk later. Right now I've got to line up a handball court and find someone to pound the hell out of."

He bolted for the door and was gone.

Struggling to get hold of myself, I decided not to say anything to Joan until later. Without a word, I took Michelle into the bedroom for her nap and stretched out next to her, totally drained.

Above us the ceiling appeared to move in the same undulation that swept over me while reading the bishop's message. Within moments I drifted off, smelling the salt air of the Irish coast. This time the waters were savage, as the cresting waves lashed at the rocks upon which Joan and I sat laughing, her hair dancing in the wind. A gale came up. Suddenly, out of nowhere, a dark wave rolled high and crashed down, sweeping us into the deep. Through the spray I saw her float by, lunged for her outstretched fingers, and missed as an eddy pulled us both apart and into oblivion.

I woke in a cold sweat, clinging to Michelle's tiny hand, curled within my own. Unnerved, I tiptoed into the study surrounded by books, and was strangely comforted by their familiar dust jackets. I ran a finger across the cool leather of my first *Missale Romanum* and a musty copy of Bernanos's *Diary of a Country Priest*. Longing for what seemed far simpler times, I hesitated, then dialed the bishop's residence. He answered on the first ring.

"Bishop here."

The receiver shaking, I asked him about the Roman Congregations. His response was flat. We might have been discussing the weather.

"I ran into the delegate in Chicago. He passed on the news. Said he's never seen the Vatican so adamant on anything."

"What'd he do? Call in the Curia?"

"No, not at all. He's just an errand boy in this one, like I am. It's over both our heads."

Impatient with the matter-of-fact conversation, I lashed out.

"You act like it was a surprise, when all along you've both been on our trail like a couple of bloodhounds!"

"It's all I could do to let you stay on till the end of June. They wanted you out at once!" he spat back.

"Well, it's what you wanted. You probably invited them in!" I blurted seething with frustration.

There was a stony silence. For an instant I thought he'd hung up.

"I'll let that pass. You're not the only one hurt by Rome's intervention. Nothing good can come out of it. Not for the church. For the parish there. For the diocese. Nor for me."

"Not for you! Are you kidding? You'll get a medal!"

"How do you think this makes me look? It's my diocese and the Vatican has to step in and handle it for me. Imagine!" he bellowed.

The whole episode was too much. My emotions spilled out in a series of fragmented questions, brought up short when Curtiss informed me that Pat Langley had also been swept away in the wake of things.

"Because of me?"

"Sure. I called him a few hours ago. The poor guy's devastated. He was just getting started and now he's out, too. I tried to tell him that he wasn't the target. You were."

"Jadot should've known that."

"Rome's point is that he can't stay working in the same parish he once served in as a priest. Whether he was just doing the music and some counseling didn't matter. When I talked with Pat he admitted that he'd hoped to eventually work his way back into the priesthood all along. He disappointed me—looks like I underestimated him."

"Me, too," I thought.

I asked if Archbishop Hunthausen knew of the Curia's action. He did not.

The bishop's voice was quiet, laced with a hint of benevolence. "Look, Mike. You have to understand the hierarchy. Many of them feel betrayed by priests who have married. They are angry and have no sympathy for such men. We're lucky to have gotten by here with your case as long as we did."

"We?"

"What?"

"Ah, nothing. Just thinking of the hierarchy you're referring to.

It's tragic to spend a lifetime preaching about love only to end up, when the chips are down, protesting against it.''

Curtiss digressed for some time on the climate among the American bishops and the concern in curial circles that renewal in the United States was unsupervised and moving too rapidly. Half-listening, I inquired about the Senate of Priests and the parish council. What did he intend to do?

"What are you talking about? You don't seem to see that it's all over. So far as the Vatican is concerned, it never happened. As a bishop of the church, I intend to follow the directives without equivocation.''

"Well, folks may have more than a little trouble with that.''

I had touched a raw nerve. At the hint of further resistance, he promised to bring the full weight of his office and the Holy See down on top of me.

"Roma locutor est?" My voice was empty.

"You've got it! Rome has spoken! I'm washing my hands of this whole mess. It's finished!'' He slammed down the receiver.

In the sudden silence, I thought of nights on the back porch with Grandpa when I was a child gazing up into black skies where stars fell like souls from the heavens.

The evening was unseasonably warm. Michelle in her crib, arms wrapped snuggly around her scraggly teddy bear, we settled onto the porch swing. Throughout the day, Joan had given me distance. Only her curious eyes mirrored a suspicion that something significant had happened. She waited. Seasoned in such waitings.

The moon was full, as if pasted flat against the horizon by a huge thumb. For a while we allowed ourselves to float back to a world gone by. Memories of the small logging community of Lincoln. A stag and a doe moving dreamily beneath another moon. When finally I mentioned the Vatican's intervention, she leaned her head against my own. By the time I finished, the moon had slid behind the clouds, carrying with it part of the woman I first knew.

She pushed away from me, the whites of her eyes glistening against the darkness.

"I hate them. Oh, dear God, how I hate them! All I can picture is a cardinal sitting behind his desk in Rome, his belly pushing through a cassock stained with yesterday's lunch. He doesn't care about you, the parish, not even Jesus Christ. Just about his damnable system with its sacred persons! I don't want any part of them, ever again!''

Though we had known our journey might someday suffer such a blow, this time Joan's reaction frightened me. Instinctively, I wanted to protect her; keep intact at least a part of the innocent affection for the church she had carried as a dowry into our lives. That same affection was now in jeopardy. Unable to tolerate its loss, I rushed to offer a series of defenses.

After all, the church was in a period of transition. Only the most naïve would have expected us to survive as long as we did. Rome was full of good men anxious to serve the church. It wasn't so much a question of malice or fault as the times themselves. From the Vatican on down, all of us were caught up in the tumult of an advancing era. Change would come, but not overnight.

No matter what I said, there was no denying that a cord deep within her had stretched too far, once too often, and snapped. Despite my outcry, her once-consuming affection for the church was forever lost.

Joan sat up on the edge of the swing, her back straight and full of resolve.

"I don't know what it is," she said, matter-of-factly, her face milked dry of emotion. "Maybe it's that I'm a woman and they've gone after my man for too long. In ways, I just expected more of them. Anyway, we'll sort it out someday. For now we have to decide what you're going to do."

My thoughts raced back to the rector's office at Mount Angel Seminary. After being reminded that the people of Resurrection would go to the wall for what they believed, the bishop-elect had hesitated not in the least. Smiling, he warned me that if they did, they had best be prepared for what they found there. We were now face up against that very wall.

When I failed to answer her question, Joan asked if Curtiss might ignore the Curia. We both knew the answer. He would stand firm, and if necessary carry through with his threat to disband the parish. Already against the wall, we were being pushed into its corner.

I reached out taking her hand, praying she at least would cry. She did not but just stared blankly at the darkening sky overhead.

We decided to inform the parish council of the latest developments and in so doing, perhaps find some light for the way ahead.

While their reactions ranged from numbness and shock to outright rage, the common denominator was a sense of betrayal. Everyone agreed there were but two options—rejection of the Vatican's mandate or my resignation. If ever there had been a middle ground, it was gone.

A clear majority sided with Kirby Walsh and Kevin Doherty who urged refusal of the Vatican's orders. A stance which they believed should be carried all the way to testing the bishop's promised retaliation and, if necessary, enduring the consequences. As a very distraught Jane Harlow put it, no other parish was in a better position to make a stand which might make it possible someday for priests elsewhere to marry and remain. In turn, she received strong support for her suggestion that running in the face of danger would be backing down on the faith itself, leaving Resurrection spiritless.

Faced with an accelerating momentum toward defiance, Esther Gilmore cautiously asked the question that could not be avoided.

"What if we do this? You know, stand up and say we won't see Mike and Joanie thrown out? What could happen?" She fidgeted, brushing away imaginary crumbs from the tabletop. "All I've ever wanted to do is live and die a good Catholic!"

Unusually silent until then, Drake Shepler suggested that it could lead to a break with the institutional church.

"Not that we'd be leaving, or even want to. Fact is, we'd be pushed out. There's a difference," he said, as one who had been pondering the repercussions for some time. Then, looking directly at me, he said, "I just wouldn't have believed this of the bishop, of any bishop, but . . . well, pardon the expression—it sounds like he and Rome have been in bed together all along."

When Esther asked Tim what would happen to him, I waited for him to tell about the personal line he had drawn, permitting him to go only so far. But he let the moment pass without comment.

Though the majority in the group pressed passionately for taking a stand, no decision was reached, contingent upon my own.

Everything within me pressed for defiance of the Congregations' decrees. If any discernment could be salvaged, it pointed toward the primacy of love over the church's reliance on coercion.

The council adjourned, giving me forty-eight hours to decide whether to resist the termination or back away from almost certain schism with the Roman Catholic Church. Somewhat desperately, I decided to seek further counsel.

I reached Jeffry Connley, who listened patiently to the summary of events, audibly wincing at the mention of the Vatican intervention.

"Once the hounds of orthodoxy got your scent they just wouldn't give up the chase. To them, getting married made you a rotten apple in the clerical barrel. Even though what's happened has nothing to do with the faith, I'm sure that doesn't make it hurt any less. As for what to do next? Things look pretty bleak . . ."

When I informed him of my desire to hold firm against the Curia and Elden Curtiss, I could picture him shifting his heavy frame uneasily.

"You can only run between the raindrops for so long. Just don't forget you have a family and a future ahead of you. There comes a point, you know, when it's time to say uncle and get on with your life."

He was right. Still, I thought . . . if we had a chance . . .

"You don't think it's worth it, do you, Jeff?"

"In a way, no. They have too many horses."

"And?"

"Well," he said, finally touching what he'd been leading up to, "I'm worried about what will happen to you. They're afraid, Mike, and I can tell you right now, blinding fear calculates and, if pushed, destroys. You defy them and they'll chew you up in little pieces."

No sooner had we hung up than Archbishop Hunthausen returned my call. Like Connley, he listened quietly, at first replying only with a pained silence. Stung, but hardly surprised by the course of events, he sought to console me before lashing out with uncharacteristic anger.

"Not all priests have a call to celibacy. This loss of talent is happening everywhere. It's scandalous. Somehow we have to put the brakes on it!"

When cautioned that he, too, was being watched, he dismissed the warning, insisting that if the law had been stretched in our case, it was in the name of a higher one.

"Archbishop Jadot never once mentioned you to me. Never! I would wager he knew about it all right, but let it pass. Elden should never have gone to Jadot," he said, his voice rising with frustration. "What'd he expect him to do, ignore it? It's easy for any of us to get tied into knots looking out for the church, sometimes forgetting those it's meant to serve. I'm sure Elden's a good and decent man. My guess is, he regrets what's happened."

In the wake of his own intense feelings, it was easier for me to suggest resisting the Congregations' mandates. At once, Hunthausen's tone shifted.

"Much as I empathize with you and the people there, I have to be honest. It would be a terrible mistake to do that."

"We'd try and keep you out of it," I said, misreading him.

"Oh no. Don't worry about me! It's just that the pain it would cause for all of you would be too much."

When I asked if he thought Curtiss would carry through with the threatened reprisals, he didn't hesitate.

"Oh yes. Sure. That's my point."

"That way they win. I resent having to choose between my own conscience and the church. Besides, what happens to us? To renewal?" I protested unconvincingly, knowing all along his loyalty would never permit him to sanction head-on confrontation with the institution.

He paused. I could hear his labored breathing.

"There's no answer to that one, except faith. Do whatever you have to. Just make sure you've prayed about it."

Then, wrestling with whether to continue, he did so with an aggrieved ring to every word.

"Why is it so hard for those in authority—and I include myself —to admit the church makes mistakes? How can we expect others to be honest if we can't even be truthful with ourselves? Dad once told me that life boils down to the choice between love and hate. Certain officials, well intentioned, I'm sure, seem to be coming down on the dark side of this one. Whatever you decide, don't make the same error."

A surge of sadness washed through me. Sadness for all the people of Resurrection; even for Curtiss and the Curia, but most of all for him. I wanted to tell him so.

"Dutch . . ." I stammered.

He waited, but by then a lump as big as a fist had swelled up in my throat.

"I know. Give Joan a hug," he said and hung up.

John of the Cross spoke of the "dark night of the soul." If ever there was such a moment in my life, it came during the final twenty-four hours as the council waited for our decision.

What did I want to do? Clearly the desire to remain in the priesthood was there, but at what cost to Resurrection? The weeks of tension and uncertainty already wearing them down would be nothing compared to what would happen if we rejected the Vatican's demands. Then again, we had to listen to the people; to their outcries of protest and firm commitment to see us remain. Yet again, at what cost? We ran the risk of Curtiss going all the way with his promised action against any and all who refused to obey. What if we did go into schism? Could I live with the subsequent excommunication of those who intended to follow me? How would separation look to us in a year, or in ten years? On the other hand, certainly Doherty, Walsh, and the others were right. If there was ever a time to stand up to the institutional church —for the sake of the church—it was now. Perhaps if we stood firm, other parishes would rally around us. The Vatican would back down or, better yet, face up to the needless loss of priests worldwide. We would win the day.

Then there was the Archbishop of Seattle. While he might support us up to a point, he could never go along with the rush to battle. Yet, what would the ensuing conflict do to him, to his future and those he served?

Above all, there was the dilemma posed by Tim O'Mera, who gave no signs of retreating from the line he had previously drawn. If we stood together, we might succeed in shaking the Vatican's resolve. Although some among the Curia would tolerate the excommunication of those in the parish who stuck with us, even the most resolute among them would shrink at the prospect of the subsequent publicity. Such public exposure could only help spur the now forbidden dialogue on the married priesthood issue and raise the equally significant questions of the role of women and the right of the laity to be heard within the powerful corridors of Catholicism. However, if Tim remained resolute—and there was no reason to believe otherwise—in the crunch, we would end up on opposite sides of the fence and the center might then not hold. The community might well become divided. The dilemma was accentuated by my pledge not to reveal Tim's bottom line to the council unless he chose to do so.

Of course, the other option was for me to step aside, thus sparing us all further trauma. Perhaps my own ego was blurring my obligation of faith. Then again, would such a step be taken out of fear rather than faith? Since fundamental gospel values were at stake, wasn't it time to stand up so that such resistance could give birth to something new?

Nevertheless, deep down within me there still remained a faint vision of the fear formed at childhood and fostered through a lifetime: Excommunication, the institution's final sanction, for most Catholics was a profound tragedy. If schism were to come, even though against our will, could I live with it? Live with it, not only for what it could mean to Resurrection, but equally so for me, Joan, and our children? As a family we would be cut off, set adrift. In my case, most likely denied even a Christian burial by the church. Though willing to go in whatever direction I ultimately followed, Joan knew full well that in the end the choice had to be my own. Could I, would I be able to pay the high price of our convictions?

While these personal instincts scraped against the grain of my background and training, I knew the answer. Though the possibility of such a severe penalty as excommunication loomed ominously, the prospect was not enough to sway my decision. Perhaps I had seen too much of the institution, recalling the words of Hans Küng, *"simul justus et peccator,"* the church was at once holy and sinful. A church composed of fallible men who in themselves were not the living God. A church that mirrored the gospel, but by no means to be equated with the Christ from whom it sprang. Indeed, Christ would find such words as "excommunication" bitter to the taste. Besides, I would be sanctioned not for denying the essentials of faith, but in the name of a law devised and enforced by the whims of man. Regardless of whether Curtiss and the Curia attempted to levy the harshest of penalties, my Catholic faith would remain intact; my heart still attached to the church which was my home as well as theirs. Whether they chose to bury me as a Christian or not seemed trivial when weighed against whether I managed to die as one. However, it was quite another question to submit those closest to me to such a prospect and, perhaps, a shared fate.

When the decision finally came together, it felt totally right, yet tragically wrong. Resurrection deserved more than ridicule and prolonged torment. Tim had stuck by us all along. To expect him now to teeter on the very edge and risk tumbling into our midnight was asking too much. Then, too, there were Joan and Michelle, their lives and futures. In the end there was little choice. Though the decision was a wrenching one, it was not accompanied by a sudden ray of light, or easy assurance, but only a long, painful ache. I could do nothing other than step aside.

In the middle of the night, still restless, I went downstairs for a glass of milk. Within a few hours the council would meet and be advised of the decision.

"Penny for your thoughts."

Startling me, Joan reached her arms about the back of my neck. I tucked her hands beneath my chin, kissed them softly without turning, and said what neither of us wanted to hear.

"You know, Gramps always thought it was a mistake for me to become a priest. Maybe it came from his time in the old country. He wanted me to be a doctor, lawyer, something like that."

"Well, he was wrong," she said, laying her head against my shoulder and swaying gently back and forth.

"Makes no difference," I said, still not wanting to face her. "Looks like it's time to cut the cord."

"End of the line?"

I nodded.

"Good. Over the course of a year your hair's turned white. They're not worth it. Not anymore," she whispered, squeezing close.

"What about the Fat Lady?"

For several moments she didn't answer, her body trembling against mine. When she did, there was a despair in her that hurt as much as the decision. "Oh, she'll be okay. She'll survive . . . she always does."

Arm in arm, we ascended the stairway to the bedroom, where for the first time in what seemed days, I fell asleep. But the night continued with a dream as dark as it was vivid.

Several of us, all men, were in a concentration camp ringed with barbed wire. Our captors, foreign yet familiar. In a random surge of violence, they stormed through the camp, slaughtering any who crossed their path. The chatter of rifle fire came closer. Falling to the ground, I felt footsteps. Sick with fear, I heard a weapon cock, then the world exploded in my head. With the concussion came the awareness that the miss was intentional—to show me they could snuff out my life if they wished. The footsteps faded away.

Kneeling up, I was next to a captive, clad in dungarees like my own. Crew-cut and frail, he planted flowers while telling me of plans for escape circulating through the camp. There was concern about Tim O'Mera, the only son of a widowed mother. We would protect him, not permit his loss in our flight to freedom.

The captive confided that the camp was doomed, even though the wardens refused to admit it. He whispered of bombers coming— "angels from a distance"—which would destroy it all, someday, somehow.

Moved, I noticed another figure, planting flowers alongside. For the first time we observed that although he was dressed as we were, he was not a brother at all, but one of *them*. Standing, he jerked my frail confidant up to face him. Knowing he had been overheard, the old man laughed uneasily. Feigned indifference.

Unconvinced, the captor slid a long, gleaming sword from beneath his fatigues, spinning it through the air in a swath of intimidation. The two men exchanged glances. I prayed it was a bluff, but with horror realized it was not as the sword descended and sliced through his skull, splitting it open with a hollow ring.

I looked away as the victim fell to his knees, grasping for his assassin's hand, only to be thrust aside. Sucking for air, he slid into the mud, his eyes locked in the surprise of death. He was wasted. Utterly and forever wasted.

It began to rain, washing the great pool of blood away. Someone covered him with a white shroud.

I woke with a start, the bed soaked in perspiration, a medieval chant still ringing in my ears.

> **Dies Irae . . . Dies Illa**
> Day of wrath. O day of mourning
> See fulfilled the prophet's warning
> Heaven and earth in ashes mourning
> **Dies Irae . . . Dies Illa**
> What shall I, frail man, be pleading
> Who for me be interceding
> Spare O God your suppliant groaning
> **Dies Irae . . . Dies Illa**

With the choice to step aside, the dark night of my soul was over. In another sense, though, it would never be.

When advised of my decision, Tim was both enormously relieved and shaken. He would not have to stare blankly any longer into the no-man's-land of schism.

The council gathered in the same room in which they would meet with the bishop the following night. I felt the walls closing in, smelling of sweat and coffee grounds. Much like the initial step to the edge of a cold pool, I didn't want to take the plunge. There was little choice.

They listened solemnly, the only interruption being when Jane Harlow thrust a hand to her mouth protesting, "Oh no. Mike . . . no!"

Removing his glasses and rubbing his eyes, Drake Shepler looked as frayed and worn as he sounded.

"I knew it would go this way. Knew it all along. I suppose most of us did."

He then managed an optimistic note. Whether clinging to an instinctive faith in things or simply in the throes of denial, he was utterly sincere. Time was all we needed. They could write an impassioned paper of protest. Seek dialogue with those in authority at every level. There was reason to hope that within a year or so, Joan and I would be back in the parish.

"Who's kidding whom?" Kevin Doherty shot back through pursed lips.

Refusing to accept the decision, he stared across the table with such fierce intensity that I could not look away.

"They're out to get you . . . as you yourself said . . . to sweep it all under the carpet. Give the word and ninety percent of us here and most of the parish will tell Rome to drop dead. Believe me, if you bow out now, you'll never preach another homily, never work as a priest again. For godsakes don't do it!"

Perhaps he was right, though like Shepler I found comfort in denying what was happening.

"Mike?" Doherty pulled me back into the conversation.

"If you want to stay, then we'll write papers and dialogue till we're blue in the face. If that doesn't work, they'll toss you out of here over my dead body! On the other hand, if you want to hang it up, fine. Just don't do it for me, okay?"

I nodded emptily.

"I have something to say," Terry Doherty said, her voice nearly inaudible. "I'm approaching the ultimate disillusionment. We know Mike and Joan are doing this to save our skins."

Bill Carkulus, a sandy-haired, normally reserved professor, interrupted to advise her not to lose faith in a God who would always be there.

Fighting back tears, she pushed back from the table.

"Bill, I know where you and Esther are coming from, but you're in the minority. Besides, if I'm losing faith in anything, it's my fellow Christians. Just watch. If we back off, they'll pick away at the flesh of this parish until it's nothing but a heap of dry bones! Curtiss has indicated all along he doesn't care for this place. After Mike's gone, he'll tighten the screws bit by bit."

Carkulus was not to be denied.

"We can't fight against our own church. I love it too much to go along with that."

"You're not the only one who cares for it," she exclaimed sharply, then added with barely a whisper, "though sometimes I wonder if it hasn't lost its soul."

There was a pregnant silence, then Shepler asked me if the decision was final.

Again I nodded. "Unless you can pull off a miracle and talk them out of it."

"Well, you can be sure that tomorrow night we'll do everything we can. And I for one, and most everyone else here, will go a lot further than that if you change your mind."

Once again, it was Stephanie Moss who startled us all with her dogged persistence.

"We'll try to talk him out of it, but not if we have to handle him with kid gloves. Curtiss has to know that if conformity is the price we have to pay for acceptance in the church—if all he wants is for us to be docile and submissive—then he's barking up the wrong tree. He's got to know what we think and feel!"

Without hesitating, she went on about growing up in Catholic schools that stressed humility and submissiveness. Fostering an atmosphere which led her to assume she must always be in the wrong whenever she questioned authority's wisdom against her own.

Kirby Walsh waited until she finished.

"Whoever's after Mike and Joan won't be interested in what we think. Folks like that are only keen on what we ought to think, and that's not the same at all."

He swallowed a couple of times, fighting off his emotions.

"I'm with Kevin. They'll go through with this outrage over my dead body. I'd ask Mike and Joan to stay but we can't. Good God, they've suffered way too much as it is. So have the people in this . . ."

The tears began streaming down his cheeks. Overcome in the face of his anguish, Joan rushed into my office, closing the door.

Shepler called for an adjournment, leaving everyone thankful the ordeal was over. Kevin Doherty came over to me at once, saying that while he didn't agree, he understood.

*   *   *

That night, Joan's eyes were still bloodshot from emotion, I reached across the bed for her. She came to me quickly, with a sense of urgency. Just before we surrendered to each other, I wondered if instead of celebrating love, we were in fact denying death.

The atmosphere had that particular hushed stillness which comes just before a storm. From the conference room, Drake Shepler looked out at hundreds of empty chairs encircling the altar, row upon row, their stark white backs spreading across the green carpet like a field of tombstones. He turned away, leafing through an ever-present notebook of odds and ends with such determination that one could presume its contents contained a hidden solution to the puzzle before us. Bill Leason doodled pensively on one of the yellow pads placed before each council member. Still others, like Jane Harlow, simply stared straight ahead, lost in their own thoughts.

Before long, Tim opened the glass doors and walked in with Elden Curtiss. While someone took the bishop's coat, Tim settled next to me.

"It's funny. The guy has no idea how close this thing came to blowing up in his face. In his mind the fact that Rome has spoken means it's all over. It hasn't dawned on him that anyone would resist after that—you least of all."

Curtiss moved casually about the circle, oblivious of the anger boiling just beneath the surface. A volcano of feelings rumbled within me. He was probably off the hook, and I resented that nearly as much as I now resented him. Then again, I struggled against myself, fearful that my vision was clouded and unfair. After all, I thought, there were good qualities to the man. He, too, was a victim of a church which moved slowly, leaving all of us little more than footnotes in its vast history. I remained on the outer edge of the circle, sipping a cup of coffee. It was bitter, burning my tongue. The bishop brought up the Vatican's intervention. Subdued and official, he might have been presiding at a wake.

The Sacred Congregations had cut short his willingness to consider proposals to salvage my ministry. Like us, he too had been slighted. In an effort at reconciliation, a priest of their liking would be assigned in my place. He trusted they would understand.

Kirby Walsh loosened his tie. It had been a long day with counseling appointments stretching back to back. He waited until the bishop finished.

"Maybe you ought to hear what we have to say. It would be refreshing to have the official church not only dictate but listen for a change."

Curtiss's apparent resolve to come not as an adversary but a mutual victim folded at once.

"I didn't come here to debate the wisdom of the termination, just to inform you of the reasoning behind it. Besides, I know what you all feel," he sputtered, obviously furious. "I've read hundreds of letters from here, many of them insulting and ill-informed. It's you people who need to do some listening. You have no idea what it means for me to get orders from the highest levels of the Vatican. All you think about is your own little corner of the world!"

An impatient frown spread across Walsh's face.

"You want us to believe that you had no idea that the Vatican was waiting at the door like a hound on the scent? That even though you've been on our case from day one, that it all came as a bolt out of the blue?"

"Facts are facts!"

"There are facts and there are truths. Facts oftentimes obscure the truth."

Curtiss insisted that he had nothing to do with the Congregations' actions.

"I'm sorry, Bishop," Walsh answered, with just a hint of the head of steam pushing him along, "but I flat-out don't believe you."

For a moment, I wanted to intervene. Rescue the bishop. Tell him we understood—at least in a way. Yet he appeared to take an odd pleasure in what was happening, as if accepting a penance not altogether unexpected. If the brief scenario immobilized me, not so Jane Harlow who poured out another volley of helpless anguish.

"Rome is thousands of miles away. If it weren't for a few clergy around here who've been yelping because a priest had the honesty to do what had to be done, none of this would've happened!"

Curtiss glared at the mother of two who, in her blue jeans and plaid blouse, struck me as about as far from the inner chambers of the Curia as one could possibly get.

Everyone in the room jumped when the bishop slapped his hands together like a cymbal.

"Ah, but you people are naïve. When the Congregation of the

Clergy and the Congregation of the Faith speak, they do so in the name of the Holy Father. I'm a bishop of the church, carrying out orders from the pope himself.''

Unruffled, Gay Pomeroy lit a cigarette and, exhaling into the sudden stillness, calmly introduced herself as the wife of the physician who had delivered Michelle.

"Forgive me, Bishop, but every time Rome speaks, you make it sound like Moses coming down the mountain with the tablets. Correct me if I'm off-base here, but I thought all of us made up Catholicism. Is all that business about the church being the 'People of God' just empty words?''

Bristling, he waited for her to continue.

"Just because the pope says something doesn't always make it right. A few years ago it was a mortal sin to eat meat on Fridays, then the law changed. What happened to all those people who ate meat before it was okay? Are we supposed to believe they're in hell?''

"If they ate it over a long period of time. Yes. They probably are,'' Curtiss answered coolly.

Pomeroy's voice began to crack. "Our present pope is the same one who keeps saying birth control is a mortal sin. If he can blow it on that one, he can be wrong about what's happening here, too.''

"We can't just go off choosing between some rules we like and those we don't,'' he answered, just as John Barry caught his attention.

"If that's the case, Your Excellency, then it should apply to you, too,'' he snapped.

Neither the bishop nor any of us knew what he was getting at. The recently fired attorney for the diocese continued.

"We had nearly fifty kids ready for Confirmation this spring. They'd been preparing for months and were really up for it. Then with no warning, you decide you won't confirm them because we have a married priest.''

"That's right and they won't be until this mess is resolved,'' he answered steadily.

Barry might have been addressing a jury.

"But as I understand it, the law forbids you from holding the sacraments over our heads. You know, as a punishment or reward. Near as I can tell, you were way out of bounds denying those kids the sacraments.''

"Don't talk church law to me!" Curtiss snapped, his eyes darting toward Tim.

Taking the cue, Tim intervened.

"All of us have strong feelings. We just want to be honest with you tonight, Bishop. Seems to me the church can't be honest in public if we can't be in private."

Reaching over to touch Curtiss's arm gently, Yvonne Shepler glided to center stage.

"Bishop Hunthausen always listened with his heart. Maybe all of us can do the same."

"I'm not the archbishop and I get tired of being compared to him everywhere I go," he said matter-of-factly.

Undaunted, she continued.

"Maybe what I'm saying is we aren't used to following along blindly. We won't be putty in your hands or anyone else's."

For the first time all evening, Curtiss looked over at me, at once perturbed and pleading.

"Mike? Don't they understand they're talking with a successor of the apostles? I'm the chief teacher of the diocese and am tired of tearing my hair out over all this."

"Well, God's got to be bald tearing his hair out over it, too," I answered quietly, not prepared for the laughter which rippled through the room. Though he didn't join in, the bishop seemed to settle back just a bit.

Bill Leason, always one to choose his remarks and their timing carefully, took advantage of the moment to point out that the issues before us were larger than celibacy and the squabble over a married priesthood. Issues which touched upon fundamental values—above all, on the right of Catholics to question the status quo and receive a proper hearing from the hierarchy.

"You're talking about collegiality," Curtiss replied. "It doesn't apply when people simply fly off half-cocked, disregarding the law and . . ."

Leason ran a hand through his curly hair, shaking his head.

"If that's how you see us, then you don't know us at all. It's like you, or somebody out there, is using this community as a lightning rod to vent frustration over changes in the church."

I lifted my hand to back Leason off, but I was too late. Curtiss slammed his fist on the table.

"Listen! I'll be out that door in two seconds rather than sit here and be subjected to this kind of disrespect. I will not tolerate revolt in this parish or my diocese. You hear? I won't have it!''

Normally placid, Leason pushed on, propelled by a passion larger than himself.

''We do respect you, but it's hard when all along you haven't seemed to respect us. This so-called decision of yours—or whoever's —is a slap in the parish's face. All you say is 'stay in line or else.' What are you going to do, send us to eternal damnation, too? I'm so tired of this constant coercion.''

Frustrated, he waited for someone in the obviously nervous group to say something. When no one did, he stood up and went over to the coffeepot.

Tim suggested we all take a break, but no one moved. When Leason returned, he was silent, nonchalantly stirring sugar into his cup. He might have been home at the breakfast table.

Shaken but subdued, Curtiss repeated his resentment at being accused of doing anything but what was best for the universal church, to which he was committed as a husband to his bride.

Calmer, Leason nonetheless could not let it pass.

''That's my point. You're not the only one committed to the church or responsible for its future. But you can't expect us to let that be a substitute for faith in God.''

''There's no use going on with this,'' the bishop said, waving him off. ''We all have to let the dust settle a bit.''

A few around the table appeared to agree. Kirby Walsh was not one of them.

''You won't live long enough to see the dust settle on this one,'' he said before going on to denounce a system that focused on what the Curia wanted, apparently ignoring the gospel itself.

Curtiss toyed with his pectoral cross until Walsh finished.

''You keep saying 'gospel, gospel.' That's not the point here.'' He sighed, shaking his head. ''Even Protestants have the gospel! That's not what makes us different. We're bound together by tradition and the law. That's Catholicism, mister. The law is our true cement, and it leaves no room for a married priest!''

Exasperated, Kevin Doherty flipped a pen across the tabletop, where it spun like an arrow on a game of chance.

''Can't Rome see the priesthood is dying? Even though the average priest in America today is over fifty years old and the bottom has dropped out on vocations, you're still willing to dump people like

Mike. The whole thing is hypocritical. More than that, it's sick!''

"Not if you're committed to celibacy as a norm for the priesthood, which I am," the bishop shouted back, but without nearly as much force as earlier in the evening.

The arguments swung to what the termination would do to the young people of Resurrection, to converts, and to the image of Catholicism in general within the city. Walsh estimated that as many as a quarter of the parish could leave the church over the episode.

Curtiss shrugged. "It sounds to me like inordinate pride. A holier-than-thou attitude. If they want to leave, let them."

"Could be the church is leaving us."

The bishop rotated his ring, speaking to Walsh as a teacher might to a student unfamiliar with the nuances of Catholicism.

"That's absurd. Anyway, we can never stop loving her."

"Even if she tears our heart out in the process?" Walsh said, the punch all but taken out of him. "It's madness. Utter madness. You, or whoever is responsible, spend so much time trying to milk the fear out of tomorrow that you're squandering the present."

We had been over it a dozen times before. I was tired of witnessing their torment, their thrashing about like boxers punching at the air. Seeing the despairing looks around me, I began to resent the discussion, knowing the protest had run its course.

Curtiss turned to me.

"Mike, something's going on here and I'm not sure what. You're not considering going against Holy Church on this, are you?"

There was alarm in his eyes, which now clung to mine. In that fraction of a second he must have seen something, for the alarm faded as we both recognized that for me, it was lost.

Next to me, Joan, who had long since crossed the threshold of toleration, scribbled a note on her pad.

"Better kiss the Fat Lady good-bye."

Numb, almost without feeling, I did just that, telling the bishop that enough was enough. As I had informed the council earlier, I would not defy the Curia's decrees.

Immediately he thanked me for being a "real churchman," for a willingness to accept the will of the Holy See for the sake of the larger church. About to say that it wasn't that at all, I let the moment pass.

In the lull, Drake Shepler broke out of his pocket of silence, suggesting that I be placed on sabbatical for a year with the hope of someday returning to more acceptable work within the church. In turn, the bishop promised that the council's white paper documenting Resurrection's experience with married priesthood would not be ignored by the hierarchy.

With that, Bishop Curtiss rose to leave, but not before Gay Pomeroy took a deep breath, looking him square-on.

"With all due respect, one last thing for the record, Your Excellency. I was born and raised in Philadelphia. Talk about Catholic! It's Cardinal Krol territory. I went through Catholic schools all my life; so did my husband. I jumped through all the proper hoops, but never have I been part of such creative liturgies as here. And that's due in no small part to Joan's efforts. Nor have I heard a priest preach like Mike. He knows what it's like to live day in and day out closely with another person—what it's like to feel a child kick against its mother's womb, and what goes through your head when you sit up all night with a sick child. Most of all, he relates faith to what we go through in our families, jobs—in other words, what we come up against in the trenches. Having a married priest has made a definite difference. Maybe in itself, it isn't that big a deal, but having the one you are tearing away from me and my family, it sure as hell is." She started to falter, but straightened up, taking another breath.

"Excuse the language, but this is hard for me. What you, or Rome, or whoever are doing is destroying one of the best things that's happened in my life, and something which could happen in other parishes, too. I've always been proud to be a Roman Catholic, but right now all I feel for the church is shame—a terrible, burning shame!"

I wanted to reach out to her. Say something, anything, but felt limp and drained. When the council adjourned, she was the first one to leave the circle, dashing into the starlit night.

As he was about to leave, Curtiss pulled Tim aside, asking for her name, mentioning he thought she was totally out of line; promising she had not heard the last of him.

Though the news began to trickle out, we put off informing the entire parish that the battle was all but over. It was far easier to swim around in a pool of denial than face up to the fact that the chances of returning to the ministry were no better than those of the biblical camel passing through the needle's eye. However, events themselves began to force their way through the cracks of our fragile defenses. In mid-May, the Senate of Priests provided the first jolt of several tremors to come. One which would repeat itself time and again within me, playing over and over like the reel of an old movie.

Originally scheduled to discuss alternatives to the termination, the Senate convened at Resurrection, Elden Curtiss announcing a change of agenda. The rules of the game were altered. There would be no discussion of options. When he began reading the mandates from Vatican City, I felt like the sole occupant of a theater watching a play unfold on a distant stage. From the last row I could see the outlines of characters, hear voices without faces.

Unprepared for the surprising action of the Vatican Congregations, the cast is paralyzed, left only to lament my sudden passing and spread flowers over the dead.

The bishop mentions Cardinals Wright of the Congregation of the Clergy and Seper of the Congregation of the Faith. He has no alternative but to comply. Any delay could be misinterpreted at the Vatican.

A far-off voice, that of a friend, calls the same cardinals "wooden headed," "popcorn farts." An apology is demanded. Given. Another asks why it all had to happen. The bishop points out that the "experiment" has to be stopped for fear that it might spread. Then, too, there is scandal, confusion, abdication of the law. The same voice suggests that his tone is not one of a man offended but rather of one vindicated; wonders indeed if the bishop hasn't found a way to get off the hook. Others rush to Curtiss's defense. After all, the man did what he could. . .

The next voice is my own. Strained, flat, with a hint of piety, it irritates me. All along, my cause—that of Joan and the parish—has been the gospel. While we are for a married priesthood, the issue was always secondary. There is alarm in my words. Alarm for the church which Michelle and generations to follow will inherit. Alarm that the Vatican's action reveals a soul ringed with steel. Fear, too, that we are victims of a witch hunt designed to remove from the Book of Life the names of priests who have strayed. Nevertheless, we find comfort knowing that a precedent has been established. Perhaps someday I will again live the life to which the Holy Spirit calls me.

Bishop Curtiss assumes center stage. Once again he laments the mistake at Resurrection, one destined to be taken apart piece by piece. It is all beyond his control. He will be loyal, as must they. He cautions paternally against expecting sympathy from the College of Bishops. Warns that the majority of his colleagues feel betrayed by priests who have become hooked up with women, view their choice to marry as morally unsound. He will wash his hands of the Miles affair, as must they.

The Senate decides to write the apostolic delegate and the Curia in protest. The banishment is unfortunate. There is a motion calling for a task force. It is tabled.

From the back of the room, I excuse myself as the chairman moves to the next topic on the agenda.

It was the first Sunday in June; rumors were rampant, with only a few in Resurrection aware of the Vatican's intervention. The parish would have to know at once.

Throughout the week, in preparing to make the announcement, I drew a blank. Felt utterly stymied. Time was running out; try as I might, the words refused to come together.

The question did not lie so much in what to tell everyone as how to do so. While it was our choice not to resist further, it was a begrudging choice, heavy with feelings of resentment, anger, and loss. The problem, then, was not so much protecting the community from the facts as how I could avoid sucking people we cared about into the swirling whirlpool of my personal feelings. After all, the university students still had a lifetime to live out with the church. There were all too many families who relied on us for direction in reaching for the elusive hem of the garment of Christ. In telling them of our loss, how could we avoid jeopardizing their faith and confidence in Catholicism? It all came down to trying to protect them while not concealing the truth. The dilemma left me with hundreds of words but nothing to say.

From the outset of our relationship, Joan provided a mirror for my own feelings. With only a few hours remaining before the first mass, she reached beyond my ideas and the words I had scratched out, tapping the restless part of my soul where the Fat Lady sat on her porch swatting flies.

"You can't protect them," Joan admonished while I paced back and forth in our living room. "There are already people out there who are angry and hurt deeply by the church. There's no way it could be otherwise after what's happened. The harm's already done. It's out of your control. Let the bishops, the congregations, or whoever 'they' are, be responsible."

"Maybe," I argued, increasingly frustrated with each passing moment. "But it would be too easy just to go after them, grinding an ax. It just seems wrong."

"You don't need to keep wet-nursing that big thing out there called the church," she said impatiently. "People in the parish know the difference between the institution and their faith. They can see when the emperor doesn't have any clothes! There's no need to attack any-one. You don't even have to tell everything. Just do what you've always done and talk about the gospel. It'll do the confronting.'' She wrapped her arms gently about me. ''Then just let the chips fall where they may.''

She was right, as once again I found myself through her. With less than an hour before mass, what was so elusive now seemed terribly obvious. In the announcement I would focus on the gospel, with its own persuasive force. At the same time there would be no need to conceal the well of feelings which lay just beneath the surface of every word—nor should there be. After all, I thought, ten years to the very day I had knelt before Raymond Hunthausen to accept the priesthood and was now moments away from confirming its loss.

Throughout the entrance rite, the admonition authored years earlier by Hans Küng, and signed by Catholicism's finest theologians, fluttered through my consciousness. If efforts at renewal were thwarted, those entrusted with proclaiming the gospel could not in conscience remain silent.

''Silence out of opportunism or lack of courage makes one just as guilty as those persons who were silent during the time of the Reformation.''

Draping the microphone over my flaming-red vestment marking the season of Pentecost, I leafed through the pages of the Gospel of Mark. The story was a familiar one of the rising tension between the carpenter's son and those entrusted with the religious establishment. The Pharisees were disturbed that the disciples of Jesus did not follow the tradition of the elders who never ate without washing their hands up to the elbow. When confronted, Jesus castigated them with the words of Isaiah.

> This people honors me only with lip-service,
> while their hearts are far from me.
> The worship they offer me is worthless,
> the doctrines they teach are only human regulations.

Iron-faced, Tim took the book from me, slapping it shut. Stepping through the usual cluster of children gathered on the steps in front of the altar, I began with the story in Mark, then shifted gears.

''There's something else to say this morning, but it's going to be difficult. However, in case I'm not strong or forceful enough, we need only lay hold of the church's own center and foundation—the gospel of Jesus Christ.''

All at once the normally effusive atmosphere turned leaden. Through the windows in the back, a puffy cloud floated against a pale blue sky. I thought of Michelle and her request the day before for a pet cloud. We laughed then; not so this day.

"Ironically, today is the tenth anniversary of my ordination to the priesthood. Although none of us feel worthy of the call, I can say that the years here have made me more appreciative of it. Because of you, I understand far more than a decade ago what it means to have the hot coal placed against one's lips. Once the fire to share God's word touches, its heat won't go away—at least not for me," I said, my throat dry and raspy.

From then on, the words tumbled out in spite of me.

I spoke of the twin loves—those of the priesthood and of Joan. Of human regulations clung to with the force of a death grasp, as if they were of divine origin. How the law forbidding priests to marry was such a regulation, now strangling the spirit of far too many around the world, a regulation which would have kept the apostles themselves from the ministry. In our case, we tried to reach beyond it to a tradition deep within the church, but one obscured by the sands of time.

Suddenly I felt a need to be closer to the people themselves and stepped into the center aisle. Approaching the subject of the Vatican's action, I needed to touch them, feel their warmth and remember it had been real. My fingers brushed against the hair of a teenage girl and settled on the coarse tweed of someone else's sports coat.

"Serving here has been a joyous experience, but as you know there were always dark clouds on the horizon.''

I went on to mention the council's closed meetings with the bishop, avoiding any reference to Rome until there was no alternative.

"Just recently the Vatican entered the scene. I'm afraid they are in support of the human regulations which . . .'' My voice began to falter before I was able to go on about the Roman Congregations. Once again the words began to flow freely, but this time into a pained silence.

"I won't be able to preach the gospel any longer among you, for that matter, anywhere else in the church. I'll join the over twelve thousand American priests—Lord knows how many worldwide—who in the decade since I was ordained are now gone. Most forced to leave alive vocations for the fault of falling in love. And all for what? What justifies this horrendous loss and permits the official church to gnaw away at the psyches of such men while allowing their gifts to wither on the vine?'' I asked, taken back by the shock of hearing my own wounds expressed in words.

Directly in front of me an elderly woman quietly began to cry as throughout the center, the initial shock of realizing that efforts to roll back the termination had failed began to set in. Initially concerned about controlling my own emotions, I was totally unprepared for the anger and grief spreading across the sea of faces in front of me. I rushed to finish.

We would leave the parish lest innocent people get hurt. Of course, Resurrection would survive; proving along with other communities scattered across the country that the Spirit is stronger than the folly of man. Joan and I were sad, and angry. We were not bitter.

Toward the back I saw Joan set Michelle down and wrap her arms about a normally reserved public accountant who began sobbing unabashedly against her. It was a scene which would repeat itself with any number of people in the weeks to follow. Whether at grocery stores, on campus, on city streets—everywhere and anywhere—it would be the same. I looked away, fighting back my own sudden rush to tears.

''We have only two regrets. Certainly that those outside Resurrection, though quite possibly sincere, have inflicted so much pain upon so many people. I'm tired of seeing your tears! No one has a right to hurt you that way. And one more thing. I regret the two years I waited trying to get permission to marry the wonderful woman who is now with me. I regret giving that two years to the church and not marrying her right away.''

I turned back to the altar, stunned by the deluge of grief all around me. For the remainder of mass, I was unable to look at them, choosing instead to stare blankly at the puffy clouds floating lazily by.

Faced with a defeat almost everyone had felt would never happen, the people of Resurrection were left with little choice but to wander through entirely personal corridors of anger and despair. Whenever we could, Tim and I tried to reach out, offering comfort, suggesting avenues of hope. Every so often we had the haunting sense that the damage inflicted was, for all too many, irreparable. Jessie was no exception.

An amber glow of twilight bathed the parking lot in front of the parish as the university junior approached me. Jessie was shy and somewhat retiring. Her oval face with brown fawnlike eyes was familiar around Resurrection. Though normally keeping herself in the background, this time she was up front.

Like so many others, she needed to talk and did so at first with measured control, twisting the end of the red ponytail spilling across her shoulder. Before long, tears spotted her cheeks as she approached the core of the trouble festering within her.

"I know you said we can get along with another priest. Still, if we lose you, then we lose not only your leadership and your preaching—which incidentally along with Father Tim's got me out of bed and up here Sunday after Sunday," she said, trying to smile, "but we lose lots more than that. Just when I started to believe again, any suggestion that I count as an individual to the official church just goes twirling down the drain."

In a way she was right, echoing sentiments repeated throughout the week since my announcement. Only this time there was a bloody wound lying open between the lines. Anxious to protect both her and the church, I spoke of the future, of promises yet unseen. I knew by her blank look that my effort was unconvincing.

"Father, all of a sudden it feels like my world's starting to come apart. You and O'Mera want to put a kindly face on things, when all I see looking back at me from the Vatican's chambers are ghouls' grins," she said, rubbing her eyes.

I leaned back against the cold metal of the Volvo, shivering. Over the past few days, in order to tolerate the curtain falling on my own hopes, I had unknowingly survived as if encased in a suit of medieval armor. Whatever protest and anguish others threw at me bounced off like so many pellets of popcorn against the chain mail. Now this timid and somewhat frightened girl was clawing away at that armor, seeking to grab hold of me lest she slip away from all she held dear.

"You always told us to ask what Jesus would do before we made judgments. Fair enough. Can you imagine him striking out like the bigwigs in the church are doing? Do you think he would kick you, your wife, and baby girl out? Or that he'd ignore my feelings and everyone else's in the parish?"

Her voice was hollow, but the question hung over me like a blade; the same one which had ripped open the wound within her.

Even as a slight smile stretched across my face, I resented falling back to such feigned ease. It was difficult to swallow.

"No, Jessie, I don't think he would."

"You know darn well he wouldn't, Father! So do I! If that's the case, then the church is pretty corrupt, isn't it?" she asked, her question falling away like a leaf swept along in the wind.

I didn't answer. She was right, yet in a way also wrong.

"The average human being shows more concern and respect for his dog than those who did this have shown to any of us. Well, they should quit prattling so sanctimoniously and check out the blood on their hands. Not just yours, but mine, too."

Suddenly she threw herself into my arms and began sobbing like a child. Eventually steadied, she pulled away.

"I intend to leave the church for good," she muttered. "Trouble is, I don't know where to go."

Wanting to cry out to her and tell her not to leave so much of what was good, I felt the protest die within me as she turned away and went down the hill into darkness, leaving me with an overriding guilt for having failed her.

The following Sunday just after communion at each mass, Drake Shepler spoke to the congregation. For him as well as for many of us, the first time he did so was the most difficult.

Impeccably dressed, his silver beard groomed to perfection, Shepler might have been announcing a bake sale in any parish across the nation. His voice was steady, each word carefully crafted and delivered, as he spoke into the microphone.

"We're all anxious to have a chance to declare ourselves to Bishop Curtiss, the apostolic delegate, and to Rome. So the council has prepared a statement to witness what strikes most all of us in the parish as an immoral affront to the people of God. We have to believe they'll listen like the Lord. He never refused the petition of anyone."

The aroma of fresh flowers lining the altar carried with it the memory of the hospital room last year when Drake, following a second heart attack, managed to bounce back once again.

"Let me read the paragraph to you," Shepler went on, unfolding a single sheet of paper. It was the first time all of them had heard it.

> Standing on the firm foundation of the Gospel of Jesus
> Christ and the rich traditions of our apostolic faith, we, the
> undersigned, wish to express herewith our heart-felt support of

the ministry of Michael Miles; to declare that we have enjoyed
a truly gospel experience under his ministry and to indicate our
deep sorrow, dismay and protest at the prospect of his ministry
being terminated.

He stopped and, hands trembling, folded the statement carefully
back into his pocket.

"I, we of the council, want to invite all of you to sign this if you
choose. There are copies in the back following mass, along with a
more detailed document we will forward to the authorities. Don't feel
you have to, but if you want, please do. We want to be able to tell
those in authority how much pain this. . ."

Again he halted, this time placing a clenched fist against his lips
to muffle an unexpected sob. He tried to speak again.

"So, if you want to sign, please do. Much more important, pray,"
he stammered before returning to his place alongside Yvonne.

That Sunday, although the university was already starting summer
recess, approximately two thousand persons attended mass at Resurrection. Over 1,800 of them took the time to stop and sign the council's
statement challenging the termination.

When finally we were alone, Joan and I read over the entire statement.

An Open Letter To Those United In Catholic And Apostolic Faith From The Community Of Resurrection.

. . . Our words are addressed in love, with the deep conviction that as laity the church is also ours to claim and preserve
for now and in the future. We must speak, for to remain silent
would be an offense against our parish, the church, the gospel
of Jesus and ultimately ourselves.

May this document stand as a strong dissent against Mike's
termination, but even more may it raise a voice on behalf of a
hunger within us and possibly beyond us. To suppress the gifts
of this one man, to silence his most effective voice in proclaiming God's word, only because he has a beautiful wife and
child, is to lose sight of the desperate needs of the People of
God in these our times . . . Are we all not one in our hunger
and hope for God's word and the church's life? Are we all not
lifting the same cross toward freedom?

. . . Following his marriage witnessed within our parish,

we all realized that an unprecedented step forward had been taken in the American church. While we lamented the limitations placed upon Mike's ministry and fervently prayed for the day he would be restored to full priestly faculties, we rejoiced that so much had been saved.

. . . In an age when university students seem all too absent from the church, we have observed an overwhelming response . . . Many of those once alienated from the church have returned. From infancy to ninety, from the campus and beyond, from widely divergent backgrounds, we have become a happy people . . . while far from perfect, many of us, perhaps for the first time, have found the church we longed for . . . that is, until this dark hour overcame us, . . . haunted Mike and eventually us.

. . . Our parish is anguished and angry, and many of us have wanted to openly resist the termination order . . . out of our desire to remain in unity with the church . . . we have reluctantly obeyed the order. Obeyed, though strongly believing in our hearts that such a decree is a tragic violation of our experience and the promptings of the Holy Spirit.

. . . Why, we ask, at a time when the church is experiencing an irreplaceable loss of priests . . . can anything so good and so right be judged so wrong? How can effective ministry and preaching be dashed against the stone by the very institution called to preserve us all in hope? . . . We are scandalized at this waste and loss.

What are we to do? We have written hundreds of letters to church authority; we have signed our statement. But to what avail? The lack of response is deafening. As always, we, the laity, seem powerless except for God's ever new Spirit . . . Meanwhile for a church which does not recognize the voice of its people, we weep.

We who have been deeply touched by the gospel ministry of this priest, now married these several years, simply cannot condone what is tragically taking place. Where do we go? Thankfully, the Lord Jesus will be the final judge of what has taken place . . . we turn most especially to those in leadership within the church. We plead with you . . . to listen to us—to talk with us—to pray with us. As the flock must love its shepherds, so must the shepherds love their flock.

The manifesto witnessing to the sentiments of nearly two thousand souls was immediately sent to Bishop Elden Curtiss and the apostolic delegate, with a request that copies be forwarded to central officials within Vatican City. It was destined never to receive an acknowledgment, much less an answer, from anyone.

As I wound to a stop in front of the chancery, a robin scurried across the summer grass, dashing back and forth beneath the wide arch of a water sprinkler. I thought back to far simpler days when as a budding seminarian, I had mowed the same lawn, cared for the daisies which still lined the walkway. After parking the car, I circled around the south wall, running my fingertips over the massive stones quarried from the nearby hills at the turn of the century. Baked by the morning sun, they were already warm. Walking along the clay pathway, which led to a backyard sheltered by rows of lilacs, I heard faint echoes of Raymond Hunthausen's nieces and nephews who used to spend hours batting a volleyball through the summer sky. The net was gone now; so, too, their voices, but a small statue remained nestled at the far corner of the yard. No sooner had I stopped before the Madonna, searching for a way to pray, than a voice startled me.

"Elden's waiting. He saw you drive up," Caston Broderick said apologetically. "His emotional winds are howling, so watch out."

"What about? We're just supposed to pull a few loose ends together. Hell, it's all over."

He smiled, threw up his hands as if to grab an answer out of the air. "Who knows? We've had another avalanche of mail and the guy's paranoid about you. He wants this thing behind him. Come on. You don't want to miss this last party."

Broderick closed the door, leaving us alone. Livid, the bishop started in before I sat down, as if we had been in midsentence just seconds before.

"I'm starting to get letters again," he thundered, going over to the desk and clasping a few pages in his hand. "It's dreadful. That parish is now estranged from me, thanks to you. For godsakes, I'm their bishop!"

I started to reply, then backed away from our familiar pattern as he continued in a rage.

"I'm going to write a few of them back telling them they'd better reassess their participation in Catholicism. I will not have bitter, vindictive people around. I won't have anyone out of step with me!

They can't be alienated from me and remain part of the church! Besides, the Vatican ordered you out, not me. Don't they know that?''

We had been over it all before, only this time I felt less attached, as if the umbilical cord connecting me to a source of life had snapped. I looked up noticing for the first time his eyes were hazel gray, the color of Michelle's.

"You were probably their hatchetman from the start. Let's not forget that you made the decision to get rid of me in this very room, Bishop. You'll never be able to blot that out of conscience. Never.''

At once, he flopped down in the heavy lounge chair, looking by any account exhausted.

"It's Rome I'm concerned about. We can't have everyone viewing the Curia as a bunch of fuddy-duddies.''

It was a term I had not heard for years, certainly never in reference to the bureaucrats within the Holy See. For a split second, I wondered if what tickled a nerve within me had done the same to him and we would break out together in an overdue peal of laughter. The moment passed, leaving an edge of disquiet knifing across his face.

"Look, Mike. You've got to help me hold the lid on. The next couple of weeks are critical and could still spell trouble," he said, nearly pleading while pointing through the window to the asphalt driveway. "All we need are pickets out there. Pickets and press! It would be a nightmare!''

"It won't happen.''

"We've got to make sure," he muttered quietly, acting as if we were standing together arm in arm, protecting the palace gates.

As before, flashing hot then cold, he cooled down and half-grinned.

"So far you've surprised many of the old bucks in the clergy by not stirring up a hornet's nest. Metzner, Sexton.'' He stopped, catching himself before deciding to go on. "There are some of the priests who thought you would fight this all the way. They don't understand what I do. You treasure the unity of the entire church as much as me. You're loyal. It's a virtue I prize.''

"We can be loyal and still disagree with what's going on," I said, citing the example of Andrew Greeley, a priest who, though often highly critical of the church, remained fiercely attached to its faith.

At the mention of Greeley and his writings, Curtiss came unglued. Waving a finger in my face, he referred to him as a "SOB," pledging to write the bishops to ensure that "we get him.''

As abruptly as he erupted, he settled down. It was a chance to turn a corner and knock on a door neither of us had opened.

"What about us, Bishop?" I asked. "Where are we, you know, personally?"

Curtiss shifted, seemingly thrown off yet warmed by my question.

"Light years apart on some things. Gerald Himmler warned me of you the day I stepped into this office. You'll always be stubborn about this marriage business. I love Holy Church; see her as my spouse as she is the Lord's. Quite honestly, I can't help but see you in an adulterous relationship separated from your only true bride."

His forthright sincerity deflected an impulse to object gnawing within me.

"You're not a realist, Mike. It's one thing to want to change the discipline of celibacy through legitimate channels. Quite another to refuse to accept it."

"Channels? There aren't any! Besides, we weren't on a crusade. We just fell in love. The church made it an issue."

"Well, then, call it the luck of the draw. The Vatican Congregations figured you were notorious, and so . . ."

"Notorious!" I flared.

"In the sense that you saw your whole thing as the wave of the future. Anyway, as for where we stand? We'll consider you on sabbatical this year. The diocese will help out a little financially and who knows"—he leaned forward, palms up as if cradling my future—"maybe we can find something for you someday. Not in this diocese, heaven knows, but somewhere. In the meantime, your replacement will only be able to help out part-time this first year."

"Why's that?"

"I knew you'd ask," he said, checking his watch. "We're a bit short of priests, but Tim talked with me about having a Protestant minister in now and then to help out with sermons and the like. I don't especially care for it, but it'll be okay for now."

"Better than having a married priest contaminate things," I shot back, most of my energy dissipated.

He seemed not to hear, bringing an abrupt end to the conversation.

Just before leaving, I advised him of inquiries from the press, regretting it at once.

He went rigid, his fragile fingers rotating an episcopal ring as if in search of a combination, then he leaped from the chair and moved to a portrait of Paul VI.

Standing there, locked into Paul's unseeing eyes, he struck me as terribly small. Suddenly spinning on his heels, Curtiss advanced in my direction. Later that night, his ashen face would awaken me, look back at me from the bathroom mirror, follow me into a restless dawn.

Grappling for control, he shouted, "I'll say this only one more time. Don't shoot your mouth off to the press or anyone else. Learn a lesson from others who've decided to wash their clerical linen in public. They've been burned but good!"

His lips tight and purpling, he came closer, warning me against letting the lid off Resurrection.

Suddenly I saw that Curtiss, too, was caught. That he, too, was a victim of the same institution we both sought to serve. I wanted to reach out and touch him. Say I was sorry for him. Sorry for us all. But my body felt heavy, as though full of sand.

With that, the bishop threw open the door and stormed out of the office.

Outside, the sky was sheathed in lead as the wind tore repeatedly at a tree branch, whipping it back and forth against the windowpane. Though the sprinkler continued its monotonous twirl, the robin was gone.

Set in oversized bold type and blocked out for special attention, the notice read like an epitaph. Released and printed in Montana's press, it came as a complete surprise.

DIRECTIVES RECEIVED FROM ROME

The following directives concerning the ministry of Michael Miles at Resurrection Parish, Bozeman, have been received from the Roman Congregations for the Doctrine of the Faith and for the Clergy, through the office of the Apostolic Delegate, Archbishop Jean Jadot.

1. Michael Miles . . . may not remain in active ministry.
2. He may not be active in lay ministry.
3. He may not exercise a ministerial role reserved for those in Sacred Orders.

The comments carried a by-line from Elden Curtiss.

Priests who are dispensed from the duties and obligations of priesthood, including the obligation of celibacy, are to be considered laymen in the Church. They are like lawyers who have been removed from the bar and no longer have a license to practice law. They are still lawyers, but they cannot practice

law. The Sacrament of Holy Orders cannot be reversed or lost
once received. However, once a priest is dispensed, he no
longer has a license to function in priestly ministry. This is the
case with Michael Miles.

The anger which I had unwittingly buried surfaced like a gusher
breaking through crusty desert topsoil. At the sight of the article, I
was seething but in a strange way also set free. Despite the bishop's
pledge of assistance, it was certain there would never be a ministerial
light for me at the end of Catholicism's tunnel. In the minds of those
at the top of the hierarchical scale, I was *persona non grata*, and had
been all along.

The task of explaining the release fell on Caston Broderick. Apologetically, he admitted being offended by the tactics employed.

"I don't think Curtiss saw it as splashing your name before the
public," he said wearily. "He just wanted it out as insurance."

"Like a coup de grâce?" I replied angrily. "So he slanders us!
The business of comparing me to a disbarred attorney is ludicrous.
Meanwhile, this diocese is growing stiff in the joints. It's in a rut,
going to seed."

"The fact is that you people are the target and he has to suggest
you're guilty of something to justify the punishment."

"Guilty of what?"

"Oh come on, Mike. Staying in the priesthood!"

"Am I guilty?"

A long silence.

"Caston?"

"In the church's mind, of course. That's their whole point."

"And?"

"I'm sorry. Maybe we were all a bit too naïve. It's more than the
fall of the cards. At the top of the heap they play for keeps."

"Hardball, as they say?"

I didn't wait for a response, knowing in that moment that not only
the present but the future too was lost.

As the few days remaining before my final mass fell away, I was
all but convinced that saying a public farewell to Resurrection would
be an impossible task. All thought of the prospect left me tight and
uncertain.

Saturday afternoon was hollow, seemingly empty even of the presence of God. Alone at the center, I busied myself removing books from shelves, packing away photographs from more promising times. Momentarily I glanced up, staring into the large canvas face of Jesus suspended over the sanctuary. His lips mute, eyes expressionless. A terrible scream rose within me with no way of making its sound heard. Then the dam broke. Spasms of grief quaked through me, shaking loose feelings which until then had lain like an anchor hooked around my soul. Once over, the siege left me purged, enough so that Sunday's gospel finally penetrated and, with it, the strength to go through with the last good-bye.

Other than being fiercely hot, the day started out like any other in a lifetime of Sundays. Slightly thrown off by the normal banter of the community waiting for the liturgy to begin, I wondered aloud to Tim if they had forgotten.

"They haven't," he answered, adjusting a cincture about his alb. "They're just like me. Pretending it isn't so."

Weren't we all? Joan reached out, gently stroking my cheek, then pulled her hand away to cover her mouth. Wordlessly, I headed for the altar, looking back at her just one more time.

Throughout the entrance rite of the mass, I felt as if I were enclosed in a bubble, hearing and seeing, yet insulated from everything outside. Only when I started to read the Scriptures did the bubble burst and every face in the room come breaking through. Even a fleeting glance was enough to convince me that Tim was right. They hadn't forgotten at all.

Luke's story of the transfiguration struck me as more than coincidental. Hours before the crucifixion, while on the road to Jerusalem, Jesus invited Peter, James, and John to climb with him up the mountain. Only a few years earlier the three men had been wandering on separate paths in which the power of the divine played little part. Not until drawn together by the young Jew from Nazareth had those paths crossed. Just how much their lives had changed was about to unfold in the stirring drama of the mountaintop.

Whatever happened there among the clouds and lightning, the lesson was profound. Not until much later—through a simple yet profound story—would they seek to paint a picture of the indescribable for generations yet to come.

They found themselves on the mountain with the prophets. Elijah, who belched fire while castigating oppressors enslaving his people.

Moses, who saw farther than he would ever go, calling a whole people to burst their bonds and strike out in the name of a promise.

The mountain—where an aging fisherman and the Sons of Thunder were at last to look upon Jesus for whom he really was, glimpse his face, etched with lightning. There they would hear that he truly was the Messiah of their God.

The mountain—where they would see that without him religion would be little more than an empty vessel—all else leading to nothing else.

The mountain— where Peter, with typical abandon, pleaded that they might remain forever, never to enter the dark valley again.

Yet Peter, out of his head, had to be drawn back to the sight of Jerusalem far below. Jerusalem, the holy city over which Jesus wept, the object of their descent. The sight of their destiny. Jerusalem, which threatened to swallow them up. Jerusalem, where Skull Place beckoned, and where in the days ahead, when the air tasted of metal and their nostrils were filled with ash, they would in their desperation need to remember what they had seen and heard on the mountain.

As in a bottle, Luke's story washed across the shore of Resurrection's desolation. Before intersecting, our lives—like those of Peter, James, and John—had once taken independent paths. For some, Catholicism was nothing more than a club or an experience of guilt and fear. Others, finding religion all but meaningless, had placed an uneasy distance between themselves and the church. While for many more, Catholicism was vital but lacked the fire which Jesus prayed would sweep across the earth. A poignant message and one which I now sought to unravel.

"Thanks to the Second Vatican Council, we, along with parishes throughout this country and the world, felt invited to journey up the mountain and catch a glimpse of who we might yet become."

Whereas earlier I had feared breaking down in front of them, I immediately felt more assured, recalling our own buoyant, often painful climb up the mountain. A trek which produced its own share of wrong turns and mistakes, but one guided in part by the voice of a prophet who, like Moses and Elijah, had visions of freedom.

I wiped a glaze of perspiration from my forehead.

"Raymond Hunthausen has to be one of God's prophets. Surely he will emerge in the years ahead as a central figure in the history of the American Church. Whatever direction his future takes, it is bound to be prophetic because he has seen the fire. He's not only a man of faith and courage; most especially he's one who never lost sight of his own humanity.''

For an instant, it felt as though it was not my last mass; that the entire episode was a momentary mist soon to be evaporated by the same blazing sun which had blinded Peter. However, like him, none of us could presume to remain on the mountain.

"Looking back over five years of married priesthood, perhaps I should have known from the outset we were living on borrowed time. Even so, I consider the voices which call us down from the mountain to be tragic. Not only for me—for Joan and Michelle—but for the Catholic Church we all love. It is a tragedy of priorities, but we can find comfort knowing that the Lord Jesus himself will be the final judge of what's happened here.''

Increasingly aware that all around me the atmosphere was one of barely contained pain, I began in a threadbare voice to list my personal reasons for hope.

"Personally, there is so much to be thankful for. To come here eight years ago in love with the priesthood, and in the course of time to find that complemented by your love and then to be blessed with Joan and Michelle. Well, we leave with all that still alive.''

All around the tears began; among the most difficult to witness, those of Tim. In the back Joan held on, her face a stony mask.

"I want to say it has been a joy to serve among you for these years. It has indeed. I don't want to say I'll never break bread and preach the word again . . .''

Turning back to the altar, I started to choke up, but felt compelled to add something more.

"Only one thing Joan and I would ask of you. Even though we go down the mountain into the dark valley, always remember what you saw up there. Don't forget the all too fleeting moment, unique in the American Church and perhaps the world, which took place here. Please don't allow the memory to die. For if any of us do, Jerusalem will have swallowed us up.''

The rest of the mass was a blur. After the final song, instead of standing outside in the hot breeze to say good-bye, I went directly into my office, closed the door, and began rocking Michelle until she fell asleep.

Just seeing the story splashed across the front pages of the state's newspapers was like a kick in the stomach. There was the brutal sting of reality behind the headlines.

MARRIED PRIEST IS SILENCED

The stories spoke of the end of a religious Camelot and the ensuing anguished reaction throughout Resurrection.

Although Elden Curtiss's promise of repercussions if I responded to reporters' queries remained branded in my memory, there were temptations to ignore the warning. Such was the case when a friend, forty years a priest, urged us to speak out in defiance of possible recriminations. Fully aware of how subtle the restraints on truth could be, he pleaded with us to tell the story. Urged us not to be part of a silence falling like rain over Catholicism.

However, it was Jeffry Connley's compassionate counsel that convinced me to say nothing. The pain was too close, the desire to lash out all too real, for us to offer anything resembling objectivity. Someday perhaps, but not until scar tissue covered the gaping wounds.

In opting for silence, we permitted a vacuum which the official church moved at once to fill, then gloss over. With minor variations, the statements from the bishop's office were consistent. After marriage, my duties at Resurrection consisted of little more than counseling and some teaching. Rome, however, did not agree, being sensitive to the law restricting men from working in any capacity in parishes where they had once served as priests. The universal church had to be considered. I would be transferred to another area of the vineyard. Purely a matter of administration.

The cover-up was complete except for a journalist from a national tabloid who sensed something askew. Day after day he called, pushing at our walls of silence, eventually going right to the point.

"Father, we know you've been removed; the question is why? We also know the damn chancery office is sending out a smoke screen. If what we've heard here in the East is even remotely true, it's a major story in the American Church. You have a Rembrandt painting there which will turn into a Mickey Mouse if you continue your silence. Think about it. I'll call back."

That night, after looking in on Michelle, I kissed her good night, then went downstairs to disconnect the telephone. Nevertheless, the reporter might have broken through the silence were it not for a story far overshadowing our own, which unexpectedly called him away.

The towering cottonwoods surrounding the Sieben Ranch rustled gently in the afternoon breeze. Horses, their tails sweeping lazily at flies, stood scattered throughout the pasture as young lambs scurried through shoulder-high alfalfa. A close friend since childhood, Max Baucus was in the final months of a heated campaign for the United States Senate. Certain we were anxious to escape the preoccupation with our circumstances, he invited Joan and me to be part of a gathering at his ranch and meet the vice-president of the United States.

Walter Mondale had been gracious, holding Michelle in his lap, sharing stories of his own children. Later, seated on weathered fence-poles soaking up the August sun, Joan and I watched him baste a side of beef rotating over a charcoal pit. Rome and the termination were far away.

An athletic figure, looking slightly uncomfortable in new Levi's and cowboy boots, approached Mondale, his role of protector divulged by the earpiece protruding from the side of his head. The secret-service agent whispered something to the vice-president, who in turn passed it on to those around him.

Moments afterward, Max brushed the sandy furl of hair from his eyes, looking around until he spotted us. Walking across the field, his boots kicking up small puffs of dust, he moved with the same gait he'd had as a child. Joan slid off the fence, assisting Michelle in her losing struggle to keep the nipple of a milk bottle in the mouth of an impatient lamb.

"Mike," Max said, taking her place next to me. "Fritz just got word that the pope is dead."

"Paul the Sixth?"

He nodded. "The very same. Didn't you say he'd been pretty ill and his aides were supposedly running things?"

"Yeah, that's been the rumor," I replied limply, a picture of the frail and harassed Giovanni Montini springing to memory.

"Now that he's gone, who runs the shop?"

I needed to let the news settle.

"Not the Curia. As soon as the pope dies, they're dissolved until the conclave selects a new one."

"Geez." Max whistled, looking younger than his thirty-odd years. "Weren't they the ones who came after you? What if he'd died just a few weeks earlier? Would that have canceled your pink slip?"

Before I could come up with an answer, Mondale called out to the future senator to help slice the beef, and he jumped down, leaving me with his question and so many more.

That afternoon, a couple of people asked if a new pope might reinstate us. One jokingly offered to adopt Michelle, since she was part of the problem. My reaction was always the same. A slight wince, a slouch of the shoulders, and a swallow of cold beer, which wouldn't wash any of it away.

The ensuing weeks were dominated by news of the pending Vatican conclave and by speculation as to who might become the 263rd successor to the Chair of Peter, now vacated by a figure appearing more serene in death than ever in life. In the face of such drama and much to our relief, the trauma besetting Resurrection sank like a stone from public view. Still, there was no escaping the looming hole left in our personal lives by the loss of ministry. That wound was raw and most sensitive on Sundays, which Joan and I came to dread.

From earliest childhood, both of our lives had been stitched together with the strong thread of Sundays. The Lord's Day, a sabbath to keep holy. Despite the urging of Elden Curtiss that we stay away from Resurrection, there was really nowhere else for us to worship. Initially we attended mass in the parish, hopeful that we might recover a semblance of normalcy. It didn't take long to discover that neither we nor the community were prepared for the adjustment.

There were the familiar faces. The usual smiles and handshakes. Yet just behind our attempt at pretense lurked a common past, and after a few seconds of idle chatter we would run out of things to say, for fear of touching upon memories none of us wished to dredge up.

However, it was during the celebration of the liturgy itself that any pretense inevitably unraveled. Anxious to remain inconspicuous, we would sit in the back, but there was no way to check our feelings, raw at the vivid reminder of all that had been lost. While we needed to be there, it was all but impossible to be. Even in the simple act of joining the lines to receive the Eucharist, we could feel remorseful eyes like hot irons on us. Eventually their heat began to sear through the fine membrane of our charade. Somehow it didn't seem fair to inflict the community with our presence, which only rubbed salt into their wounds.

If it was painful to attend the liturgy with those we had been so much a part of for so long, remaining at home was equally so. Whenever just the two of us celebrated mass over the dining room table, a feeling of emptiness enveloped us like a yellow fog. The only remaining option, Holy Rosary—with a clergy we believed supportive of the termination—really did not exist.

So the Sundays passed, each a day to endure, opening upon a week during which we might try to forget, only to be pulled up short by still another Sunday—the Lord's Day, with nowhere to go.

With the rush of speculation over Paul VI's possible successor, I nearly forgot about one of his final episcopal appointments. With the day of installation of Thomas Murphy as Bishop of Eastern Montana growing near, it was confirmed; the apostolic delegate would be the presiding prelate.

Jean Jadot—the Belgian-born archbishop and seasoned diplomat. Jadot—one of a handful of men on an intimate basis with Paul VI. Jadot—though involved in the nuances of my personal life, a stranger still. His presence in Great Falls was opportune. I requested an appointment, suggesting he might offer insight into what remained a confusing scenario.

Bearing the pale blue seal of the papacy, the reply to my request was immediate. The delegate would welcome an opportunity to explain the unanswered questions surrounding our case. Next to the tiara and keys of the Fisherman, a number: Ours was case 2339/78/6.

It was a balmy August afternoon, the sidewalk leading to the Redemptorist monastery hot beneath my feet. When an aged housekeeper answered the ring, the bright glare of sunshine reflecting off the door transformed her into a silhouette without a face. Inside, she ushered me quietly into a cool parlor, the same sun shielded by long lace curtains matching the doily upon which she placed a glass of iced tea. Scattered around the room was walnut furniture smelling of mothballs. Just above a brass floor lamp, its shade singed with a brown spot from a bulb which had gotten too close, was a faded painting. It depicted a young boy, clad in a dusty apron from another era, leaning over a worn workbench, chiseling a statue of the Virgin Mary. So caught up in the finishing touches of what must have been a lengthy labor of love, he appeared oblivious to the arms of the statue, which spread above his sandy hair with a tender blessing, protecting him from the harshness outside. Sipping tea, I longed to lay hold of the feelings buried within his world and find there the comfort absent from our own.

My head reeled with a long list of questions to which Jadot might hold the key. Though the Vatican decrees contained the signatures of Cardinals John Wright and Franjo Seper, was it really their hands which stretched out to trap the Word now dead in my throat? What of the delegate himself? Was he, as Curtiss said, nothing more than an errand boy carrying out the Vatican's directives, or was he, too, fully involved? If so, then how explain his silence throughout most of the five years of our venture into married priesthood? Reputed to be the most enlightened representative of the papal throne sent to America in the twentieth century, he may have looked the other way until forced to act.

In the cool darkness, I sought again the comfort of the painting, in which a pile of wooden shavings lay scattered at the boy's feet. So also I thought was my life—Joan's, too and even our daughter's—scattered before us in a heap. Jadot might help pick up those pieces. We would talk as one priest to another. He would listen, picking up the notes of the joyful sound which once was Resurrection.

The parlor door swung open.

"Mr. Miles?"

A young cleric who except for his suit and collar might have stepped off Madison Avenue stood in the doorway.

"I'm Father Richard Purtell," he said cordially.

Diplomats carry an entourage of associates around like so much luggage. The delegate's personal secretary seemed comfortable with his role, striking me as too neat, too sharp around the edges.

"His Excellency will see you now."

Passing through a narrow hallway, we emerged into a spacious community room cluttered with stuffed, off-pink furniture. The apostolic delegate, peering over wireless glasses, loomed like a giant crane draped in black. A tall man, he approached with a stoop, warmly taking my hand.

"*S'il vous plait.* May I call you Michael?" he asked as we sat on opposite ends of a sofa.

Surprisingly, Purtell drew up a chair and remained. When he withdrew a note pad and began writing before either of us spoke, I stiffened. Jadot noticed.

"Let me assure you," he said in broken English, "Father is only here to help with my faulty memory."

Jadot, too, held a pad, and looked up with kindly, milk-blue eyes.

"Please proceed."

"Perhaps you would like to begin, Archbishop. I really need your observations and feelings on my . . . ah . . . case. Or maybe you just have some questions."

"No. We know all we need to. There's nothing at all we wish to say to you. Carry on," he said matter-of-factly with a wave of his thin, bony hand.

I hesitated, wondering why he had agreed to the meeting. In the silence the persistent scratching of the secretary's pen pricked away at my inflated expectations. Unsettled, yet not willing to allow the chance to slip by, I started to spill out our experience. Midway through, the secretary interrupted my monologue.

"When did you leave?" he asked, a slight furrow beneath his wavy blond hair. "We need to get it clear—for the record."

Like a caller at the wrong door, I felt out of place, my headlong plunge reined in abruptly.

"Leave?"

Purtell noticed the quizzical expression spreading across my face, sighed patiently, taking another tack.

"A moment ago you mentioned your marriage to . . . what's her name? No matter. We need the date of your marriage. You know, when you left the priesthood."

Marriage meant leaving the priesthood; obviously they were one and the same. I wanted to reach over and take his pen, rewrite the script. Wanted to shout out, "Can't you see? That's the whole point. I never left anything!"

Instead, my candor wound down like a top. It was clear; they were seeking information. But evidence for what and against whom?

Jadot peered up, the window behind him casting a soft glare over his naked head. As from a prepared text, he began to speak, now and then revealing a gentle, pious soul but one immersed in the brine of conviction.

"When you married you gave up the presbyterate, Michael. You knew that."

"But that's what I'm trying to tell you. We examined the law and saw there was room to . . ."

"You were in clear violation of the precepts of the Sacred Congregations all along!" he replied coolly.

"Bishop Hunthausen gave us permission. We tried to observe the limitations on my priesthood, but without tossing it away."

"Frankly," he interrupted, "that was a permission your former ordinary was not at liberty to give."

Though the actors and stage were different, it was the same script. I started to disagree, deciding against it in face of the sheer futility.

"If that's the case, Archbishop, why did you let it go for so long?

You didn't disagree until we'd been married for years," I said, struggling against any suggestion of argument.

He paused, reaching into a vest pocket for a thin gold case. With one motion he snapped it open, extracted a cigarette, and lit up. As he exhaled, a brittle edge now laced the delegate's voice.

"It was never a case of agreement. We simply didn't know about you and this . . . this . . . scandal for at least two years. Not until priests from here informed us and wrote the Holy See."

He yawned, leaning back against the sofa to stretch his long legs.

"The last time the Holy Father and I talked, he lamented how you Americans don't seem to appreciate the needs of the universal church. You don't realize how other countries can be affected adversely by your actions. The Roman Catholic Church is not ready for a married *prêtrise* whether or not your *paroisse* might be, which I doubt."

"*Paroisse?*"

"Excuse me, I mean to say 'parish.' "

Once a whirlwind, my mind settled into an uneasy calm as the pieces scattered about us started to fall into place.

The delegate returned to his conversation with Paul VI, repeating the pontiff's adamant opposition to any suggestion of a married priesthood. Nevertheless, at one point Jadot hinted that the future might contain a change for the universal church if precedents were established.

"For example in nineteen thirty-five in Brussels, there was a boy who worked in a bakery all night. In those days we had the eucharistic fast and no one could have so much as a *verre* . . . excuse me, a glass of water . . . after midnight if they wished to receive holy communion. So . . ."—Jadot leaned forward, slapping his slender hands together, causing the secretary to sit up with a start— ". . . the boy petitioned Rome and Pius the Eleventh personally gave him permission to have water during the night. Twenty-five years later, after I was chaplain to the École Royale Militaire, the law was changed for us all!"

"That's what I'm trying to say and why our precedent might contain an important lesson for the whole church," I said, nearly pleading.

"Perhaps, but there is a difference. Celibacy is a special treasure. It allows the *pasteur* to be available to his people," he answered softly.

Moving closer to him, I forgot for a moment the rapid pen strokes of Father Purtell.

"Maybe it's special. So is marriage. Besides, for many priests celibacy isn't a treasure but a cross. All too often they end up filling in the time they'd normally spend with a family on golf, television, trips or booze.''

"*S'il vous plait* . . . Booze?''

"He means alcohol. Whiskey and such, Excellency,'' Purtell interjected.

"Oh yes. You say 'booze'?'' Jadot shook his head. "A problem, no? Yet you miss my point, Michael. Regardless, I'm opposed to a change in the law.''

"The cost is high. Just take Great Falls. It's growing while the number of clergy is shrinking. There are only a few of them for nearly one-hundred-thousand . . .'' I stopped. It was an old tape.

Resolute, the delegate peered straight ahead. "If ever there were a change, priests who broke their promise to Mother Church would not be forgiven.''

His tone was benevolent. Detached.

"What you did was very wrong. It had to be stopped. Now you have to live with the church's just punishment.''

Try as we might, a vast difference of age, culture, and perspective continued to separate us. I edged back to my own side of the couch.

"Punishment? Just throwing us and our dreams into the Tiber with so many others is more like banishment, Excellency. Meanwhile, what are we supposed to do, just walk away from everything we believe in?'' I asked vehemently.

"Promenade?''

Again it was Purtell who picked up his question.

"Walk away . . . he's asking for Your Excellency's recommendation for future employment,'' he said sharply.

"Oh yes. Well, you must move out of the West. Perhaps to the East. Somewhere where you are not of notoriety. Then, maybe you could find such work as, say, counseling delinquent children.''

If he hadn't been utterly sincere, I might have laughed.

"Of course, whatever you do, there can be no publicity. It would only inflict suffering on you and Mother Church,'' he added good-naturedly.

The secretary's pen was scratching furiously, grating against me like a fingernail against a chalkboard. Suddenly it stopped as Purtell pointed to his watch.

Jadot stood, his stoop resembling that of a tall tree, deeply rooted but bent from the battering of a relentless wind. For the first time he struck me as being not only a sentinel at the church's gates, but also a victim. Maybe in our case his hand was forced. It was no secret that certain well-placed figures in the Curia saw him as generally too permissive, sought his removal. Was the apparent weariness within him partially a sadness?

"Archbishop?" I asked, desperate for any straw of encouragement. "Do you have anything at all to say to the people of Resurrection? They're devastated by all of this. There are so many people simply shattered."

The delegate paused, ever the guardian of Vatican City. At that moment it dawned on me that in a sense he didn't care; couldn't care.

"Say to them? No, Michael. I have nothing to say to them. Nothing at all."

One question continued to plague me. With little to lose, I decided to try once again.

"You said you only knew about us two years after we were married?"

"*Oui.*"

"But you see, that still leaves three years. If, as you said, I shouldn't have been able to remain in the first place, why did you wait so long?"

Jadot didn't hesitate.

"When your new bishop was appointed, he was told to take care of your situation. He agreed at once, but was advised to take his time."

He chuckled, speaking to me as a comrade whose inside view of the church would help me comprehend.

"The problem was how? After all, we couldn't just stand outside your parish, tossing rocks. I'm sure you would agree, these things take time. Prudence and time. The church is seasoned in both."

I thought back to the painting. The Virgin. The child scattering chips across the floor.

"You're saying Curtiss knew all along? I was a marked man from day one?"

The gentleness melted from his eyes.

"That's much too strong. Let's just say he's a man of duty. The Holy See had to put a stop to it all before it started to . . ."

"Spread?"

"Please now," he said, adjusting a scarlet sash about his cassock, "I must ask you to leave."

The secretary's pen moved to dead zero on case number 2339/78/6.

On my way out, I stopped by the painting, once again longing for the simplicity of a child's faith. Instead, the words from the Apocalypse drifted through the corner of my mind.

Then I saw the Lamb . . . When he broke the second seal, . . .
out came another horse, bright red, and its rider was given this
duty: to take away peace . . . He was given a huge sword.

In that twilight it was all too obvious. Even as I spoke the first
words of love to Joan, the second seal was fracturing. Soon after, we
were to be stalked by the horse of blood red, its rider sent forth wielding
a sword, hell-bent on carrying out his duty.

Albino Cardinal Luciani emerged unexpectedly from the conclave
as the 263rd pontiff—John Paul I. Most of the world, let alone its 800
million Roman Catholics, had never heard of him, yet from the outset
there was admittedly something special about the man who wore his
papal *zucchetto* slightly askew atop his cropped hair. Even while im-
parting the solemn *"Urbi et orbi"* blessing over St. Peter's Square,
he revealed a contagious smile. Displaying a sense of purpose unob-
scured by his own gentle shyness, the pope pledged at once to continue
the reforms set in motion by the predecessor he most admired—
John XXIII.

The idea first came to me on a misty afternoon in Seattle while
the archbishop, lying back on the carpet of his office, was tossing
Michelle into the air as she squealed for more. "Dutchhausen," as
she now called him, was about to leave for Rome and his *ad limina*,
a visit required every five years of each bishop within Catholicism.
This time, Raymond Hunthausen would have an audience with the
new pontiff.

It was a long shot, but when I broached the subject, he didn't
so much as pause in the game with Michelle, adding he had in fact
been thinking of it all along. During the audience, Dutch would attempt to discuss our circumstances, not to erase the termination, which
would be next to impossible, but share an experience of benefit to
the universal church. The precedent established at Resurrection might
be of assistance to a pope inheriting an increasingly acute crisis in
the priesthood. In Dutch's mind, since the suppression had come at
the hands of the Curia, it was appropriate to bring it up with the
Holy Father. The timing was opportune; he hadn't yet appointed a
new Curia.

Once again we found ourselves waiting for news from Rome. Joan
cautioned against exaggerated expectations, since the system he in-

herited would be far stronger than the short, bespectacled Luciani. Still, in our own way, we truly wanted to believe in the system and felt again the stirrings of hope that we and subsequent others might swim against the tide.

The swim was terribly short. While Hunthausen managed to see the pope, the audience was combined with one given to an unexpected entourage of American bishops. Luciani spoke briefly of the importance of family life as a mirror of God's love. In the pope, the archbishop recognized a man at once untouched by the burdens of the papacy and utterly at ease with his ego. Confident he would be approachable in our case, Hunthausen arranged to see John Paul later in the week. There would be no such opportunity. The next time they met was during the funeral for the gentle man, whose reign of thirty-four days was cut short in tragic and clouded circumstances. Luciani had passed from the scene like a meteor.

Jan Cardinal Willebrands of the Netherlands spoke for many, when he admitted to sensing that with Albino Luciani something fresh had been about to happen in the Roman Catholic Church—neither he nor any of us would ever discover what it was.

Saddened by the death, Hunthausen returned home, pending the results of still another conclave. He did not have to wait long for the puff of black smoke to reappear over the Sistine Chapel.

A massive crowd stirred in the piazza below him as Pericle Cardinal Felici stepped out onto the floodlit balcony of St. Peter's Basilica, his trembling voice ricocheting off the Bernini colonnades.

"Habemus Papam . . ."

He paused as a roar rose, fell, and rose again from the throng below.

"Carolum Sanctae Romanae Ecclesiae Cardinalem . . . Wojtyla!''

Karol Wojtyla, the craggy-faced Cardinal of Krakow, stepped forward onto the center stage of church history. His arrival was a surprise for a church desperate for such surprises. Even though his first official pronouncement upon taking office was emphatically to link priesthood to celibacy, we wanted, indeed needed, to reach out to him. While we had no idea where our efforts would lead, there was nowhere else to turn and little to lose.

The archbishop again agreed to be of assistance, promising to forward my intimate message to the pope along with the statement signed by the people of Resurrection. As a follow-up, he would address a personal letter to John Paul II. To ensure that our efforts would actually reach the pontiff, we required the assistance of the apostolic delegate. Jadot agreed, at the archbishop's request, to forward our message in the diplomatic pouch marked for the pontiff's personal attention. The delegate declined to say whether he intended to discuss case number 2339/78/6 with John Paul II.

Hunthausen's communiqué was nearly as moving as the fact that he was willing to do it.

> Your Holiness:
>
> I ordained Michael to the priesthood and have known him well for several years; more than that I have grown to respect him greatly as I have observed him minister with love and dedication to God's people. He is an extraordinary young man with great love for the Lord and a burning desire to make the Lord known and loved.
>
> It is my humble opinion that his thoughts are deserving of a careful hearing. I know that he will be grateful for any attention you are able to give.

My own message, relying heavily upon Resurrection's statement, sought to convey the heart of our experience, thereby seeking a way to ensure that the lessons gained surrounding the question of married priesthood might touch John Paul II and someday open doors for others.

> Your Holiness:
>
> I am your brother Joseph, in exile from much of what I hold dear. It is from this painful exile that I reach out confidently for you.
>
> My story in many ways is the Church's story. I come not to seek a reversal of the Curia's decision, nor even to question the good will of the Congregations involved. Rather, I approach you as our new Pontiff who stands at the dawn of the next century. I come out of hope that a positive and creative lesson may not be lost to the Church I love.
>
> I know that you too, Holy Father, must weep over the crisis in ministry and the drastic reduction of qualified priests and vocations. Yet before us lies a treasure, a pool of talent and faith which the Church is tragically neglecting. It is because

of the light which our experience at Resurrection gives to such
a problem, that I come to you.

You alone are the shepherd who may initiate a process in
the future toward the reconciliation of thousands of your priest
brothers now suffering in exile.

How then can I share with you? I long for a way. Please
help us find that way.

The letter concluded with a desperate shot in the dark: the suggestion of a personal audience, if desired, to fill the pontiff in on the
positive aspects of our experience. Hunthausen would accompany me
if the request was granted. Together we waited for a reply.

We were to wait a long time. First weeks, then months, as Wojtyla
traveled the world, admonishing nations against enslavement of the
human spirit and violations of basic rights and dignity. At last, nearly
a year to the day of my dismissal, the letter arrived. By then, all
anticipation of its contents and the prospect of a morning star rising
above the Eternal City during John Paul's pontificate had long since
vanished.

The papal coat of arms was embossed above the Secretariat of
State's message.

I am directed by the Holy Father to reply to your letter,
which he received some time ago. What you wrote about your
experience has been noted and the sentiments which prompted
you to share your thoughts with the Holy Father are appreciated.

His Holiness will remember you in his prayers.

That was it. Nothing more. I folded the paper carefully inside a
worn copy of the Scriptures given to me at ordination. Though the
pontiff would embrace his would-be assassin, Mehmet Ali Agca, before the clicking shutters of the world's press, we could expect no
such gesture.

That same afternoon, Joan went into labor, giving birth to our
second child. A son.

# EPILOGUE

Invent the future! . . . The future
is not given . . . It is taken, taken . . .
Take it!

—Rhoda Lerman,
The Book of the Night

Michelle nestled her hand within mine as we walked through a light drizzle toward home. The first week of the first grade for our firstborn had gone well, punctuated throughout by her excited chatter summarizing a collage of events. This day she was as quiet as the rain. With the clamor of parents and children fading behind us, she tugged at my trouserleg.

"Dad?" Her dark eyes reached out to me from beneath a pale blue raincoat. "Are you a priest?"

Only as she asked the question a second time did I realize that the dampness on her face wasn't from the weather.

"Holly and Katie said you were a priest just like Father Haefield."

Reaching down to wipe her eyes, I sensed how dangerously close I had come to failing her. We stopped beneath a birch tree, stood upon a cushion of fallen leaves. Michelle told me of the morning.

Halfway around the get-acquainted circle it was her turn to share about her family.

"I told them you weren't. That you worked for a senator or some-one like that. Holly said you didn't. Katie said you were a priest. Mrs. Swenson said you used to be but weren't anymore."

Her tears had stopped. She looked away, examining the tiny drop-lets shimmering like diamonds on the leaves.

"At lunch Katie said her grandma told her you once were but some people made you stop because of Mom and us kids." She turned, looking up at me. "We didn't do anything, did we?"

I had seen the same expression of evaporating innocence on her face once before.

It was a spring morning when the earth seemed to burst with promise. We had just finished planting a row of peas when she stumbled across a young meadowlark, the life crushed out of it beneath the grass. Michelle would hear nothing of my discourse on nature's way, even less of divine providence.

"It's just not fair," she protested. "Why does something so pretty have to die?"

Now the same shadow of perplexity swept over her. I felt an erosion of trust; knew she doubted me once again. What could I say?

For an instant I found myself thinking back to a time before Michelle's mother and I were married. Hans Küng had just expressed his fear that enforced celibacy would lead to a mounting crisis. The crisis he foresaw was now pressing in upon Catholicism with a vengeance.

I was now but one of about 125,000 men in the intervening years to be put on a shelf and labeled an ex-priest; thousands upon thousands of us in America alone. Statisticians were beginning to speak of the priesthood as a geriatric society. Whereas the average age of the functioning priest was already fifty-six, by the time Michelle reached her teens there would be fewer than half as many as today, and those for the most part would be over seventy years of age. Meanwhile, seminaries nationwide were boarded up and "priestless" parishes were becoming commonplace.

The major reason given for the staggering losses and dismal projections remained the Vatican's refusal to give priests the freedom to marry. An issue Rome felt as strongly about as that swirling around women and full equality. In the end, I thought, two sides of the same coin.

Michelle began tugging at my sleeve. Her question had not gone away. One having precious little to do with statistics and multicolored graphs. A question asked instead about me. About her father. She stood there, eyes upon mine, waiting for an answer.

It was a precious moment, and one I desperately wanted not to avoid. Still, what words would suffice? After all, she was a child. What could she possibly comprehend about the whole affair? Certainly there was nothing to hide. Yet the prospect of reliving the pain and confusion was something I had sought for a long time to avoid. I told her something about having been a priest until she was three years old, before being told by a man far away in another country to stop being one; that it was all hard to understand, even for big people.

We walked on in the rain, the chasm between us spanned by a slender thread of silence. Only once, as we waited for a traffic light, did she look up at me with the same hollow eyes as before. I offered nothing more. That evening, just before falling asleep she said to her mother, "Please tell me why they made Dad quit priesting. Was it because of me?"

Michelle's question, but more so the whisper of doubt behind it, has shaken loose the walls of resistance so carefully built up, brick by brick, within me. She deserves an honest reply. Anything less would be to risk failing her and ultimately myself. In response, I have thrown off the shroud of silence and herein attempted an answer for the day when she is mature enough to understand.

As I write these final words, it is Holy Week. We have fled from fond memories of the season, now laced with the fine edge of despair, to a secluded cabin overlooking Canyon Ferry Lake. Holy Week— once a touchstone, now laden with reminders of a priesthood forever lost.

During our days here, it is as though we have dropped off the planet only to fall into its center. With the children asleep—there are three now—Joan and I slip outside onto the deck. There, cradling steaming mugs of coffee, we await the sunrise.

Gradually, shafts of purple and orange stretch their fingers across the sky, racing ahead of the sun. Canadian geese, so low we can hear the flap of their wings, soar through the canyon, their cries calling forth the dawn. For a moment it feels like we are in a time warp. The first man and woman witnessing the unfolding of creation. When I tell her this, Joan laughs, the sound skidding across the water. In her laughter, the echo of a free and conquering spirit. Still, it is a freedom scarred with the lines of memory.

The mood of our conversation shifts; drifting along the pathway of the intervening years. In reaching down within ourselves, tugging at nerve ends buried by time, we have answered our daughter's question, while unearthing others. Others which grind like flint against our souls. Has our experience unalterably changed Joan and me? Are we today only shadows of what we once were or might have been?

Certainly she is different from the day of innocence captured in a faded photo buried in a dresser drawer. The first communion portrait

of a child destined to come up against a powerful institution; there to
see too much and to be forever wounded.

Joan's father died recently, but not before his true feelings for her
overcame a stance he believed his church demanded. After a decade
of strain, he called his daughter home. There, surrounded by family,
he asked for and received her forgiveness. In his final words he sought
to assure her of his affection and that at last he understood.

Whether or not Joan will be able to forgive those who hold the
reins of power in Catholicism is a question for the future. Not that she
didn't know that in marrying a man who needed to remain a priest
fierce opposition was to be expected. It's just that she may have seen
too much for too long. May have asked, "What would Jesus do?" of
the ecclesiastical bureaucracy once too often. In any event, there is
little doubt that those dark brown eyes staring out from beneath the
communion veil saw something in our experience that ravaged her
innocence.

Most definitely we have both been changed in our journey which
led us to the church's wailing wall. While the list of contradictions
within Catholicism rise like Jacob's ladder before God, it is nonetheless
the home of our faith and our children's to inherit, though indeed we
fear for them. Perhaps someday as the church recovers its soul, we
will once again discover in it our own.

For now, neither of us knows whether in looking back we can ever
truly feel at home again. Still, it is the joy of our children and the
ever-flowering love between the two of us that continue to lend form
to chaos. Joan's expression assures me she knows this, just as the
waking sounds of our infant daughter puts an end to our conversation.

Hours later now. Joan is inside reading to the children, and I have
returned to be alone on the deck. The wind is up, blowing in a storm.
Dark clouds cover the cliffs surrounding the lake, as a gale tosses the
porch chimes back and forth like church bells—another reminder that
it is Good Friday. Calling to mind two men, no doubt at this precise
moment in two separate cathedrals. Raymond Hunthausen, enormously
popular among his own own people, yet living with unrelenting pressure from the Vatican. Checked at every turn by the Curia, denied by
John Paul II any voice in the choice of his expected successor, he
looks toward a tenuous tomorrow. Informed predictions of Hunthausen's forced retirement remain as persistent as those anticipating the
elevation of Elden Curtiss to higher episcopal office.

Suddenly, a familiar melancholy sweeps over me. Try as I might to suppress it, the sense of loss—the inability to do what the Spirit still prompts me to do—surfaces. Why must the Word that I and so many priests like me have been ordained to speak lie strangled in our throats? Why, despite our banishment over love, does our terrible passion persist? How can anything which was so real simply vanish?

I want to shout into the void, in one voice with the countless women who, like Joan, share daily in our loss, and their children who, like our own, must live forever in its shadow. Where in all the madness is the promised presence of our God?

Across the lake the storm clouds billow, hurling jagged arrows of lightning. A furious blast of thunder rattles the rafters. Startled, my eyes fall upon a naked tree. Worn and gnarled, silhouetted on the hillside against the sky, its lifeless branches stretching out like the arms of a cross. It might have been another cross looming atop another hill on that first black Friday afternoon. For an instant I can almost hear the hammers, the screams of searing pain. Smell the sponge of Golgotha's bitter gall. Abandoned, strapped against a blood-stained tree, where, I wonder, was the Crucified's God when he needed Him so?

It starts to sprinkle. Shivering, I wrap a slicker over my shoulders when, quite unexpectedly, the ghost of the Fisherman rises from the water below. The face of one to whom I had bidden farewell, haunting me still. Peter, with his own doubts, failures, and clinging attachments. Peter, who long ago peered through the raging storm, to guess at something dancing over the waves. Peter the Apostle who made a choice and, stepping out upon the deep with salt swelling his tongue, stinging his eyes, risked himself only to find himself.

As the rain begins falling in silver sheets, I peer through them into his imagined face floating above the whitecaps, wondering whether in the hour of testing he suspected there would come another time, as indeed there did.

Surely, Peter, with the savage afternoon of Skull Place behind you and the tomb empty, you were home free. John's gospel pictures you squatting comfortably on a tranquil seashore, feasting on grilled fish and broken bread. You were in a festive mood, laughter rolling like a hoop from your mouth. After all, the questions were over, or so you might have wished. But then it didn't go the way you expected. You knew it when the eyes of Jesus sought you out and seized your own, holding them close.

"Simon, son of John. Do you love me?"

How ill-timed of him. How embarrassing, such intimacy in front of your friends. Feigning lightness, you shrugged it off.

"Of course I love you."

It wasn't enough. I know what you must have felt when Jesus persisted, asking a second time.

"Do you love me?"

Damn, how nerve-wracking! Not so much the question as his bloody persistence. I can see you glancing around at the others, none of whom forgot it was you who had denied the Christ three times. Nervously, with trace of impatience, you answered once again.

"Yes, Lord. You know all things. You know I love you."

That should have done it. When Jesus stood, inviting you to follow him, it seemed a bit too much. Why should you go traipsing off into the unknown while the others remained behind? You protested loudly, as only you were capable of, but in the end you gave what was perhaps your most important yes. Pulled by an attachment stronger than yourself, you went along.

I can imagine how hard it must have been saying good-bye to it all, let alone setting out on that second journey. Trudging along the seashore behind Jesus, could you ever have imagined what the future would hold? A future which would find you humiliated once more, only this time before the mocking crowds of Rome. There, crucified upside down with blood thundering in your ears and pushing out your eyes, you would at long last meet your end.

This afternoon, the wind has many faces. Among them that of Peter's ghost. The hounding presence—outside and yet within me also—sways back and forth over the lake below. Somehow I know that the two of us are about to say good-bye, but not before I, too, accept the final query once asked of him. That which in the last analysis may truly be the only one which matters.

I wait, sensing the question which now tumbles from the lips of the Fisherman's God.

"Do you love me?"

Framed within the rain-splattered window, Michelle is watching me. In that fractured second, I know she is change itself. The droplets silhouetted against her forehead call to mind her baptism. A reminder that she is part of a people perhaps destined to reclaim the church as their own. Time is on her side.

Reaching over, I touch the place where her lips rest against the glass. She smiles fondly.

"Do you love me?"

Wrapping the wildly flapping slicker about me, I lean into the wind, making my way across the hillside to the naked tree. There, braced against its rugged skin, I notice the lake is suddenly at peace, raindrops falling across its surface like stars across the heavens.

"Do you love me?"

Despite it all. The dream and failure. The pride and folly. The numbing sense of loss. My response can be no other.

"Ah yes, Lord. You know all things. You know I love you."